D1213477

MUSICAL LETTERS
FROM ABROAD

Da Capo Press Music Titles

FREDERICK FREEDMAN, General Editor
University of California at Los Angeles

MUSICAL LETTERS
FROM ABROAD

By LOWELL MASON

New Introduction by
Elwyn A. Wienandt
Baylor University

Da Capo Press · New York · 1967

A Da Capo Press Reprint Edition

*An unabridged republication of the 1854 edition
published by Mason Brothers, New York*

Library of Congress Catalog Card No. 67-13035

Printed in the United States

Introduction
to the Da Capo Edition

To every person who knows his name at all, any reference to Lowell Mason (1792–1872) brings to mind a
single prominent area of activity, and perhaps a number
of subsidiary ones, depending upon the musical experience and associations of that person. To the music
educator, Mason has become renowned for his pursuit
of an ideal that all children of school age should be
taught music through singing. His introduction of a
course of study based on Pestalozzian principles was a
milestone in the long road leading to our present elab-
orate programs in music education. In the area of
teacher training, he is remembered for having brought
teachers together for conventions that were the fore-
runners of our present-day regional and national meetings. These annual meetings are not now as essential as
they were in the nineteenth century, since the dissemi-

nation of professional information is suitably accomplished by the printed word, but they still serve to generate enthusiasm and develop fresh viewpoints in a way that only person-to-person contacts can. To church musicians, he is firmly established as a critic, commentator, composer of hymns, and compiler of numerous best-selling collections of religious music. He left a significant mark upon our musical scene by introducing into his anthologies many European compositions, adapted from secular and religious sources, and translated into a comfortable kind of congregational poetry. His insistence on a high quality of performance excited the attention and admiration of large numbers of musicians, clergymen, and laymen. The higher level of performance in many churches that resulted from his efforts is of major importance in American choral history.

Other musicians to bear the family name were his sons, William and Henry, and his grandson, Daniel Gregory Mason. Their influence on American music is the most significant that can be attributed to any one family, covering the areas of conducting, composition, keyboard performance and pedagogy, book and music publishing, instrument building and merchandising, teacher training, music education, and church music. The family reputation can be criticized in several of these areas for falling short of the ideal, but the effect of the presence of these men on the American musical scene cannot be disregarded. The importance of Lowell Mason, founder of this petty dynasty, is not to be minimized simply because we think our sophistication greater than his.

Mason was one of a considerable number of nineteenth-century American musicians who made a modest fortune out of music, not by pursuit of the highest ideals of an abstract art, but by reaching a large public with a kind of music that, while not always obtaining the approval of higher criticism, served abundantly to elevate standards of public music making. His interest in vocal music and music education, and his familiarity with the organ and its use in church services, placed him in the mainstream of popular musical activity, and his abilities as an organizer and promoter of conventions and publications made him one of the most widely known American musical figures of his time. Had he attempted a career in the more severely evaluated mart of concert music, his fame would probably have been very small. As he saw fit to work with amateurs and beginners in performance, he rose to prominence on the crest of the wave of desire for musical participation in schools, churches, and community groups.

Although most aspects of Mason's life are generally known from a variety of books,[1] there is an almost unaccountable confusion surrounding his second trip to Europe. One source states that "he visited Europe first in 1837 with the view of examining the method of teaching in Germany and embodied the results in a volume entitled *Music Letters from Abroad* (New York, 1853)."[2] While it is true that he went to Europe in the summer of 1837, there was no connection between that event and the volume presented here, the title of which, incidentally, was cited incorrectly, and one must doubt that the compiler of the information had examined the book carefully before commenting on it. The *Musical Letters*

[1] Arthur Lowndes Rich, *Lowell Mason: The Father of Singing Among the Children* (Chapel Hill: The University of North Carolina Press, 1946) ; Edward Bailey Birge, *History of Public School Music in the United States* (Boston: Oliver Ditson Company, 1937) ; Gilbert Chase, *America's Music: From the Pilgrims to the Present* (New York: McGraw-Hill Book Company, 1955) ; Leonard Ellinwood, *The History of American Church Music* (New York: Morehouse-Gorham Company, 1953) ; *Baker's Biographical Dictionary of Musicians*, ed. by Nicolas Slonimsky (6th ed.; New York: G. Schirmer, 1965), pp. 1043f; *Grove's Dictionary of Music and Musicians*, ed. by Eric Blom (5th ed.; New York: St. Martin's Press, 1955), V, 610; *Die Musik in Geschichte und Gegenwart*, ed. by Friedrich Blume (Kassel: Bärenreiter-Verlag, 1949–), VIII, 1756f; Oscar Thompson (ed.), *The International Cyclopedia of Music and Musicians* (7th rev. ed. by Nicolas Slonimsky; New York: Dodd, Mead & Co., 1956), p. 1101.

[2] Thompson, *loc. cit.* The entry appears on the same page in the 1st ed. (1939) and the 4th ed. (1946). Any lack of accuracy for this entry is therefore attributable to the first editor.

are entirely concerned with a second trip; and, as Mason states in the Preface, they "are almost exclusively on musical subjects, and . . . relate more particularly to the department of church-music, or to the service of song in religious worship."

One of the most thorough of the Mason studies notes the confusion surrounding the actual date of Mason's second trip to Europe, as well as its duration,[3] but even here a later reference says that "the *Musical Letters from Abroad* and the fragmentary journal which he kept on his first journey to Europe are valuable for their accounts of music teaching and musical activities of mid-nineteenth century Europe."[4] In fact, music teaching is not an important feature of the letters at all. They are, on the contrary, concerned with public music—concert halls, church services and performances, music festivals, and virtuoso performers—and musical education is generally ignored.[5]

---

[3]Rich, *op. cit.*, p. 104.

[4]*Ibid.*, p. 110.

[5]In Letter xv, Mason undertakes a long evaluation of the Leipzig Conservatory, but most of the letter is taken up with an account written by "a young gentleman, a Bostonian, a graduate of Harvard University, now a musical student and member of the Conservatory— Mr. J. P." The possessor of these fine recommendations was probably James Cutler Dunn Parker (1828–1916), a student in Leipzig from 1851–54, according to *Baker's*, p. 1209.

Mason sailed for Europe on December 20, 1851, arriving at Liverpool on New Year's morning, 1852. His first letter was written from London on January 9th. In it, his sense of dramatic journalism is immediately evident as he reports the burial at sea of a fellow passenger who, whether or not he actually died of delirium tremens, is the principal actor in a drama that sets the tone for the entire volume and insures the reader a fair share of excitement to come.

There are fifty-four letters in all, covering a period of about fifteen months. They are not written on a strict schedule. Sometimes several are sent on successive days; at other times there are gaps of weeks between them. The relationship between the various letters, the places and events they describe, and Mason's activities at the time is not easy to see. In some cases, the letters are reports after the fact. Letter LII, for example, was apparently completed and sent from London, but it concerns a side trip to Holland, where no letter had been posted. At a few points, Mason's very itinerary is unclear, and the order of events is also clouded, although most of the inconsistencies can be rationalized by recalling that letter-writing is not always the most compelling activity of the day, and that this was the case even in an age when letters were a more common means

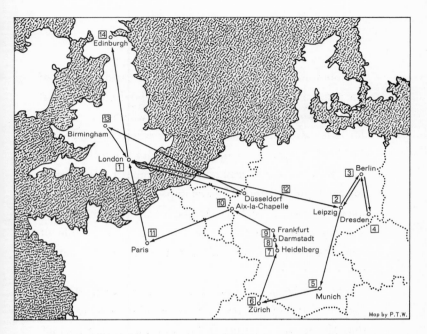

Map by P.T.W.

Map code	Letter	Dateline	Place written
1	I–III	January 9–15, 1852	London
2	IV–XX	January 22–April 2	Leipzig
3	XXI–XXII	April 5–9	Berlin
4	XXIII	April 12	Dresden
3	XXIV	[?]	Berlin
2	XXV–XXVII	May 2–10	Leipzig
5	XXVIII–XXXI	May 18–26	Munich
6	XXXII	June 7	Zürich
7	XXXIII	June 12	Heidelberg
8	XXXIV	June 19	Darmstadt
9	XXXV	June 21	Frankfurt [am Main]
10	XXXVI	June 24	Aix-la-Chapelle
11	XXXVII–XXXVIII	July 7–12	Paris
1	XXXIX–XL	August 12–[?]	[London]
12	XLI	September 18	Düsseldorf
13	XLII–XLIII	September 2–[?]	Birmingham
1	XLIV–LIII	[?]–March 11, 1853	London
14	LIV	March 29, 1853	Edinburgh

of communication. In the end, only a careful study of his itinerary, as determined from the datelines and occasional interior references, can prove whether a particular letter was completed in the place where it was begun, or whether certain breaks in continuity are to be attributed to haphazard arrangement in preparing the letters for book publication. The accompanying map and table make it possible to trace Mason's travels quickly; and a comparison with the topic sentences in the table of contents will prove rewarding in ascertaining his activities in each city.

The relatively small number of letters during the last eight months of the trip can be attributed to the fact that Mason was teaching in London during that period[6] and that he was probably compiling *Mason's Hand-book of Psalmody* at the same time.[7]

That Lowell Mason was an astute businessman can be seen from almost all of his activities. This volume of letters is no exception, for its organization shows that, at least in part, he intended to act as a latter-day Burney in describing the various stages of his journey. His main interest is religious music, but he reports on a variety of

[6]Rich, *op. cit.*, p. 104.
[7]*Ibid.*, p. 161.

concert performances, and his visits to the principal music festivals are presented in considerable detail, even to mentioning the prices of various refreshments and the problem of cigar-smoking patrons at the Düsseldorf festival. Occasional references to the discomforts of travel and the prices of food, and the general format and tone of the material, also indicate that Burney influenced Mason more than a little.

Most often, however, Mason describes church buildings, their size and seating capacities, orders of service, styles of organ playing, and, almost without exception, the amount and kind of congregational singing. His concern for quality in performance, taste in the selection of church pieces, the propriety of religious practices, and the decorum of performers, sheds a certain light on American practices as well, whether he compares them directly or simply implies that great differences exist. He is a critic of behavior as much as music, of congregational procedure as well as performance practice.

His description (Letter X) of a Sunday service at Leipzig's Thomas-Kirche shows the normal practice a century after Bach's residence there. The order of service he gives is for a Sunday in Lent and, as he indicates, no orchestra is used. However, in Letter XIV, still during

Lent, he reports on the performance of a work for chorus, organ, and orchestra at the Nicolai-Kirche. It would be interesting to know why the old practice was followed at one church and not at the other, but Mason's attention was focused on the comparison of German and American musical practice rather than on a small point of German liturgical procedure. He is careful to note the use of the same choir and orchestra at St. Thomas on one Sunday and alternately at St. Nicholas on the next, but he sees it is as contemporary practice and not as the survival of a century-old custom.[8]

Mason was a careful observer, but it is clear that he spent little time in recapitulation and comparison. When a letter was written, its story was closed. Thus, certain apparent inconsistencies are simply factual reporting without the addition of pedantic comparisons. Mason did not originally intend that these letters should form

[8]The practice in Bach's time is discussed by Albert Schweitzer, *J. S. Bach*, trans. by Ernest Newman (2 vols., New York: Macmillan, 1950), I, 128, where he says, "On the three last Sundays in Advent, and in Lent, no cantatas were given, the organ was silenced, and the motets were discontinued." Philipp Spitta, *Johann Sebastian Bach*, trans. by Clara Bell and J. A. Fuller-Maitland (3 vols., London: Novello, 1884–1885; reprint, New York: Dover Publications, 1951), II, 271, states that "the order of service for Passion week had this feature in common with the whole of Lent, that neither the organ nor concerted music were employed."

a continuous narrative, and reference to earlier happenings would have been useless to one who had missed the original discussion. And even when the letters were gathered into book form, there was apparently little effort to bring complete order out of them. The sudden appearance of a letter discussing a place visited previously, the misspelled German, the lack of careful proofreading for errors in English spelling—all point to a hasty assembling of materials for a market that would disappear if the opportunity for prompt publication were lost. Furthermore, Mason had little time to devote to this collection after he returned to America. Four new books appeared from his pen in 1854, and a like number the following year, all while he was teaching, lecturing, organizing meetings, writing articles, and presumably compiling the books that were to appear in succeeding years.

The letters were published three times. They first appeared, as Mason states in the Preface, "in various periodicals," while he was still abroad. They next appeared as a bound volume under the imprint of the Boston music publishers, O. Ditson and Company, in 1853; and they were published for the last time a year later by Mason Brothers. Regardless of the number of copies printed, however, few seem to remain extant.

Rich's check list,[9] which collates the Mason holdings of nineteen libraries, all east of the Ohio River, shows that only six own a copy of the *Musical Letters*. Such books are often even scarcer as one searches westward. This reprint provides the views of Mason on his own world of music; and it makes generally available still another document on which to base comparisons of American and European musical practices and tastes in the nineteenth century.

The copy from which the Da Capo Press reprint was made is presently owned by Mrs. Clarence R. Sharpes of Parkersburg, West Virginia, who first brought the volume to my attention.

ELWYN A. WIENANDT

Baylor University
Waco, Texas
July 1, 1966

---

[9]Rich, *op cit.*, p. 139. While a list of nineteen libraries cannot be considered representative of the United States, the ones included are some of the most significant for materials of this type.

MUSICAL LETTERS
FROM ABROAD

MUSICAL LETTERS

FROM ABROAD:

INCLUDING DETAILED ACCOUNTS OF THE

BIRMINGHAM, NORWICH, AND DUSSELDORF

MUSICAL FESTIVALS OF 1852.

BY LOWELL MASON.

NEW YORK:
PUBLISHED BY MASON BROTHERS.

1854.

STEREOTYPED BY
THOMAS B. SMITH,
216 William Street, N. Y.

PRINTED BY
JOHN A. GRAY,
97 Cliff St. N. Y.

PREFACE.

THE following letters are almost exclusively on musical subjects, and they relate more particularly to the department of church-music, or to the service of song in religious worship. There are many persons in different parts of our country, who are deeply interested in the subject of music, who are beginning to appreciate its value, and who are engaged in the cause of musical education, and especially in efforts for the improvement of church-music; this is abundantly proved by the rapid spread of music in common schools, by the steadily growing demand for good instructors both in the vocal and instrumental departments, by the higher qualifications which from year to year are required in those who are sought for and employed as teachers, and by the constantly-increasing number of associations and gatherings for musical purposes, as elementary classes, singing societies, choirs and musical conventions.

It was for the gratification of these persons, and especially for the satisfaction of the author's numerous pupils and friends, that these very imperfect letters were originally written and published in various periodicals, and for these too they have been now collected and printed in a more convenient and permanent form. May they serve as a token of remembrance from the writer, and may they in their humble way add a little to the influence of those who, regarding music as an object worthy of human pursuit and cultivation, are exerting themselves for its improvement and universal diffusion.

Contents.

———•●•———

LETTER I.

LETTER XXIX.

LETTER XXX.

LETTER XXXI.

LETTER XXXII.

LETTER XXXIII.

LETTER XXXIV.

LETTER XXXV.

LETTER XXXVI.

LETTER XXXVII.

LETTER XXXVIII.

LETTER XLIX.

LETTER L.

LETTER LI.

LETTER LII.

LETTER LIII.

LETTER LIV.

𝕸𝖚𝖘𝖎𝖈𝖆𝖑 𝕷𝖊𝖙𝖙𝖊𝖗𝖘.

LETTER I.

The Voyage—Burial at Sea—Liverpool—Worcester Cathedral—Choir—St. Nicholas—
Rev. Mr. Havergal—Psalmody—Organ Playing.

LONDON, Jan. 9th, 1852.

A VOYAGE across the Atlantic has been so often described, that I will not attempt any account of ours, except to say that it was, with the exception of a day or two, a succession of blows and gales, rough and cold. A single circumstance may be mentioned in a death at sea. We were just rising from the dinner-table, at about 6 o'clock, the fourth day out, when a messenger came in to announce to the captain that one of the passengers in the forward cabin had just died. The captain immediately went out to ascertain the facts, and soon returned with the information that a man had died suddenly, and apparently of *delirium tremens.* The burial took place in an hour afterwards. The Episcopal service having been read by Rev. Dr. Robinson, who was a passenger on board, the body was consigned to the deep as its last resting-place. Death is always solemn, but it seemed peculiarly so at sea—in a storm, just at night, it being already dark, the wind blowing, the ocean foaming and roaring, and the ship, though by the power of her mighty engines steadily pursuing her way, tossing here and there a nut-shell upon the mighty billows,

Eleven days and a half brought us safely to Liverpool, where we arrived on New Year's morning, at about 6 o'clock. Taking a hasty look of the city, where we landed, we proceeded the next day to the old city of Worcester, delightfully situated on the banks of the river Severn, where we took lodgings for the Sabbath at the "Star and Garter Hotel." This was the last city that held out against Cromwell, and in September, 1651, the decisive battle was here fought which established his authority, and which destroyed the hopes of the Royalists. The Cathedral is, of course, an object of curiosity and interest. It is in the form of a double cross, in different styles of architecture, yet exhibiting unity or harmony of design. The tower, about 170 feet in height, is very beautiful and grand. There are many interesting monuments contained in different parts of the building; that of King John in the CHOIR attracts, perhaps, most attention. A full-length effigy of the King lies on the top of the tomb. The King was buried here, (1216,) by his own desire, in a monk's cowl, to expedite his passage through purgatory.

We attended the daily service on Saturday, at 3 o'clock. The prayers, litany, &c., were all intoned or recited to the plain chant by one of the canons of the cathedral, with the usual responses by the choir. The psalms for the day were chanted by the choir, consisting of sixteen or eighteen boys and men, who also sung the canticles set in the service or anthem form, by Dr. Nares.

The chanting was poor enough, at least, for three reasons: 1st. Great rapidity of utterance. 2d. No two members of the choir kept together. 3d. The enunciation of the words was so careless, that it was with difficulty one could keep the place and follow the performance, even with book in hand. There was, of course, nothing like attention to the sense of the psalms—

there was no appropriate emphasis, or any more expression, than would be given by a hand-organ or grind-stone. The great leading object seemed to be to hurry on, and get through as quickly as possible. One good point, however, in the chanting was the absence of all drawling in the cadences. The tones were not prolonged, but were delivered in quick succession.

On Sunday morning, at 11 o'clock, we attended divine service in the parish church of St. Nicholas, Rev. Mr. Havergal rector. The exercises commenced by a few measures as a voluntary, or rather prelude, and the " giving out" the tune on the organ, after which all the congregation united in a single stanza sung to the old tune called " Tallis's Evening Hymn." The hymn was not read nor named, but it appeared to be a common thing for the worship to commence in the use of a stanza well known, always the same, and to the same tune. It was a hearty commencement, for every one seemed to join with full voice. The service was read by the curate. The chanting was done by the whole congregation, and the responding was between the occupants of the lower floor and those of the gallery—but the song was universal—men, women and children uniting harmonious voices. The Venite and the Te Deum were chanted responsively ; the psalms were not chanted but, read in the usual manner. Two metrical hymns were sung during the service. The tunes were both of the old ecclesiastical class, and were in the same rhythmic form as St. Ann's, York, &c. appear in the Cantica Laudis. The first and last words of each line being long, and all the rest short. They were sung by all the people, and in very quick time ; as fast as propriety would allow the enunciation of the words. They were sung somewhat quicker than the writer has taught this class of tunes in musical conventions and singing classes in

America. Let the tune Uxbridge, for example, be sung in
quick time, somewhat quicker than usual, and the *crotchets* will
give the time of the *minims* in the above-named class of tunes.
There were one or two organ interludes introduced in a psalm
of five stanzas; but these were very short, not more than
about two measures, or the length of the last line of a common
metre tune. " *These tunes would be popular in America,*" said
the lady who was with me, who, though not a singer, has been
accustomed for many years to give close attention to the Psalmody, and to hear criticisms and remarks concerning it.   And
indeed, they are as far from being dull and heavy as need be;
I doubt not that many good people, with us, would think it almost irreverent to sing a hymn through with such rapidity.
Yet all the people, old and young, joined—all seemed to know
the tunes perfectly, and all kept well together.

Mr. Havergal is himself, as is well known, much of a musical man, and an excellent composer.   He has once or twice
obtained the Gresham prize medal for the best composition of
a church service or anthem; and he is well-known by numerous sacred songs, published with pianoforte accompaniment.
But it is metrical psalmody and the chant in which he is most
interested, and in which he has produced some very fine specimens.   He only devotes odds and ends of time to music, and
never writes music when he is able to write sermons; but it
has been, when weary with the labors of the day, or when
travelling, that he has composed most of his popular and excellent tunes.   He has many curious and valuable old books
of psalmody, and is now himself writing, as he can find time,
some historical notice of the " Old Hundredth Psalm Tune."

In the afternoon of Sunday, we again attended the cathedral
service.   The officiating canon and the choir went through it
with the speed of railroad travelling, and if that is *well* done

which is done quickly, then this was well indeed. But the idea of worship in such a service, who would think of it, or suppose for a moment that confession, supplication, thanksgiving and adoration, had any part or lot in the matter.

We have had opportunity to attend but one public religious service in London, in the daily cathedral service at St. Paul's. It was nearly the same as at the Worcester cathedral. The choir is a little larger, but the same irreverent hurrying prevails. The manner of treating the cadences in the chant I like, for there is no singing, drawling style, but the tones are short and words quickly spoken; but with respect to the chanting in other respects, or in general, it is all confused, inarticulate, rapid and unsatisfactory—still it is not relatively, perhaps, much quicker than the other parts of the service. A company of hungry ones in a second or third-rate American hotel do not eat their dinner in greater speed than these humble confessions and prayers are recited.

It is quite astonishing that good people from America, ministers and others, should write in such glowing terms of the cathedral music of England. It is as unfit for our purposes as are their cathedrals, or their Church and State dependence and connection. One does not wonder at the old Puritans, or at their rejection of all chantings, and organ playings, and respondings, and liturgies, when he sees the very great abuses of these things here. It does not follow that they are necessarily bad things, because we see them so much abused; but it surely becomes us to guard against these abuses of them, as they are introduced into the churches of New-England.

The organ in particular, if we err not, is already sadly abused in many of our churches. Light and silly voluntaries, long and unmeaning interludes between the stanzas, loud accompaniment, fancy *stop*, and see-saw *swell*-playing, and other things, call for reformation. Indeed, unless the organ can be used as a simple aid to worship, surely it had better be altogether dispensed with.

I have omitted to mention one important point in the use of the organ, both at the parish church and at the cathedral in Worcester. It was this, viz. : the closing voluntary, in both cases, consisted of an introduction and fugue played in excellent style. How noble and elevating is the fugue ; this most learned and most interesting style of music is admirably adapted to the organ, and no person ought to be regarded as an organist who cannot play with a clear and distinct articulation, a strict fugue —yea, even a BACH !

I will also add that both organs at Worcester (as also St. Paul's here) were played in the true organ style, and without the slightest tendency to the light, frivolous, overture, polka, waltz, dance-prevailing manner so common with us. Dr. Hodges, in New York, and the elder Hayter, in Trinity church, Boston, are both fine specimens of well-educated English organists.

LETTER II.

A Sunday Service at the Foundling Hospital, London—St. Martins-in-the-Fields.

LONDON, January 15, 1852.

THIS establishment is interesting to musical people, from the fact that Handel was one of its patrons, composing for it, and performing his music for its benefit. A tablet is seen in one of the rooms, with the amount received for several years in succession from Oratorios given. But alas ! for the music now; it is anything but church music. There are nearly 400 children, about half of each sex; they all sit in the organ loft, and all sing the chants, responses, tunes, and services. They are dressed in a neat uniform, the boys in blue, with a white collar turned down, and the girls with white caps and aprons. The organ loft is so arranged, that by the raised seats every one can be distinctly seen.

The service commenced by an organ voluntary; and a lighter, more frivolous piece of organ-playing, I never heard. It was an attempt at a kind of extemporaneous overture with fancy stops, flute, oboe, &c., and great organ contrasts, staccato passages, sudden pianos, and fortes, and sforzandos, in little scraps of melody, light as the lightest of Donizetti or Verdi, without dignity, solemnity, character, or sense. Not a particle of reverence about it. I have heard the organ abused before, and degraded enough, but this was the climax of organ absurdity and degradation.

In the chanting the children kept together, and there was the entire absence of that drawling in the cadences, so common in America. The notes in the cadences were very quickly sung— very much quicker than I have been accustomed to teach them, yet not too quick. But little attention was given to words— they were not properly delivered; but the smaller words were omitted, and many were so clipped or abridged as to be decidedly coarse or vulgar, as

"Glory be t' 'he Father," &c. "As 't was 'n th' beginning," &c.

This was particularly observable in the monotone recitation of the Lord's Prayer and Creed.

The Te Deum was sung in anthem form, and was well done —*i. e.* they all kept together, pronouncing the words with the speed of an auctioneer, but without any attention to sense, emphasis, pause, and the like.

A strange psalm tune was sung. It was like an *andante allegretto*, with marked time, by Haydn. Strange indeed, to hear a hymn so sung to music so very light and inappropriate. But it was well done, that is, they all went through it together, as true as a factory wheel goes round, and with as much expression and good taste.

In the place of an anthem, an extract from the Messiah was sung. Rec. " For behold darkness," &c.; aria, "The people that walked," and the chorus "For unto us." The bass song was well done, by a fine voice, and in quite an artistic manner. The singer did himself much credit indeed, but the chorus was a failure—the little things [children] kept along and got through with it, but no character was given to it whatever. It is not children's music. Children might as well be required to read Shakspeare, as to sing Handel. They may hit the tones, but they cannot sing the music.

The organ accompaniment was here excellent—orchestra style was required, and orchestra style was played. The staccato was boldly, cleanly, and most distinctly given. Indeed the organ was made a most excellent substitute for an orchestra; and very great skill indeed was manifested by the organist.

A very excellent and instructive sermon followed; the whole service occupying a little more than two hours.

We were now permitted to follow, or rather to precede the children to their dining room. We took our stand in the boys' room, and in a few minutes the two hundred little fellows marched into the room, and took their places at the tables in most perfect order. Four of the larger boys had clarionets in their hands, and, on a signal being given, the whole company folded their hands and shut their eyes and sang a grace, accompanied by the clarionets. This was the most affecting song of the day; it was indeed much aided by sight, but the effect was to "enforce tears" from many an eye. This being over, the music of knives and forks was heard—and the nice roast beef and boiled potatoes appeared to be gratefully, or certainly gladly received. We also passed through the girls' room, and saw them at their dinner.

In the afternoon we attended church at St. Martin's-in-the-fields; but as this communication is already sufficiently long, we will only speak of the organ-playing. It was in legitimate style, and formed a striking contrast to the Foundling Hospital organ. The true organ style was here given; like the organ at St. Paul's and at Westminster Abbey, there was nothing light, trifling, and silly, but the lofty diapasons told their story with a dignity and a grandeur becoming the house of God. Truly the organ is a noble instrument, but it may be awfully degraded and sadly abused !

LETTER III.

London Thursday Concerts, Exeter Hall.

London, January 15, 1852.

THIS is a series of concerts for the people, at a low charge; the prices being four shillings, two shillings, and one shilling, according to the class of seats. They consist of vocal and instrumental music, but without orchestra. They employ some five or six solo performers, and a choir of about forty-five choristers. Glees and madrigals are sung by the choir, and songs, duets, &c., by the solo voices, with piano forte pieces, violin pieces, or other instruments as it may be convenient to obtain for the different concerts. I attended the second of the series on Thursday last. The large Exeter Hall was full of people, who seemed to be much delighted with the music; indeed I thought that there was more warmth of approval exhibited there than we usually see at the best concerts with us. The solo performers were Miss Pyne, Miss Louisa Pyne, Miss Binckes, Mr. Swift, (a new tenor,) Herr Jonghmans, Mr. Cotton, and Mr. Whitworth. Miss Goddard played serenade (Don Pasquale), by Thalberg, and also an *andante* and *rondo caprisioso* by Mendelssohn, on the piano forte, and Mr. Richardson played an air with variations on the flute. Miss Binckes has a very fine voice, and sung to the great acceptance of the audience, and Miss Louisa Pyne sung quite a difficult aria by Rode, which called forth a most enthusiastic *encore*. The pieces for full choir were performed without accompaniment, not even the piano forte being played; and although I have heard a better chorus at home, yet this was truly good. The concert was conducted by Mr. T. H. Severn. The programme contained the music to the National Anthem, printed in full in four parts, and the whole audience joined in this the closing chorus:

"God save our gracious Queen,
Long may VICTORIA reign;
God save the Queen!
Send her victorious,
Happy and glorious,
Long to reign over us,
God save the Queen!

"O Lord our God arise,
Scatter her enemies,
And make them fall.

Confound their politics,
Frustrate their knavish tricks,
On Thee our hopes we fix,
   God save us all.

" Thy choicest gifts in store
On her be pleased to pour,
   Long may she reign ;
May she defend our laws,
And ever give us cause,
To sing with heart and voice,
   God save the Queen !

There is but little music in London just now : it yields to the Christmas holidays, which are hardly over as yet. There is to be a grand performance of Mendelssohn's hymn of Praise and of Athalie on the 28th of January, and of Elijah on the 30th, but before that time I hope to be in Germany.

LETTER IV.

Gewandhaus Concert—Mendelssohn—Crowded hall—Beethoven's Symphony No. 8.— Overture by Gade.

LEIPSIG, January 22, 1852.

I HAVE this evening had an opportunity of attending one of the famous subscription concerts in this city, known as the Gewandhaus Concerts.

The concert room is not large, but convenient, and good for musical effect. The centre of the room is occupied by ladies, and the outer seats mostly by gentlemen. A narrow gallery, in which are a number of private boxes, runs round the room. The first object of attraction, after entering the room, is a fine large medallion of Mendelssohn, back of the orchestra ; there is no other bust or picture in the room. It makes one feel sad when looking at this fine representation of the great modern composer, in the very room where he has been, and still is, so highly appreciated, and where he has so often triumphed gloriously, to think that he was cut off in his youth, and that the musical world, after so short a time of enjoyment, was deprived of the talents and learning of one who promised to do for music, perhaps, more than any man living. At almost every concert, more or less of his music is performed ; his memory is cherished, not only here, where he was so well known, but by all the musical world, and his name shall be held in everlasting remembrance.

A crowd of people were waiting round the door, when we arrived ; and, although it was an hour before the time for the performance to commence, the room was filled, (save the reserved seats in the gallery,) in a few minutes after the door was opened. One must be on hand at an early hour to get a good seat. In about half an hour the members of the orchestra began to make their appearance, and as all the people in the house were talking loud, so the musicians, as they came in, one after another, began to tune, to try their instruments, and to amuse themselves by running over the scales; so that by the time they were all there, thus employed, the room was filled with sound; the more so because, as the musicians began to exercise themselves upon their instruments, the talking and laughing grew louder and louder, and at a quarter of an hour before the commencement of the music, it was a perfect Babel in the concert room, and as difficult to hear one speak as it is in a railroad car, with all the windows open, in summer. But a few minutes before the hour, the room began to grow quiet, musical expectation began to awaken, and when, as the precise moment arrived, the conductor's signal was heard, everything was still, and perfect silence took the place of noise and confusion. Another signal, and the whole band, as one man, were heard interpreting and presenting to a most attentive audience, one of the great works of the immortal Beethoven.

It was the Sinfonie No. 8, F major. This is not regarded as one of Beethoven's greatest triumphs; but, although it is light and playful, it abounds in each of its four movements, with the most fanciful and imaginative melodic figures, contrapuntal points, and instrumental contrasts. Ever lively and ever new, it never tires, but holds one in a kind of musical ecstasy from beginning to end; there seems to be no place where one can relax attention, or cease to be filled with musical delight; so that at the close of each part, a good long breath naturally comes in as a relief; and one becomes conscious of the intensity of the application he has been giving to the discourse.

The very first thing which strikes one, on hearing such an orchestra as this, is the perfect oneness of the violins. They do, indeed, constitute a perfect chorus—ten or more persons are playing the first violin, and as many more the second; but they are all *artists*, and, therefore, each one loses himself; no one is heard above the others; but all so beautifully blend as to constitute one perfect whole. This is the perfection of a chorus, be it vocal or instrumental; and this effect is produced by the Gewandhaus Orchestra.

Another point, immediately noticed, is the proper proportion of wind and stringed instruments; but perhaps the most striking point, as contrasted with our American orchestras, is the perfection of the wind instruments. It is too often the case in our orchestras that some wind instrument is wanting; thus the oboe or the faggotto is often missing; and again, it is not unfrequently the case that, although there may be some one to hold these or other instruments in the hand, or up to the sight of the audience, a tone is seldom permitted to escape from them; they are seen but not heard. Not so here; every instrument is not only represented to the eye, but is in the hands of a master who makes it speak to the ear. The consequence is, that such combinations fall upon the ear as are not heard with us. The brass instruments too are made to tell their story without any impediment of speech; whereas, with us, they stutter, or falter, or hem, or cough, to the no small disturbance of the equilibrium of one's temper. We do not know that in this concert every instrument is played in all respects right; we do not know but some notes may have been omitted, or wrong tones produced, but certain are we that we did not discover any such imperfections. There are four things, (technical points,) that we have seldom heard well exhibited elsewhere, which were exceedingly well brought out here, viz.: *Piano, Crescendo, Diminuendo* and *Fortzando.* These, with the other technicals of playing were so well observed, that added to the pure tone peculiar to each particular instrument, and connected with a most perfect amalgamation or blending of all the different elements of the orchestra, they seemed to produce, not a mere musical performance to be listened to, but a living being, or moral, spiritual existence, capable of expressing the deepest feeling, and of calling forth the strongest sympathies of humanity.

The Sinfonie being over, and a few moments for rest having been given, old Handel visited us in an Arie from his Opera "Aerio"—" *Folle é colui che al tuo favor si fida.*" It was sung by Herrn SALVATORE MARCHESI, who was the only vocalist for the evening. The song was well sung; but we sometimes hear quite as good singing across the Atlantic. Belletti is decidedly his superior. The third piece was a Flute Concerto; it was a tiresome affair. A Flute Concerto is a Flute Concerto, whether in the Gewandhaus, Hanover Square rooms, Tripler Hall or the Melodeon ; and although it may not be always played by Herrn *W. Haake*, (who certainly did his duty well,) it is always the most dry and uninteresting of musical performances.

In part 2d was given, 1st, the beautiful overture Echoes of Ossian, (often played in New York and Boston,) by N. W. GADE. 2d. Arie from Zauberflöte, by Mozart, " *Qui sdegno non s' accende.*" 3d. Mendelssohn's concerto for the piano forte, in D. Minor. 4th. Arie from Don Giovanni, by Mozart, " *Madamina, il catalogo é questo,*" and 5th. The very fine overture to the opera, " Der Wassertrager," by Cherubini.

Gade's overture may be regarded as a sacred piece. It speaks of greatness, and calls forth emotions of the sublime. Something like an Old Chorale pervades the whole, which seems to tell of worship, and to call forth humble adoration. With what grandeur this subject was given out, and oft in the course of the piece alluded to by the brass instruments, or exemplified and illustrated by the others, cannot be told. The overture is known with us, but it requires and deserves close study.

The Piano Forte Concerto, D (not G) Minor, failed for want of a performer ; a highly promising young lad of the conservatory attempted it, but he had neither grasp of mind nor of hand enough for Mendelssohn. Herr MARCHESI sang both airs well, gaining for himself decided applause.

On the whole, here is a highly-talented and well-regulated orchestra. The conductor for the evening was Julius Rietz, well known to the musical world.

I will mention one or two things about the audience :

1st. Gentlemen took off their hats before passing the door of the hall, all of them, without a single exception ; and this, al though they were there an hour before the performance con menced. There was not a single man standing under the galleries or near the doors, uncovered. The *ungentlemanly* act of standing or sitting in a concert room with hats on, could not be seen in the Gewandhaus.

2d. Ladies were all in full dress.

3d. There was silence during the performance of music. The moment the music ceased, then indeed there was a perfect buzzing of voices, and very loud talking all over the room; but at the signal for the commencement of the music, all was still; and we were not prevented from hearing the music by those whisperings so annoying in some places.

On the whole, this was a very fine concert; the orchestra playing was as near to perfection, I doubt not, as can often be found; and that constitutes the great attraction of the Gewandhaus. Every man seems to be able to play on his own instrument well; every man seems to give undivided attention to the music, and to endeavor to observe carefully, not only the time, as given by the conductor, but all those little gesticulations by which expression is indicated. Our orchestra playing in America is fast improving. The *Philharmonic* of New York, the *Musical Fund* of Boston, and may I not say, especially the *Germanians*, have each done much to advance this cause. We must indeed be dependent upon foreign artists for generations to come; so it is even in England, where no small portion of the performers are Germans; but we shall run faster when once fairly started, than the English. The cause of musical education has already taken deep root with us; our music teachers are more numerous and more competent than they were a few years ago; many promising young men are entering the profession, and the work of teaching children and of teaching in schools is constantly on the advance. Better music, too, is being published now than formerly; the sonatas

of Mozart and Beethoven, for piano forte, and Gems of German
song in the vocal department, are only specimens of what is being done in this way. But I must not enlarge. I only add
that at the concert of which I have tried to give some account,
two young Bostonians, students in music here, were seated beside me, (J. C. D. P. and W. M.,) both of whom, it is to be
hoped, will ere long be engaged in the work, doing their part
to advance an art and a science so important to human improvement and happiness.

LETTER V.

Concert of the "Musik-Vereins Euterpe"—Symphony by Westmayer—Von Weber's
Oberon—Mdlle. Marie Wieck—Old and New School of Piano Forte playing.

LEIPZIG, January 27, 1852.

THESE concerts are similar to the celebrated Gewandhaus
Concerts. They are held in a somewhat smaller room, and at
a small subscription price, and are given only once in two
weeks. The orchestra consists of about sixty talented musicians, and if Dreyschock and David are not seen leading the
violins here as at the Gewandhaus, they, together with the other
instruments, string and wind, are in the hands of artists of deservedly high reputation. The selections are also of the highest order, and the Euterpe presents its patrons with the works
of the great masters in a style worthy of a Leipzig concert.

At a quarter of an hour before the time of commencement,
the members of the orchestra were in their places, talking,
tuning and getting ready. This, together with the general conversation of the people assembled, produces a *buzzing* chorus of

great power—a chorus with which the Leipzig concerts commence. Every ticket was sold at an early hour, and of course every seat was occupied.

The concert commenced precisely at the hour appointed, with a new Sinfonie in E flat Major, in manuscript, by W. Westmayer, who conducted the performance. He is a young candidate for fame, who has been educated at the Conservatory here, and who is regarded as already a successful composer. The Sinfonie consisted of four parts, and occupied in its performance exactly thirty-eight minutes. I dare not attempt anything like a particular description of it, or comparison of it with other like compositions; it was listened to with good attention by a discriminating audience, and met a favorable reception. It seemed to me, however, to want light and shade, and variety in the treatment of the different subjects introduced. Parts of it were exceedingly interesting, considered in reference to modern combinations and contrasts of the different orchestral elements, but there was a too constant *forte*, and a too frequent reiteration of the tonic and dominant harmony, with brass instruments, in military rhythm—this, indeed, is a general resort of such composers as are sometimes at a loss for an idea, or in a similar condition with the public speaker who is obliged to speak, but has nothing in particular to say. I do not mean that Mr. Westmayer was *minus thought*, but still there was not such a flow as we often find in a Mozart.

The Sinfonie was truly good, and seemed to give much satisfaction—and yet I could not help thinking that it was an excellent preparation for the high appreciation of the next orchestral piece, which was no less an overture than the celebrated No. 2, C Major, to Leonore, and which was given with an effect far beyond what can be often heard.

The overture by C. M. Von Weber, to Oberon, was **also**

played with such an energy and brilliancy as to take one's breath away. The stillness of the *pianos*, the gradual and immense range of the *crescendos*, the thundering power of the *fortes*, with instantaneous *contrasts* and startling *sfortzandos*, were enough to work up the feelings to a perfect phrenzy. Wonderfully effective were these ever favorite overtures by Beethoven and Weber.

It was no small attraction of this concert that the piano forte was played by the Fräulein MARIE WIECK, the sister of the celebrated Clara, wife of Robert Schumann. Mdlle. Wieck is a very superior player; she has not the strong hand of a DeMeyer or a Listz, but she has a most finished touch, and plays with great elegance and expression. Her first piece (hear it, oh ye of the exclusive modern school,) was nothing more nor less than Dussek's 12th Concerto in E flat major, the Adagio and Allegro movements of which she played—a most beautiful composition, elegant and tasteful in the highest degree, played both by the principal and by the orchestra as near perfection as such things can be done. There is nothing in the music to astonish, or to excite wonder or surprise, but there is that in it which is adapted to call forth perfect delight. It is full of peace, and innocence, and purity, and joy, and it is from beginning to end a constant appeal to the perception of the beautiful. I am no enemy to the modern school; it is indispensable to an accomplished pianist, and every well-educated musician will delight in it; but they err who suppose that in *Clementi* and *Cramer* and *Dussek* and *Pleyel*, there is nothing good or worth being saved. The fact is, the pianists, previous to him who is generally regarded as the head of the great modern school, had worked out a very satisfactory solution of the problem of piano forte playing, or certainly so if considered with reference to the more natural and legitimate powers of the instrument. Thal-

berg, Listz, and others, have certainly much enlarged the
boundaries, or the available capacities of the piano, but some of
their followers have gone to extremes; so much so that there
has seemed to be danger of losing altogether the ordinary effects
of piano forte playing, or that they would he swallowed up in
the extraordinary feats of left-hand melodies, flights of octaves,
and the various methods by which amazement and wonder are
excited.   Thanks for the signs of returning soberness and good
sense; we greatly mistake if other authors like Dussek are not
yet to be brought back to the concert room, and to the parlor,
to fill with delight the spirit of the true lover of music, and
of the most beautiful of all keyed instruments, the piano forte.

A word to another class.   There are some who condemn altogether the modern school, and who seem to suppose that all
true musical genius left the world with Haydn and those of his
day.   Fräulein WIECK is not of their number, for while she
played Dussek, in the first part of the concert, she played not
Thalberg, or Listz, or DeMeyer in the second part, but Pagan-
nini!   Yes, the Carnival of Venice, arranged for the piano, and
if music pleased legitimately in Dussek, the *Fräulein* excited
no small degree of feeling by her exquisite touch, and facility of
execution in the composition of the Prince of violinists.   What
if it be mere trickery; a dexterous artifice will always, at least,
call forth admiration, and one does not always want to sit in
sober judgment, and decide on the grounds of intrinsic musical
merit—relaxation must be indulged, the beautiful give way to
the ornamental, and true pleasure to mere amusement.   If
there is a time for all things, surely there is room enough for
the old and new school of piano forte playing—yes, and for
both schools of organ playing too, although this is not the place
to dwell upon the latter.

There was still another interesting feature in the Euterpe

Concert—it was the singing of Mdlle. LOUISE WOLFL. She sang an air from Stradella by Flotow, and also two German songs, the latter by Franz Schubert. A pretty singer, but not superior to several American vocalists.

The principal point of interest in the concerts here, to an American, seems to be the excellence of the orchestral performance. This satisfies.

LETTER VI.

Gewandhaus Concert—Julius Rietz—Harman's new Symphony—Cherubini—Beethoven —Rossini—Mendelssohn.

LEIPZIG, January 30, 1852.

PERHAPS there is not a series of subscription concerts in the world of a deservedly higher reputation than that of the Gewandhaus, Leipzig; and this is equally true both in relation to the character of the music selected, and the manner in which it is performed. The circumstances under which these concerts are produced are highly favorable, and cannot fail, ordinarily, to lead to the most happy results. The room is neither too large nor too small, though, perhaps, its dimensions might be somewhat extended without injury. The concerts are universally popular; the lovers of music are always there; everybody who loves music, and can procure a ticket, is engaged on Thursday evening, and the many professors of music (including those of the Conservatory), the musical students, and the critics, with all the piano forte ladies, and all other musical ladies, are there. They go, too, for musical purposes; not so much to see or be seen as to listen to the productions of the great composers, or to those of some young aspirant for musical fame, who is so fortunate as to obtain the consent of the government to the performance of his works. Expectation is awake, and good music, well done, is looked for and demanded by the large and intelligent audience. Indeed, the Gewandhaus Concert is a kind of high school, where taste is formed 'in the young, and perfected in the old, and where the knowledge of musical science, the appreciation and love of musical art, and the general state and progress of both, are made manifest.

It may be regarded also as a tribunal, the approval of which is a sure passport to the young performer ; for he who can give satisfaction here, need not fear to appear before any truly enlightened audience in the world. This last remark, however, it may be necessary to receive with some restriction applied to the students of the " *Conservatorium der Musik*," to whom there is sometimes an indulgence extended amounting almost to partiality or favoritism, They are as children, and what parent can see the faults of his child ? The members of the orchestra may all be regarded as solo players ; every instrument is well played, and every performer is capable of executing the most difficult passages at once, so that a single rehearsal only is necessary, even for a new complicated symphony—and that not for anything belonging to the technics of art, but only for the higher points of taste and expression. The Conductor (Julius Rietz) is a thorough musician of the German school, a man of much experience, who has the full confidence of the members of the orchestra and of the musical community. He is well acquainted with the works of the best composers, and knows how to bring them out in the careful observance of all those little nice points of delicacy and taste, upon which the highest and best effect depends. The rehearsals are private and exclusive ; they are *thorough*, but not *tedious*. Indeed it is but necessary to name the point, or to describe with accuracy the effect desired, when the *finger*, the *bow*, or the *embouchure*, responds immediately to the conductor's conception of the passage, and the *ideal* becomes *real*.

The orchestra being well prepared at the rehearsal, the conductor's duty becomes a very simple one at the performance; hence there are no violent gesticulations, stampings, bowings or see-sawings of the head, scraping of the feet, or showing off of the baton, but all is calm and quiet, and a simple indication of the time, with some slight occasional variations for different forms of dynamic effect, is all that is necessary. A thorough knowledge of music and of composition, an acquaintance with the capacity of every instrument and its proper use and effect, a perfect control of time, decision, firmness, entire self-possession and control, gentleness of manner, affability, courtesy—these are among the indispensable requisites in a conductor, and these our Gewandhaus conductor seems to possess.

Are not the circumstances then (some of which have been mentioned) so favorable as to justify the patrons of these concerts in expecting and demanding a high degree of perfection in the performances ?

The concert last evening was, perhaps, inferior to the general average. A principal point of attraction is always found in the *Symphony*, and on this occasion it was not a Mozart, a Beethoven, or a Mendelssohn, but an original manuscript composition of a member of the Orchestra, Ferd. Hermann, that was performed. Herr Hermann directed his own Symphony. It did not meet with a very warm reception, though sufficiently so to afford good encouragement to the author and his friends. There is always so much caution and incredulity, and sometimes suspicion, envy and jealousy abroad, that the path to fame, even to true merit, is rough and beset with difficulties.

Our author, we suppose, could not complain of the manner in which his work was received, and probably a young composer does not often obtain greater approbation. There were undoubtedly fine points in the Symphony, indicating talent, taste and judgment. Its themes were concise and clear, and there seemed to be a considerable degree of the effusion of genuine feeling, without dry detail, commonplace thoughts, or tedious repetitions. The instrumentation was quite well balanced, though the Oboe was, perhaps, somewhat too prominent in the melodic passages; a greater variety of coloring in this respect might be an improvement. The thoughts were easy, natural and chaste, but yet never so striking as to call forth a rapturous or involuntary exclamation of delight or applause. The interest too was well sustained through the four movements, and although we suppose that the critics will not allow to this Symphony a higher place than mediocrity, yet the young author may be well contented with the award bestowed, return to his study, and try again.

Signor Stigelli, a Tenor, from the Royal Italian Opera, London, sang with approbation ; Carl Deichmann, a Violinist, from Hanover, played with entire success, a Concerto, by Vieux Temps ; an aria by Julius Rietz, (Conductor,) was charmingly sung by Miss Mayer, coming seemingly fresh from the heart, on the tones of a sweet voice.

The omission to send the above by the last week's mail, enables me to add a word in relation to the concert of last evening, the *sixteenth* of the season. Owing to the fact (I suppose) that there were several distinguished solo singers here, the first part of the concert consisted more of vocal music than usual. A chorus of men's voices was also introduced, and large extracts were given from Cherubini's opera of " Ali

Baba," and from Rossini's " Wilhelm Tell," also an aria from
Don Juan by Mozart. Two overtures were admirably played,
viz. : Leonore No. 2, Beethoven, and William Tell, Rossini.
The fine chorus of men's voices added much to the interest of
the concert, but the principal piece was the charming A minor
Symphony No. 3, by Mendelssohn. I have often heard this
magnificent production of Mendelssohn performed at home, but
it is no discredit to our orchestras to say that it is quite a different thing when given with the precision of the Gewandhaus
orchestra. I will attempt no description ; suffice it to say that
it was the perfection of orchestral music—so soft and so loud,
so melancholy and so joyful, so exciting and so soothing, so expressive and so effective—imagine it, ye who have no opportunity of hearing it.

LETTER VII.

Sketch of Moscheles, the celebrated Pianist.

LEIPZIG, February 16, 1852.

This veteran of the piano forte, who has established for himself
so high a reputation, and who was for many years the prince of
the piano in London, has resided for the last six years in Leipzig as professor in the " Conservatorium der Musik ;" in this
institution he occupies the place for which he is so eminently
qualified, and is the principal teacher of his favorite instrument.
Mendelssohn was his particular friend, and it was at the great
composer's urgent solicitation that Moscheles gave up his lucra-
tive situation in London, and came to Leipzig, to devote the
remainder of his life, in connection with his young friend, to the

cause of musical education, and the building up of a high school for music here. Mendelssohn was young, but Moscheles was already past the meridian of life. Little did he expect to survive his talented friend; but while the elder of the two still lives, the highly-gifted Mendelssohn was taken away while yet in early life. While the musical world most deeply mourns his loss, every mouth is filled with his praise, and his name seems destined to live with those of Bach, Handel, Mozart and Beethoven.

We well remember when, some thirty years since, Moscheles, Kalkbrenner, and Ries, formed the great trio of piano forte composers, performers, and teachers. Cramer still lived, though he had mostly retired from public life. No man had ever stood higher as a pianist than Cramer; no one has since stood higher, and probably no one ever will. His works are among the musical classics, and must be studied by every one who would excel. But this trio of writers who immediately succeeded Cramer, seemed to enlarge the compass of the instrument, and to cause it to speak, if not with a more chaste, beautiful, or better language, yet with a more extensive vocabulary. Ries and Kalkbrenner too, after having obtained a high reputation, passed away—*they are not*—and Moscheles seems now almost the only remaining link of connection between the old and new schools. He is the enlightened and warm advocate of improvement, and he has done much not only for the piano, but for music generally; but he goes not with those who, by new systems of notation, or by any mechanical training of the hand, rather impede than accelerate the progress of science or art. The Hand-Guide of Kalkbrenner he never approved. He well knows that all dexterity of finger must be achieved according to the natural laws of exercise; industry and perseverance in the proper use and training of the muscles can only insure success.

He knows of no short, patent, or royal road to musical excellence; but insists upon the same drilling or training now that he did when he commenced his professional career in London.

Moscheles stands very high not only as a teacher and composer, but also as a performer. I well remember being at a select music party at his house in London in '37. Several distinguished pianists were there, one of whom now fills the world with his praise, and has been called the king of the piano forte —himself once Moscheles's pupil. The Chevalier Neukomm was there, and in the course of the evening, being in conversation with that distinguished man, I asked him the question, " Who is the greatest living pianist ?" " I think HE is," replied the Chevalier, pointing to Moscheles.

M. Moscheles retains his powers, and is still fresh and young. He is always busy, as he is full of teaching, and has much to do in connection with the conservatory ; yet he finds time to entertain a stranger, and to amuse and instruct one by many musical anecdotes and reminiscences. He knows with familiarity, the history of music and of musical composers, vocalists and instrumentalists, for well nigh half a century. His position in London as teacher, composer, and conductor, brought him into connection with many of the first musical men, and he profited well by his experience. He was the friend, and is, as is well known, the biographer of Beethoven ; and he has many relics of the great symphonist, which he shows with pleasure to those persons who are interested in such things. Among the manuscripts which I saw, was the first sketch of the great Mass in D, (Beethoven's Second Mass,) the leading thoughts merely being written down in a character not easy to decypher, and which would be as unintelligible to many a one who thinks he understands music, as the hieroglyphics on an ancient Egyptian monument. This sketch is contained in a sketch-book, in which *first thoughts* of several of Beethoven's compositions appear. Such a sketch-book he is said always to have carried with him, in which he made a hasty record of passing thoughts. From these he selected, in study hours, the most worthy, and elaborated them in such form and connection as his excellent taste and good judgment dictated. The sketch-book, as Mr. Moscheles told me, clearly proves that Beethoven did not always rely upon first thoughts, but that he frequently modified them according to the dictates of a careful judgment. This is probably true of all the great writers. It was so with Mendelssohn, whose after thoughts were often preferred and adopted, even although the composition containing them was already published. Hence the disagreement that sometimes appears between the English and German copies of the works of Mendelssohn; for after a work was published in one country he would sometimes alter and improve upon it, before it was allowed to appear in the other.

The sketch book of Beethoven contains first thoughts of other compositions, and especially of variations upon a waltz of Diabelli, in respect to which Moscheles related to me the following circumstances. Diabelli, who was a publisher of music in Vienna, a friend and companion of Beethoven, and also a good musician, composed a waltz with which he, the composer, was much pleased, and which, though of a popular and taking character, was truly chaste and elegant. The idea occurred to him of getting from distinguished composers to the number of fifty, variations, and then to publish his waltz in connection with them. Accordingly he wrote letters to eminent musicians, sending his waltz, mentioning his plan, and asking from each a variation. Moscheles was himself one of the number to whom application was made. Diabelli called on Beethoven, and made known his wishes to him. Beethoven, amused with the novelty of the project, promised to do his part. After some months,

and when returns had been received from many to whom appli
cation had been made, Diabelli called on Beethoven for his
contribution. It was not ready; indeed it had been forgotten,
but Beethoven promised it in a week. A week passed away
and a second call was made, and a second disappointment experienced, the variation had not been written; he was promised
however that without fail it should be ready on a certain day.
On the day appointed Diabelli called for the third time, when
Beethoven coming into the room with his paper said, "Ah, my
dear Diabelli, you asked me for one variation, but here are
thirty-three," and he actually presented him with thirty-three
variations instead of one. They were immediately published,
extensively circulated, and much admired. (See Beethoven's
120th work.) The other fifty variations were also published,
but those by Beethoven obtained the decided preference.

Moscheles has original manuscripts of many of the great
musical composers; but nothing that he can produce will be
looked upon with more interest than his letters from Mendelssohn. These he has very carefully bound together so as to
preserve them in safety; they are between seventy and eighty
in number, and are on various musical, literary, and artistic
subjects. They are beautifully written, sometimes embellished
with illustrative drawings with the pen, and are full of humor,
wit, and good feeling. One of them, for example, after the
words "Dear Moscheles," begins with an *intrada*, or trumpet
salutation. It is carefully written, on a staff made with the pen
at the moment, without a rule, in small notes, and a more
joyful or heartfelt greeting cannot be conceived. Another, a
congratulation on the birth of Moscheles's son Felix, (now pursuing his studies in Paris as an artist,) commences with various
orchestral instruments hastily sketched with a pen, with a host
of violins descending as angels of music from heaven; a most

beautiful design indeed, which Mendelssohn proceeds to explain, when leaving his musical symbols, he has recourse to letters and words.   Moscheles Piano Forte Pastoral Concerto (op 96 in D) was composed for Mendelssohn and dedicated to him. In Mendelssohn's letter written in acknowledgment of the receipt of the Concerto, and which is highly complimentary to the author, he has drawn a landscape representing pastoral life, with mountains and valleys, flocks, herds, houses, &c., including a village church with its joyfully ringing bell, as illustrative of the ideas suggested to his mind as he played over the music of his friend.   The letters are here, too, in which Mendelssohn first opens his mind on the subject of the conservatory, and in which he urges Moscheles to come to Leipzig and join him in carrying out his favorite project.

During a visit to Moscheles, when I gathered the materials for this communication, as well as many other pieces of interesting information which I cannot now mention, he was so kind as to play to me for half an hour or more, various piano forte studies and other music, illustrative of the powers and progress of the instrument.

Moscheles's own works for the piano are much used; his printed studies are as follows—24 Studies for piano forte, op. 70; 12 Characteristic Studies, op. 95; 2 Studies originally published in Beethoven's album, op. 105; 2 Grand Studies, being part of a complete method by Moscheles and Fetzs; 4 Grand Concert Studies, op. 111; Daily Companion, or practical and progressive exercises for two performers, op. 107.

He has recently published (by Kistner, Leipzig,) a grand Sonata (op. 121 in E) for Piano Forte and Violincello.   The Concertmeister David, (the well known Violinist,) has adapted the Violincello part for the Violin, as he has also done with Mendelssohn's Sonatas.   Moscheles, although a very popular

performer, has retired from all public playing; yet he is not
slow to encourage young aspirants for fame. His influence is
on the side of truly scientific music, like that of Beethoven and
Mendelssohn, nor will he do anything to patronize a more
superficial style or flippant taste, either in composition or in
playing. As a teacher, it is as well his object to form the taste
as the hand. Would that his example in this respect were followed by all teachers, and that our young pianists would practice with diligence and perseverance his studies, and other
similar works, rather than spend their energies upon the many
mountebank trickeries of some modern writers.

LETTER VIII.

Seventeenth Gewandhaus Concert—Ferdinand David—Gluck's "Iphegenie in Tauride"
—Madame Sontag—Central Hall Concert.

LEIPZIG, February 21, 1852.

THIS Concert was particularly attractive to the musical people of Leipzig, from the fact that the singer was *Mad. Sontag*,
by marriage the Countess Rossi. The weather was unfavorable, being rainy, and the streets were muddy. I took my place
at the door of the Gewandhaus at half-past four, where the
people were then gathering. By five, when the outer door
was opened, a multitude had assembled, and immediately
rushed into the house, filling the long stairway and entry.
Here was another interval of waiting, until half-past five,
when the door of the hall was opened, and the room was
immediately filled. We had now to wait another hour, or
until half-past six ; when the performance commenced with
a symphonie, by Joseph Hadyn in C, very light, playful,

and pleasing, but lacking the depth of a Beethoven or a Mendelssohn. It is so easy a composition, that it seemed to be quite children's play for the orchestra, who yet rendered it in the most perfect manner possible. This was followed by an Arie from "*Rinaldo*" by Handel; a most charming song indeed, and as charmingly sung by Mad. Sontag. Of Mad. Sontag's singing, I dare not speak now. I will only say that *no one can have a more perfect execution;* but to say in what her excellence consists, as a singer, or what are the peculiarities of her style, must not *now* be attempted.

The third piece was "*Romanze for the Violin*," by Beethoven; performed by Herr Concertmeister, *Ferdinand David.* This is the *David* whose compositions for the violin are so well known, and whose reputation as a player is so extensive. Mad. Sontag then sang "*Bel raggio lusinghier*," from Rossini's Semiramide, a song requiring the greatest powers of vocalization; this was perfectly given by the inimitable artist.

The second part consisted of the Overture and a long scene from Gluck's famous "*Iphigenie in Tauride;*" the principal vocal part being that of Iphigenie by Mad. Sontag. Gluck has not been heard with us, but he ranks in the very first class of composers here. The overture is a magnificent concert piece, and it was performed by this fine orchestra with wonderful precision and effect. Beethoven's *Overture to Egmont* closed the musical entertainments of the evening, and well repaid one for his *Two Thalers*, (cost of a ticket,) and for all the previous waiting, wetting, and crowding necessary to secure a place to stand up.

Mad. Sontag is gone, and the Gewandhaus Orchestra is thrown upon its own strength and resources; but it fails not, neither is it faint or weary. The Eighteenth Concert was (save the charming singer) one of the very best of the season. The Orchestra (said one who has often heard) never played better; well might they feel the inspiration of their author, for they played *Beethoven's* 4*th Symphonie*, than which he has not written a better. It is not so well known in America, but it cannot rank second to anything which Beethoven has composed.

The *adagio* (sextuple movement) is as perfect in design and as beautiful in coloring as in any work of musical art. Fräulein *Anna Klassig* sang a *Recitative and Arie from Sphor's Jessonda.* Herr *G. Krüger*, from Stuttgart, played two pieces well on the Harp; and a well-trained choir, *Pauliner Sänger-Vereins*, of fifty men's voices sung three pieces, two of which were by Mendelssohn, and one of which may be found in the "Fireside Harmony" (*Waserfahrt.*) Mendelssohn's Overture "*Melusine*," as fine an Overture as exists, was played; and the performance was worthy of the composition.

These Concerts are very popular and fashionable. The Musical Professors are all there, expectation is fully awake, and I believe almost always fully gratified.

Mad. Sontag has left Leipzig for Dresden, where she will undoubtedly create as great a sensation as she has here. I hope to notice her more particularly hereafter.

The next evening (20th February), I attended one of the cheap, *eating, drinking, smoking, talking, sitting-round-the-table, wearing-hat*, &c., &c., &c., Concerts. The Orchestra numbered about thirty performers. It was really a fine Orchestra, though it appeared feeble in strings, (having only four violins on a part,) after listening to the Gewandhaus band. Beethoven's Sym. No. 7, was played, and also Weber's Overture to Oberon —with other music, including a very excellent new overture (manuscript) by W. Herfuth. The contrast was really a very excellent one, but it suffered in comparison with that of the preceding evening ; and the room was too much filled with to-bacco smoke and noise for comfort.

LETTER IX.

Mad. Sontag—the two *Styles* of Singing Compared—Mara—Catalani—Wagner—Lind—Sontag.

LEIPZIG, February 28, 1852.

How shall we speak of this vocalist, or to whom shall we compare her ? The power of language has been exhausted on inferior or commonplace artists. Excellent, beautiful, charming, delightful, and other like adjectives fail ; and words cannot give an idea of Sontag, because by their common use they have lost their significance, and because it is really quite impossible for any one to imagine what her singing is who has not heard her, or some one of the very few real artists who take rank with her. Those, however, who have heard Jenny Lind (and she is, perhaps, the only person living to whom Sontag can be likened), will be prepared to understand what may be truly said of Sontag, and to appreciate and enjoy her singing. Both these artists belong to the same general school, and both excel in the same department ; but yet they are not alike, not even when they represent the same character, or sing the same song.

Singing (so also music generally, and other fine arts), may be divided into two general classes, or styles, corresponding to the *sublime* and the *beautiful* in nature. These have been sometimes designated by the terms *great* and *small ;* or, with qualifications and exceptions, *serious* and *humorous ;* or, when carried to extremes, *tragic* and *comic ;* and singers as well as actors usually excel in the one style or in the other. There may be now and then one who does well in both, (Garrick for example;) but true excellence in both departments is not to be looked for in the same person.

It is the office of the *great* style to move the deeper feelings of the soul, or to call forth the most powerful emotions belonging to humanity ; and this it does sometimes by strains the most simple, or even by a single tone; while at others, a similar effect may be produced by an immense volume of voice, or by great executive power. The style which has been called *small*, (only, however, in a good sense of the term,) excites the gentler feelings, brings up to the imagination figures of beauty and loveliness, and fills the soul with pure delight.

The natural qualifications indispensable to any high degree of excellence in either department are very rarely found; hence there are but few *good* singers in the same age, or existing on the stage at the same time. But yet we are confined mostly to the present generation for illustration of our subject, since the singer's art, as it admits not of record, cannot be handed down to posterity, but perishes with him. But few can form any adequate idea of the great vocalists who have heretofore lived; we can but with great difficulty carry the remembrance of excellence in the singer's art for any considerable time, and we are very apt to think the *last* the *best*. It is safe to assume, however, that *Mara*, for example, excelled in the *great* style ; for history tells us that she gave a character to the sublime songs of Handel and other old masters, that no one since her time has been able to do. But how shall we get an idea of what Mara's rendering of "I know that my Redeemer liveth," really was? We cannot. Or rather, every one will form an idea in accordance to the materials he has accumulated, or to what he has heard of the power of song. Every one says the song which we have mentioned is *great ;* but every young lady who has spent a few years in vocal music, thinks that she can sing it, for she has taken it month after month for a lesson, has sung it to her teacher for years, and he has often told her that she sings it well, and this has been fully confirmed by her parents and friends ; and still she may not have any adequate perception of the song—of its immensity, or deep spirituality, or of the extensive natural powers both mental and physical, thoroughly developed, necessary for any just rendering of the mighty conception of *Handel* and *Job.**

Catalani was also *great,* or belonged to the *great* school, if we may credit the reports of those still living who were familiar with her manner ; and she is said to have produced the most sublime effects with a very simple melody. A gentleman who heard her, told me, that she would sing the national anthem, " *God save the King,*" calling forth the deepest reverence and awe, hushing to perfect silence a mixed multitude who had assembled to hear her, and filling the minds of all with an overwhelming idea of greatness and immensity. But although *Mara* and *Catalani,* both belonged to the *great* school, it does not, therefore, follow that they were alike. Perhaps it may be safe to say that it belonged to *Mara* to speak, in deep-felt yet simple tones, to the heart; and to *Catalani* by her immense power of voice, to excite feelings of awe and reverence, or by

* We hope we shall not be understood to discourage our young vocalists from the study of this or other similar songs. Handel must be sung; the Messiah must be sung; and wherever the Messiah is sung, " I know that my Redeemer liveth," must be sung also. We have heard it done creditably by young American singers. We would recommend the study of this, and of other songs of Handel, to every one whose musical aim is high.

the overcoming of extreme difficulties of execution, to awaken those of wonder and astonishment. Of living artists *Grisi* may be classed with those who can sing in the *great* style; though she belongs rather to that department which may be called *tragic*. *Viardôt Garcia* also moves in the same lofty sphere, and is probably the first singer in the world, in this style; and to the same class, too, belongs the *Fräulein Wagner* of Berlin.

We do not know whether we have succeeded in conveying to the minds of our readers an idea of what we mean by the *great style* in singing; but we feel quite certain that we can make ourselves understood when we speak of the *beautiful;* (*small*, technically;) for here we can illustrate our meaning by reference to one who has been extensively heard, and wherever heard admired, in America. To this style belongs Jenny Lind; and to this style also belongs the no less perfect artist, the Countess Rossi-Sontag. But while we assign to the same general class both of these inimitable artists, they are, as has already been said, unlike. We can only mention a few of the points of difference. Jenny Lind has a voice of higher compass; she has also more strength of lungs or command of breath, and can, therefore, prolong a tone to greater length, and sing with a greater degree of power than Sontag. On the other hand, Sontag has a richer low voice, and throughout its whole compass greater purity of tone. With respect to this point, Sontag's voice is perfect. And not only in their natural, but also in their acquired powers, do they differ; and the musicians, some of them say, that Sontag has the more perfect school. But we prefer not to express our opinion on this point, nor will we venture to say which has the greater execution; they are, in this respect, both stars of the first magnitude; and either of them is sufficiently bright to dazzle the eyes of a common beholder. When listening to Jenny Lind, we have thought that vocal execution could be carried no farther; and when listening to Sontag, we have felt quite sure that her's was the perfection of excellence, and have been disposed to class ourselves with those who think the *last* the *best*. One of the German critics has said that Sontag "has attained the very height of the science of song;" that "both in the technical and spiritual, she stands in a place which has not before been reached by any mortal, and that her performances may therefore with propriety be called supernatural." The same writer compares her to Jenny Lind, and says that "no one else living can claim so perfect a command over the vocal organs as these two artists."

Their favorite characters are the same; and the very parts in which Jenny Lind excelled, and out-rivaled every one else, are the same which Sontag represents better than they have ever been represented before. To her pre-eminent histrionic talent Sontag undoubtedly owes much of her great success ; her acting is certainly not inferior to her singing. But this is said also of Jenny Lind, and by highly intelligent critics, who have seen them both in the same character. In the part of Marie, (Fille du Regiment,) which was written, as we have been informed, originally for Sontag, Jenny Lind is said to have been successful in the highest degree in her acting, and to have united in a most remarkable and unprecedented manner the very simplicity of nature with her wonderful musical powers, pouring out the fulness of her soul in connection with the perfection of art in song. And following Sontag, as she did, she was thought by some even to surpass her; but now that Sontag has come up again after a retirement from public life of twenty years or more, and after having become the mother of many children, we see her rising to a point of perfection in *Marie* which it would seem has never before been attained. We see in her the bold soldier girl, (though always modest, lovely, and excellent,) having grown up with the regiment, and having deeply imbibed the military spirit, carrying with her the fruits of her education, the love of the parade, the march, the trumpet, and the drum, into the drawing-room, and manifesting her courage in strains of song the most artistic possible to be imagined: giving the boldest and most difficult passages, apparently with the greatest ease and freedom. Now, whether Sontag's or Jenny Lind's *Marie* is the better, either with respect to acting or singing, who shall determine? A similar comparison might be made of these two Queens of song, in other favorite characters, in which each in her turn surpasses the other; but we will attempt to carry it no further. Mad. Sontag is said to have resumed her profession in consequence of the loss of property, and of having a family of children to support and educate. It is remarkable that, after a retirement from public singing for so long a time, she should yet retain her full vocal powers; yet such, I am assured, is the fact. A gentleman who stands as high as any one in the musical profession here, and who heard her often during her former triumphs, assures me that so far from having lost, she has really gained, in purity of tone and in art; though her voice has undergone some change with respect to compass or pitch, having, as he observed, lost "two or three of its higher tones and gained three or four lower ones." Mad. Sontag is now traveling through Germany, with the most brilliant success. She has recently produced much excitement in Leipzig, as she does not fail to do wherever she goes, filling the houses to overflowing, notwithstanding the tickets of admission are doubled in price. Mad. Sontag and Jenny Lind are said to be the only two singers who have been able thus to advance the admission fee. She has sung here, in all, at *nine* different

performances—*eight* times in opera, and *once* in concert.   Her
characters were as follows :

Marie: "Daughter of the Regiment," (twice)............*Donizetti.*
Amina : "Somnambula.".................................*Bellini.*
Rosina : "Barber of Seville," (twice)....................*Rossini.*
Susanne : "Marriage of Figaro,"........................*Mozart.*
Martha : "Martha, or Market of Richmond," (twice).......*Flotow.*

In the Concert Room, her songs were "Lascia ch'io pianga,"
Rinaldo, by Handel; "Bel raggio lusinghier," Semiramide,
Rossini ; and a scene, Recitative and Arie from Gluck's Iphigenie in Tauride.   We have already spoken of her as Marie ; of
other characters, we will only say, that *Rosina* and *Martha* are
great favorites; and those persons who know what these are,
will have a correct idea of the principal characteristics of her
singing, and of the characters in which she stands pre-eminent—
unapproachable.   She was always greeted and recalled with
the most perfect enthusiasm on the part of the audience, amid
showers of bouquets and wreaths of flowers.   Her appearance is
highly interesting, especially after one becomes a little familiar
with her voice and movements.   She is indeed a fine looking
woman ; youthful and active, when she appears in public, as a
young lady of eighteen.   Her triumph in Leipzig was complete.

Mad. Sontag has the reputation of being an excellent woman,
a faithful wife, an affectionate mother, and a warm-hearted
friend.   She told me that she intends a professional visit to the
United States of America in the course of the coming Summer or
Autumn, naming August as the month in which she might probably sail.   She has had quite a number of propositions, but chooses
to keep herself free from all engagements by which she might
possibly be perplexed or embarrassed.   It is not true that she
has made arrangements for Thalberg, or any one else to accom-

pany her; though she may probably make provision for such aid as she may need, before leaving Europe. We heard her in Leipzig often, and we may venture to assure those who have been enraptured with Jenny Lind, that they will not be disappointed in Mad. Sontag. I know not whether she possesses the versatility of talent of Jenny Lind; but whether she has equal power to please a popular audience with "John Anderson," or "Comin' through the rye," or not, it is sure that the appreciator of perfection in the art of song must be fully satisfied with Mad. Sontag.

LETTER X.

"Thomaskirche"—Charity Pupils—Order of Service—The good Organist—Essential Qualifications.

LEIPZIG, March 1, 1852.

THE church of St. Thomas is a venerable and antique-looking building, both inside and out. The present edifice dates as far back as 1482. It is upwards of 280 feet long, and 115 feet wide. It has double galleries, as most of the churches seem to have here; besides which there are perhaps twenty or more private boxes or apartments, which I suppose belong to distinguished or wealthy persons. I have seen one of these occupied during a part of the sermon by clergymen, in their officials, several being present. At the altar, at the extreme end of the church, is a figure of the Saviour on the cross; and, during the service, candles are kept burning. Between this and the nave is a reading-desk; and in the nave, perhaps 180 feet from the altar, stands the pulpit. During the devotional services belonging to the officiating minister, or performed by him, he stands at the altar, in front of and facing the cross, and with his back to the people.

He does not remain there, however, during the singing exercises, but retires to an adjoining room. The organ loft is in the second gallery. The organ appears large, and shows in its outside front (as nearly as I could estimate) two hundred and thirty pipes. These are not gilded, as with us, but are of the natural color of the metal. The choir for the ordinary service consists of a few boys; perhaps a man or two, though I believe usually only boys. By the ordinary service, I mean that which includes no music except singing of the hymns, or chorales, which is always done by all the people. There is always an introductory motette sung by the choir, without any accompaniment; and when this is sung there is an extra choir, numbering say forty or fifty, and all the parts are represented, boys singing soprano. There is also, every other Sabbath morning, a motette by some of the great composers, performed with full orchestral accompaniments; and for this the number of the choir is still increased. But as soon as the singing is over, the members of the orchestra and choir all leave, with the exception of the boys, retained for the leading of the congregational chorales. There is, in connection with this church, a school where boys are fitted for the University. This school is large, and employs about fifteen teachers. Provision is made for the gratuitous education, and I believe support, of sixty pupils; and these charity pupils are the musical boys whence the choir is sustained. They are regularly taught music, and are required to sing on the Sabbath, on Saturday at $1\frac{1}{2}$ o'clock, and at funerals. On Saturday regularly at the hour mentioned, there is a short service, and the choir commence it by singing one or two motettes, without accompaniment. The same choir, with orchestra, alternate between the St. Thomas and the St. Nicholas Church; and the same motette is sung in one church which was sung in the other the previous Sabbath. I have heard fine pieces performed by the choir, by *Bach*, who was formerly organist here; and they sometimes sing *Palestrina;* motettes by *Mozart, Haydn*, and other modern authors, are often done. Yesterday, Sunday, 29th Feb., I was at St. Thomas. There was no motette with orchestra, on account of Lent. The services were as follows; the order is so different from ours, that I have thought it would be interesting to many to have it given in detail. I timed each piece, and give the time which each occupied.

1. Organ	2	minutes.
2. Motette, without accompaniment	9	"
3. Organ	1	"
4. Chorale	4	"
5. Liturgical service	2	"
6. Reading	2	"
7. Organ	½	"
8. Chorale	6	"
9. Reading	2	"
10. Organ	½	"
11. Chorale	14	"
12. Sermon (about)	35	"
13. Chorale	2	"

The motette (2) may be found, with a free translation of the words, at p. 290, CANTICA LAUDIS, "Though all earthly joys should perish"; and this will give some idea of what kind of music is done by the choir *without accompaniment.* The liturgical service (5) was chanted by the minister at the altar, with responses by the choir. The reading (6) was also at the altar, but the minister turned and faced the people. The reading (9) was from the reading desk. Sermon (12) from the pulpit. The ministers all wear a black robe, with a white surplice over it, as well in preaching as in prayer; also a large ruff, say two and a half or three inches wide, round the neck, as is seen in portraits of the Reformers and clergymen of 300 years ago. No fires in the churches, however cold. The service begins punctually at $\frac{1}{2}$ past 8 o'clock in the morning, and it requires something of an effort to be up and ready on the morning of a short and cold winter's day.

The following leading qualifications of a good organist, have been suggested to my mind, and may find a place in this letter :

1. He must be able to play his instrument. The degree of execution requisite will depend much upon the peculiar local circumstances of the congregation. In some churches, both in Roman Catholic and in Protestant countries, an ability to play difficult music will be required; but in general, in our New England churches, no very great execution or command of the instrument is indispensable ; and organists more frequently fail from other causes than from a want of skill in the technicals of their instrument. If called upon for some criterion or standard by which to try one's powers of performance, we might name Handel's choruses, or say the series of Handel's choruses. One who can play these has an abundant command of his instrument. It must be understood, too, that we have taken a standard which is rather high; indeed, higher than is often necessary ; for we have known very successful organists who had not the ability to play Handel. In fact, no great power of execution is necessary for the common purposes of the church service ; and it may be also true that one who can merely play psalmody and perhaps easy anthems, so as never to trip or touch the wrong key, will be a more successful church organist than one who can play John Sebastian Bach. Let it be understood that we object not to great power of execution, but only say that it is not essential.

2. A most important, nay absolutely essential qualification,

of a good church organist is, that he should have not only a true knowledge of his office, its nature and design, but that he should also possess a true feeling of sympathy and fellowship with all, be they cleric or lay, who are engaged in the promotion of the work in which he is called to take a part. The organ (like the minister's voice or powers of eloquence) is to be regarded only as a means to an end. This end should be kept constantly in view; and in proportion as this is done, the organist will feel that both himself and his instrument, with all musical science and art, occupy only a secondary place. Any true musician will have a sufficient love of music, and sympathy with *knowledge in science* and *skill in art;* but this is not the sympathy we mean, though often mistaken for it. In short, if a man has this sympathy, it will manifest itself in the love of the Sabbath, the ordinances of religion, and the parts of public service other than the musical. An organist who, after singing is over, leaves the church, or gives no attention to prayers or sermon, whatever other excellencies he may possess, has not this of which we speak, and cannot therefore be qualified for his work; for though one may have the gift of musical prophecy, or teaching, and understand all mysteries and all knowledge, and though he has faith to remove all mountains of difficulties, and has not charity, or this love of the work to which he is called, and sympathy with those who are also engaged in it, though in another department, it profiteth him nothing. Shall I furnish another *name* for the *thing* of which I speak? " *The fear of the Lord is the beginning of wisdom.*"

3. An organist, in order to be successful, must be a man of good judgment; or he must have good common sense in the application of the powers of his instrument to the circumstances of his situation. To be able to seize upon the surrounding circumstances, and when moved by them, to put forth the mighty

powers of his instrument, under the direction and control of a well-regulated judgment, is a high qualification indeed; nevertheless it is one without which no one can succeed well. Let the organist then seek for that wisdom which is profitable to direct.

4. An organist should have that control of himself which will enable him to exercise self-denial. Any one who is fit for an organist will, of course, love music; his soul will delight in it; but yet, in the church, certainly, it should never be the object of supreme devotion; and one will find it often, very often, necessary to make musical sacrifices to the great end of organists and ministers, and churches, *religion* or *religious improvement*. Mere musical effect, the exhibition of Handel or Mozart, be it repeated, is not that at which the organist should aim. I know there are musicians who assert the contrary; there are both organists and conductors of choirs with whom music is supreme, and who openly contend for the doctrine that the best musical performance *in itself considered* is the best adapted to church purposes, or, what is the same thing, the most acceptable to God. That the best musical performance, *all things considered*, is indeed the best, of course we admit; but there may be a very high degree of musical excellence without any appropriate religious adaptation, and a man may be a most excellent musician and organ-player who, for want of judgment or self-control, or self-denial, is but a poor church organist. Simple and unpretending strains, comparatively uninteresting in themselves, will often be the most effective in religious worship; indeed, if we are not mistaken, it will be found, in general, that as religious feeling prevails, and is intense or all absorbing, it seeks only for that musical expression which is most simple and natural. A good organist must therefore be able to deny himself the gratification which

musical science or art in itself affords, and seek and obtain a higher satisfaction in the promotion of the spiritual good of his fellow men.

We need not proceed further; for where the qualifications already pointed out exist, there will be no danger but that others will exist also, and that the individual possessing them will succeed, and be useful and happy in his profession. Where these are wanting, a Handel's genius, a Bach's skill, or a Mendelssohn's learning, will not be sufficient.

We add a simple remark. If congregations would take these things into view when about engaging an organist, seeking for other qualifications than those which are merely musical, many difficulties would be avoided, and occasions would much more seldom occur of trouble between organist and singers, or organist and ministers or people.

LETTER XI.

Musik-Vereins-Euterpe—Gluck—Cherubini—Bach—Part-Songs by Men's Voices—Beethoven.

LEIPZIG, March 12, 1852.

AN excellent concert was given by the Euterpe on the evening of the 9th inst. This orchestra, though regarded as inferior to that of the Gewandhaus, is, nevertheless, fully competent to put life into any of the compositions of the great masters; it can expound Beethoven, make clear his meaning, and bring one into communion with his spirit, as was abundantly manifested on the present occasion. It numbers ten violins on a part, five double basses, an equal number of violincellos, and a complete set of wind instruments. A perfect knowledge and command of his instrument, a clear perception of the music to be performed, and the will to do the exact thing necessary, in the best possible manner, seems to belong to each performer. A universal determination to succeed seems to prevail; every man is not only competent to the discharge of his duty, but is at his post, watchful and ready, heart and hand, to put forth his whole power, according to the circumstances, at the indication of the *baton*. Why should not the result be satisfactory ?

A rich programme was presented this evening. The concert opened with an overture which is a great favorite here, and often played in public, though I have not heard it in America,— " *Iphigene in Aulis*," by Gluck. It is a charming overture, and any one's musical reputation might safely rest on the production of a single piece like this. Its subjects are at once natural and beautiful, and they are always treated in a most masterly manner; with elaborateness it is always intelligible, and with copiousness it is never diffuse. There is no departing from the main topic of discourse, no wandering in the mazes of thick darkness, or searching for ideas, but the leading thoughts are kept ever before the mind, presented now in *this* form, and now in *that*. Its analogies are perfect, its contrasts are striking, and its light and shade are applied with the hand of a Raphael or a Turner. It is full of pleasing melody, yet always subject to the laws of good taste, and manifesting both genius and science ; it is in the performance, perhaps, equally satisfactory both to the musician and to the mere unstudied lover of song.

The second piece was an extract (first and second movements) of Cherubini's Requiem, written for male voices. This, which is one of Cherubini's great works, was written under circumstances somewhat exciting, as I remember to have heard years ago. On some funeral occasion when a Requiem was desired, that which he had previously written was rejected, because composed for a mixed choir; this caused him to put forth his energies in the production of a mass for men's voices only. The music throughout is of a very high character, though it would not much interest those who desire musical gratification only from *pretty tunes* or *pleasant voices.* The first movement, " *Requiem aeternam*," with its accompaniment of violoncellos and double basses, is plaintive and sad, and tells only of sorrow, penitence and grief. In the " *Dies irae*," the full powers of the orchestra are brought into requisition; and uniting, as was the case on the present occasion, with sixty well-trained and fearless men's voices, the effect was awfully grand and commanding. The majestic movements, the severely dissonant harmonies, the wailings of the strings, the frightful appeals of the instruments of blast and percussion, and the cryings out of the voices, all combined to produce an effect which was, at times, truly terrific and overwhelming. The nineteen stanzas, however, have furnished an opportunity for musical contrasts which have been well introduced, affording variety and relief.

The third piece was the very unique but, to the musician, highly interesting " *Concert für* 2 *claviere* (*c moll*) *Von J. S. Bach*. Following the Requiem, it was like a delightful calm after a storm, enabling one to realize where he was, to breathe easily again, and put on a cheerful countenance.

Several part-songs were then sung by the " *Mannerchor*" without accompaniment.

The second part consisted of the " *Sinfonie in C minor, by L. Von Beethoven*." What a symphonie this is? We have often heard it, and it is well known in America. We will not attempt a description; we listened with intense interest to the whole of it, hardly daring to breathe in the *piano* and not having the power to do so in the *forte* passages. Is it strange then, that, whether "in the body or out of the body" at its close, we should not be able to tell?

LETTER XII.

Robert Schumann, the Composer—Clara Schumann, the Pianist—Their Great Concert.

LEIPZIG, March 13, 1852.

THE concert was given in the saloon of the Gewandhaus, by
Robert and Clara Schumann. The conductor was Robert
Schumann himself; the pianist was his wife. The orchestra
was large, and the best that Leipzig could furnish. Robert
Schumann has great celebrity, and especially in those cities
where he has resided and has brought out his music under his
own immediate direction. No one since Mendelssohn's death
stands so high in the estimation of the German musicians.
There are places where he is not known, because his music is
not understood; but even in these, and throughout Germany,
he is regarded as standing at the very head of his profession,
and no one commands as he does the universal attention of
scientific men. Some go so far as to regard him as the greatest symphonist that has ever lived; but time can only determine
this.

The concert had been advertised for some time, and the expectations of the lovers of music were fully awake. Not only
were the musicians and lovers of music of Leipzig present, but
literary and scientific men of the various professions, and the
beauty, and wealth, and fashion of the city came to do homage
to talent of so high an order, and to learning so extensive.
Like the people at Lystra, so here, they lifted up their voices,
saying, not in the speech of Lycaonia, but in that of Saxony,
" The gods are come down to us in the likeness of men."

I suppose that in no part of the world is greater respect paid
to men of genius, talent or learning than in Germany; and certainly nowhere else are musical gifts or attainments so fully

appreciated and so highly honored. Mendelssohn was wor-
shiped while he lived, and since his ascension his mantle seems
to have rested upon Robert Schumann. But it was not only
from this city that the audience was gathered on this occasion;
it had been noised abroad that this concert was to be given, and
musical men of high standing, *Kapellmeisters* and *Concertmeis-
ters*, from the region round about, came up to Leipzig. Berlin,
Dresden, Weimar, and other places were represented. At the
head of this foreign company, and indeed at the head of the
whole company, was LISZT ;—*the very* LISZT *himself* came from
Weimar to listen, and to pay honor to greatness. But Robert
Schumann is not alone, he has a "help meet" indeed. *Clara
Wieck* was perhaps the most distinguished female pianist who
has ever lived; and, unlike many ladies, she did not give up her
instrument when she became *Clara Schumann*, but rather devoted herself with greater assiduousness under her new instructor, than she had previously done under the teachings of
her father, to the profession which had been the choice of both
her husband and herself. No wonder that the people should
assemble on the occasion of a visit from this far-famed couple.
But they came not to hear any one *sing* or *play on an instrument*, for although the *wife* is indeed a most accomplished pianist, yet the *husband* neither plays nor sings; but they rather
came to hear the new music that the master had produced.
They looked for some new musical revelation, for new chords
(if possible), or new progressions; at least some new method
of treatment, or harmonic development was expected. It was
not to be the same tune over again. They went away satisfied;
for, not only was the musical performance pronounced to be
one of the very best, but the music, or the principal piece of
attraction, was regarded as worthy of its author.

The first piece was the " *Overture zu L. Byron's Manfred*

von R. Schumann." This is an overture in the true learned
German style, and as unlike the overtures of the modern Italian
and French schools as can be imagined; of course, it cannot be
popular, that is, it cannot take with the people generally; on
this occasion, however, it was fully appreciated and listened to,
by one of the most intelligent musical audiences that could be
brought together in Germany, with unmingled delight.   The
second piece was " *Concert No.* 2, *F moll, für Piano Forte mit
Begleitung des orchester, von F. Chopin,*" performed by Clara
Schumann.   This is said to be in Chopin's peculiar style, and
one of his most difficult productions.   Mad. Schumann played
it with apparent ease, and with a delicacy of touch and distinctness of articulation not to be excelled.   She has not so great a
power as some; in this respect she resembles Chopin himself,
but in everything else requisite to the perfection of piano forte
playing she is fully accomplished.   The third piece was a song
by Herr *Behr*, necessary for variety's sake; after which Mad.
Schumann played most charmingly two pieces—" *Andantino
von W. Sterndale Bennett,*" and *Lied ohne Worte* (F major), von
F. Mendelssohn Bartholdy."

The second part of the concert (and here was the attraction)
consisted of " *Die Pilgerfahrt der Rose*" (the pilgrimage of the
rose), a new composition for voices (solo and chorus) and orchestra by Robert Schumann.   This has been performed here a week
or two before, and was noticed in a previous communication.
Anything like an analytical notice of it from one who has heard
it but once or twice would hardly be expected, and in the present case it would be quite absurd.   It will be known in a few
years.   The orchestra never played better; the idea of playing
under Schumann inspired every man with new life and energy,
and the improvement in the performance of the music under the
direction of the composer (there having been a previous rehearsal

also under his teaching), was said to be very apparent. We can hardly imagine a musical occasion that would be more interesting or exciting especially to the *truly enlightened musician* than this. For the few details here given we are indebted to others, for we did not attend this concert ; we neither saw the sight nor heard the sound thereof. Why ? *It was given on Sunday Morning, March 14th, at 11 o'clock.*

LETTER XIII.

The Concerts—Gewandhaus—David—Dreyshock—Rietz—Robert Schumann—Quartette —Dupont.

LEIPZIG, March 14, 1852.

THE last Gewandhaus concert was one of peculiar interest. The band was in the most perfect order, and the programme was unusually attractive ; though great variety of music, both with respect to authorship and character, is always presented to the patrons of this celebrated series of concerts. The *Symphonie* was by Mozart in Eb major ; it is less noisy, flighty and diffuse than some more modern compositions, but not less intelligible or beautiful. The *adagio* is particularly melodious, elegant and attractive.

A *scene* and *arie* from "Orpheus," by Gluck, followed. Gluck is a decided favorite here, and especially as a dramatic writer stands among the very first.

The third piece was a *concerto for violin*, by Beethoven, performed by Herr Concertmeister F. David. This concerto, worthy the reputation of its author, was finely rendered by the violinist, and received with a hearty applause. It is very long, but it does not tire for it is full of variety, and there is enough

to admire, both in the principal and in the accompanimen'
Two quite long *cadenzas*, composed by the performer, contair
ing each an ingenious recapitulation of the thoughts, or ratho
allusion to the various figures of the movement in which th<
cadenza occurred, were introduced, with excellent taste an/
skill.

The second part of the concert consisted of "*Die erste Wa
purgisnacht,*" a ballad by Göethe, set to music by Mendels
sohn. A choir of about one hundred and fifty voices sang the
choruses (and there is much chorus in the piece) with admirable promptness and energy. The music is difficult, both for
vocalists and intrumentalists; it is one of Mendelssohn's
strong pieces, and is full of his peculiar harmonies. It is
mostly very loud, with an abundance of instruments of noise,
and extra double drums for earthquake, volcano, and thunder;
though there is most acceptable relief in occasional piano passages. Although Mendelssohn does not belong to the noisy
school, yet he has shown in the *Walpurgisnacht,* that if he had
chosen to do so he might have cast quite into the shade, or
thundered out of existence, all the Verdis of modern times.

A charming Quartette performance was recently given by a
few of the very best artists here, as David, Dreyschock, (violinist,) Rietz, and others whose names are less known. They
were assisted by a pianist from Munich, Herr Speidl. The
following pieces were played. 1st. Trio for pianoforte, violin
and violoncello, by Beethoven, (op. 70,) by Speidl, David, and
Rietz. 2d. Quartette for strings, composed by David. 3d.
Variations for pianoforte, by Mendelssohn. 4th. Quartette by
Beethoven, (op. 59,) performed by Dreyschock, Rongen, Hermann, and Rietz.

There are only four of these concerts in the annual series, so
that they are much more rare here than in Boston. They seem

not to be so popular as the concerts by full orchestra, yet they draw out a musical audience of great intelligence, and on this occasion the *learned ones* were there. It is indeed a great luxury to hear these choice works of Beethoven and others, so perfectly given. The Quartette above mentioned (op. 59) is well known, is always a favorite, and was on this occasion the crowning piece.

Another recent musical performance of much interest was on the occasion of the anniversary of a Singing Academy (Society) of this place. But one piece was sung, and that was a new composition by Robert Schumann, "*Der Rose Pilgerfahrt*," (Pilgrimage of the Rose,) an allegory by M. Horn, to which Schumann has written music. The choir consisted of about one hundred voices, well balanced as to the parts, with an efficient orchestra; the whole directed by the Concertmeister David.

The music is mostly solo, though some fine chorus effects are produced, especially in a funeral scene, the "burial of a miller's daughter." It is, throughout, highly scientific or learned, and of course difficult. A very fine musician, Mr. Richter, teacher of harmony and instrumentation in the conservatory, who was sitting beside me, said, "Robert Schumann is truly a great composer, but his music must be studied, and heard more than once, to be appreciated; we cannot understand it at the first hearing." His opera, "*Genoveva*," failed—it is too learned, and is now seldom performed. He writes for the musicians rather than for the people.

Through the politeness of Mr. Moscheles, I was permitted to listen to a private performance of a pianist, who is just coming into most favorable notice, *Mr. Dupont from Belgium.* He has, say the critics, very great execution and delicacy of touch, and is regarded as approaching nearer to Listz, than any other person. He intends a professional visit to the United States. If all the musicians who go there are treated, as far as dollars and cents are concerned, as was Jenny Lind, there will be no lack of singers and "players upon instruments."

LETTER XIV.

Church of St. Nicholas—Martin Luther—Singing by the great Congregation—Second Service—Small attendance.

LEIPZIG, March 21, 1852.

A BRIEF account of a public service, or rather two services, which I attended at the *Nicholai kirche*, on Sunday, may perhaps interest some of your readers; at least they will see it is quite a different thing from "going to meeting" in New England. This fine old church was erected many centuries ago, but it was greatly improved and enlarged in 1513, and again repaired in the inside in 1796. A church record informs us that on the 25th of May, in the afternoon, DR. MARTIN LUTHER preached in this house.

The first service commenced at $8\frac{1}{2}$ o'clock in the morning; and as the mornings are short and dark in the winter season, it requires some effort to be punctual. The church is a large one, and the stone walls and uncushioned seats are very cold, yet is there no fire found there, save the burning candles on the altar, which, though they shed some light around, afford no warmth. It is not a Papal, but a Protestant church; the Lutherans use the crucifix, candles, &c., though less than the Romanists. There are two galleries, one rising high above the other, each capable of containing, perhaps, five hundred people ; so that the church may accommodate, say three thousand, on its three floors. The organ is large, with three rows of keys, pedals, and fifty-four registers.

The exercises commenced punctually at the hour, by a short prelude, played in fine organ style, but not more than about two minutes long. This was followed by a choir piece, sung without any accompaniment, by a choir of men and boys, and without much effect. The choir had not power sufficient for so large a building. An interlude of a few minutes upon the organ followed, when a *chorale* was sung by the congregation, accompanied with full organ. The congregation was not yet large, but the people were constantly coming in, and it was fast increasing. Still the effect of the general singing was quite animating. This being concluded, the minister began his part of the service, by chanting a short sentence, which was immediately responded to by the choir ; and again the minister, and again the response. By this time the church was well filled. From an estimate that I made, I concluded that there could not be less than about twenty-five hundred people present. The organ loft, too, capable of accommodating, perhaps, a hundred, was completely filled with vocal and instrumental performers, including the common orchestral instruments, with trumpets and drums conspicuous. When the slow solemn chant was ended, the organ burst out in a loud minor voluntary, which continued three or four minutes, during which time the violins, violoncellos, double basses, and wind instruments tuned. Yet so carefully was this done, that it was hardly perceptible, for the organ was giving out its full progressive chords, so as to nullify the tuning process, at least upon the ears of the people. Tune being secured, the choir, with organ and orchestra accompaniment, sung a motette, or hymn by Beethoven. This had been announced in the newspapers of Saturday, and was, I suppose, with many an object of attention. It occupied, perhaps, fifteen minutes, and was very well done ; the drums and trumpets especially doing fine execution in the great church in the *forte* passages. It closed with a short fugue, in which the points were distinctly taken up and marked. The choir did not number more than from thirty to forty persons, and had not sufficient power for the building ; but still the performance was quite effective. I perceived that while most of the people gave close attention to the music, others were not so much interested, and one goodly-looking old man directly in front of me spent the time in reading over his psalm-book. As soon as the motette was concluded, the members of the orchestra took up their instruments and left the house, having nothing to do with the remaining service. And now came the grand singing—for the great congregation were now together. The organ gave out a choral, when all the people lifted up the loud chorus of praise. The whole house was filled with sound. It was sublime, and I found myself much more moved by this than by the previous choir and orchestra performance. The hymn (486) was indicated on tablets in different parts of the house, and every person had his book in his hand. Even the standers-up in the aisles (for there were hundrds of these) had their books and joined in the song. The singing was in unison; I could not tell, being at the opposite side of the house, whether the choir sang the parts or not; the organ did indeed pour forth full harmony, but even this was vastly overpowered by the multitude of voices—men's voices, and women's voices, and children's voices, mingled in one mighty torrent of sound, rolling through the high arches like the rush of many waters. At the end of each line of the stanza there was an interlude of a few chords upon the organ, but there was no long interlude at the end of the stanza, as in the American churches. Indeed the hymn seemed to flow along from beginning to end, as a whole, and without interruption. I observed, too, that in the hymn-singing I heard in England, the interludes between the stanzas were very short, and often omitted altogether. A very pleasing effect was produced at the close of this and every choral hymn, thus: as soon as the voices ceased on the last word of the last stanza, every head was inclined forward as in the attitude of prayer, while the organ died away *piano*, in a very short post-lude of perhaps half or three-quarters of a minute, the people retaining their position until the last sound was heard, when they gently resumed an erect posture. After this followed liturgical prayers, read by the clergyman, for a few minutes; and then the chorale was resumed, another stanza or two of the same hymn being sung to the same chorale as before. After this followed the sermon. I did not understand it, but if one might judge by the appearance of the people, it was good, for they all seemed to give close attention for at least three-quarters of an hour.

When the sermon was ended, and a short prayer offered, " Vater unser," the hymn was resumed again, and still another stanza sung to the same tune as before; so that *the same tune was sung three times in the same service.* A closing prayer of a few words, and the great congregation gradually dispersed, amid the loud rolling of the diapasons.

At half-past 11, A. M., the second service was held in the same church, *i. e.* about half an hour after the conclusion of the first. It had been previously advertised that at this hour there would be preaching by a divinity student. I attended; the service had already commenced, although there were only *three* persons in the house. These three were the *organist,* the *singer,* and one other person who was in the organ-loft (where

I ventured to go), and who seemed to be also a looker-on. The
organ was playing with some sixteen or eighteen stops out, and
the singer was singing a chorale by himself (in unison!) without a single person to hear or to be edified by the psalm.
I was the fourth person. Soon, however, two or three others
came in, and as the last stanza was drawing to a close, the minister entered the pulpit from a vestry door. By the time he
began his sermon, which was as soon as the singing closed, the
congregation numbered in all, including the organist, the singer,
the minister and the sexton (who made his appearance when
the minister came in), I believe, just *twelve* persons, *six* of
whom were seated in the body of the house near the pulpit,
and appeared to have come for the purpose of attending the
service. A short prayer was read before the preaching. The
sermon occupied about forty minutes, during which time several persons came in and others went away, so that from the beginning to the end of the exercises, from eighteen to twenty people may have been for a part of the time present. The preacher
did not seem to be in the least disconcerted from the fact that
he was almost without hearers, but went on as though the
house had been quite full. The sexton seemed to enjoy it
much, as he had nothing to do, and the singer and the organist,
too, seemed to have no particular anxiety as to the effect of
the psalmody. The moment the sermon was ended, the minister, preceded by the sexton, retired, and then, after they were
out, came the concluding song, which was a grand chorale, performed vocally by the singer (in unison!) and instrumentally by
the organist, on sixteen or eighteen stops of his organ. I suppose, too, that the six or seven persons below joined in the
song, but they did not add so much to the power of the chorus
as to enable me to say with certainty whether the singing was
by the *congregation*, or by the *choir* only.

This account of the second service will appear so strange, that I fear some of your readers may doubt whether the writer is in earnest. I can assure them that it is strictly correct, and that the service, and the whole of it, has been described just as it occurred.

LETTER XV.

The Conservatory of Music at Leipzig, Germany.

LEIPZIG, March 29, 1852.

MUSIC has made so much progress within the last few years, that the importance of a more extensive and thorough course of education is beginning to be felt; and this is especially the case with those who have made the greatest advancement. It has not been generally known in our country, that there is enough in music to occupy years of close application. The older singing books, published some fifty or eighty years ago, contained a few pages of "*Rules*," giving some directions as to finding the "*mi*," and describing the different kinds of time; and a man who could so explain these that no one could possibly understand him, was thought to be musically learned. Many a time have I heard the exclamation: "What, devote his whole time to music!" as if it was quite impossible that one could find anything to study in it for more than an evening or two in a week, for two or three months. Even now there are but very few who have any just conception of the previous preparation, time and labor necessary to thorough knowledge in the science, or skill in the art. The subject is better understood this side the Atlantic, and especially in Germany, where for many years music schools similar to our law, medical and theological schools have been established. It is exceedingly difficult, nay, quite impossible, to obtain a thorough musical education at present in America; for, although we have good musicians, they are scattered about through the different cities, and one cannot avail himself of their instructions but at great inconvenience and expense; and it is found to be a cheaper and a quicker way to come to Europe, if one is determined to make himself in good earnest a musical student.

The inquiry has often been made: What are the musical conservatories of Europe? what are their advantages? and how may one avail himself of their privileges? With the design of answering, in part, these questions, the following account of the Conservatory here has been prepared. It has been written by a young gentleman, a Bostonian, a graduate of Harvard University, now a musical student and member of the Conservatory —Mr. J. P. When young Americans, having good natural talent, favorable early musical associations, and a sufficient preparatory education, shall devote themselves, like Mr. P., to the thorough study of musical science and art, we may look for the rapid progress and success of music in our land, and may hope to realize some of the advantages for which it was designed.

" THIS INSTITUTION was founded in 1843, under the patronage of the King of Saxony, and with the valuable co-operation of the Capelmeister, Dr. FELIX MENDELSSOHN BARTHOLDY. Its reputation spread so rapidly, both in and around Germany, that at the close of the first half year it numbered forty-four pupils, thirty-three male and eleven female. At the commencement of the second term, the number had increased to sixty. These pupils are attracted thither not only from all parts of Germany, but from Belgium, Holland, Denmark, Norway, Russia, England and America.

" An institution like this, whose object is to give the student a thorough foundation in all branches, the knowledge of which is indispensable to every good musician, and to enable him to perfect himself theoretically as well as practically, has this advantage over private instruction—that by the participation of several scholars in the same immediate object of study, it awakens and keeps alive in them a true musical feeling, stimulates them to emulation and hence to industry, and preserves them from partiality or *one-sidedness* in the formation of their tastes, a fault against which every artist should be particularly cautious, during the progress of his studies.   It has also the advantage of cheapness.   Each student pays about $60 a year, for which he receives instruction in all branches.   This moderate sum, as one can readily see, must bear a very small proportion to the expense of private instruction.

" The theoretical part of the education consists of a complete course of three years.   The pupils are divided into six classes, and a new term commences every half-year; though if one is sufficiently prepared, he can enter any of the advanced classes at the time of his admission into the Conservatory.   The first year is devoted to Simple Harmony ; the second to Harmony and Simple Counterpoint; and the third to Harmony, Double Counterpoint, and Fugue.   The study of *Composition* and *Musical Form* constitutes a separate branch, being under the charge of a different instructor.   It comprises all the different forms of vocal and instrumental composition, with the analysis of classical works.   There are also exercises in playing from score and the art of conducting an Orchestra.   The Italian language is also taught to those who devote themselves principally to singing.   Lectures are given twice a week by an eminent Professor on the History and Æsthetics of Music, and the science of Acoustics, with experiments.   So much for the theoretical course.

" In the practical branch also, instruction is given in classes. No limited course can be prescribed, however, as everything here depends on the talent and industry of the scholar. The vocal department is patronized mainly by females, and for those who pursue the study, exercises in Declamation are given, to improve their pronunciation, and fit them for the stage. The instruments that are made the principal object of study are of course Piano and Violin, and each student is obliged unconditionally to devote himself to one or the other of these two. The violinists are exercised in Solo, Quartet, and Orchestra playing. The organ is unfortunately not much attended to. Those who desire to learn the common wind instruments, can do so by paying an extra fee, though it does not form part of the regular course. An opportunity is afforded to those who particularly excel on any instrument to appear at some public performance, either in orchestra, chorus, or solo.

" Besides the regular exercises, the pupils meet together one evening in the week, and those who have studied any work to the satisfaction of the teacher during the past week, perform it for the benefit of the whole assembly. These soirées are attended by the friends and families of the professors, and frequently by distinguished artists who are visiting the city. As for instance, the past fortnight, the students have been inspired by the presence of the first of living German composers, Dr. ROBERT SCHUMANN. He has twice honored these assemblies with his presence, and several of his compositions were performed in his hearing, at which he evinced great satisfaction. His wife also accompanied him, and played several pieces. This lady (formerly CLARA WIECK) ranks among the first pianists of the day, and certainly stands at the head of those of her sex.

" Two examinations are held every year, one a private one,

at which the pupils are classified according to the progress they have made,—and one, a public exhibition or concert, at which the more advanced only are allowed to appear, either as composers or performers. The privilege of attending the rehearsals of the series of concerts that is given every winter in the 'Gewandhaus,' as well as of most others, is also afforded to the pupils.

"The government of the institution is entrusted to five gentlemen, who are professed admirers of the art, and who discharge their office without compensation. The discipline is by no means more strict than every scholar who zealously engages in the study of music would willingly submit to. The regulations are very simple, viz.: that the scholars shall attend regularly the exercises, appear at no public performance without special leave, and in general conduct themselves orderly and submit to the direction of the Government of the Institution. Each pupil on leaving the Conservatory, receives a testimonial or *degree*, stating his time of study and his comparative proficiency in the art.

"As was said above, the expense is comparatively trifling, and within the means of almost every aspirant for musical knowledge. A fund has been given by the King of Saxony, by which a limited number, whose means will not otherwise allow it, can be educated free of expense.

"The professors of the Institution are such as enjoy a universal reputation, and are many of them of Mendelssohn's own selection and appointment. Among them are MOSCHELES, Instructor of the Piano, DAVID, of the Violin, and HAUPTMANN, of Harmony.

"Such are the main features and advantages of this system of musical instruction. It were to be wished most heartily, by all lovers of music, that such an Institution could be founded in every large city of our own country. The rapidly-growing taste of our good people seems to demand some such effort, and from present appearances we may certainly encourage the hope. Objections have been made to the system of instruction in classes, but these are equally applicable to other studies as well as music. To be sure, where a pupil in a *private lesson* receives the undivided attention of his instructor for the space of an hour, in the *class* he receives individually only a fraction of the same. But this comparatively trifling evil is more than counterbalanced by the advantages, as we have above hinted. The pupil becomes acquainted with many different styles, sees the beauties and the faults of each, and is imperceptibly led in this way to the formation of his own. Again, by being constantly compelled to perform before others, he cannot fail to acquire a degree of confidence, which is beneficial and necessary to every public performer. How often do we see an instance of a private pupil, when summoned unexpectedly to an exhibition of himself, completely thrown off his guard by the presence of an assembled company, and so far from doing himself justice, making a total failure. If time admitted, we might enumerate many other advantages, to the truth of which we can testify from personal experience. As it is, for the present, our word must be taken for it, and we can only conclude with the hope, that the little insight we may have given into the system and zeal with which exertions are made in Europe in the cause of this absorbing study, may be of some slight assistance in stimulating our musical countrymen to similar endeavors."

The foregoing will be read with interest, especially by such young men as are thinking of fitting themselves for the musical profession. The time is past when one can expect to succeed well, who takes up music and pursues it professionally without a suitable previous preparation. It is not necessary, indeed, that all teachers should be learned musicians ; many excellent teachers in different musical departments there may be, who have made but little progress in musical science ; but still we need such as shall be able to pursue musical investigations, and give tone to the general character of American music. Such we shall have when men like Willis, Parker, and others whom we might mention, devote themselves to the work.

In addition to what Mr. P. has said, we will remark in relation to expense, that it will cost a man about as much to live in Leipzig a year as it will to live in Boston or New York a year. One may, perhaps, live somewhat cheaper here, but this is not realized often. And the young men who come here generally find the expenses considerably more than they had been led to expect. Some live on four hundred dollars, more expend six hundred, and it is not safe for one who has been accustomed to city life in the United States, and who intends to attend the concerts, (which is quite necessary,) to make his calculations to get along with less than about eight hundred dollars per annum ; and then he must not be disappointed if he finds himself minus say two hundred dollars at the end of the year. But if a man has tried it, and finds that he can live on five hundred dollars per annum in New York, then he may safely conclude that the same sum will answer his purposes in Leipzig, or other German cities.

In addition to the names of Professors given by Mr. P. we will add the following, all of whom are to a greater or less extent connected with the Conservatory : RICHTER, RIETZ, PAPPERITZ, PLAIDY, WENZEL, BECKER, DREYSCHOCK, (violinist,) HERRMANN, and KLENGEL.

Success to the young men of America, who, *having the necessary talent*, shall devote themselves to the study and advancement of musical science and art in our land! By-and-bye, when we shall have some MARY LYON to devote herself to the work, we shall have a Conservatory, with the buildings all erected and *paid for*, like the Mount Holyoke School, in Massachusetts.

LETTER XVI.

The Nineteenth Gewandhaus Concert—Robert and Clara Schumann—Madame Tuczek-Herrenburg of Berlin.

LEIPZIG, March 19, 1852.

THE presence of Robert and Clara Schumann was enough to attract a large audience. Anticipating this, our company, consisting of three persons, went a little before the time appointed for the opening of the door; but yet we found a crowd gathered; the room filled immediately as the door was opened, but we succeeded in obtaining good seats. We had now to wait a full hour before the music commenced, but in the midst of such a multitude of good-looking and well-dressed ladies and gentlemen, all in conversation in loud and merry voices, it soon passed away. Half an hour before the commencement, the oboe was heard, running the scales, &c.; this was soon followed by *faggotti, corni, clarionetti*, and *strings ;* every man tuning and getting his instrument and his fingers in readiness. Mendelssohn seemed to look down from his bust immediately opposite the orchestra with approbation. At half-past six precisely, Kapelmeister Rietz takes his stand—the signal is given—every one is silent and attentive, and Beethoven's overture (op. 124) fills the whole company with delight. This is a very pleasing overture; it is less learned, but of a more popular character than most of Beethoven's. It is often marked with a rhythm like the music of the march or dance; and the flourishes of the brass instruments and drums almost lead one to suppose that he is listening to a military band. But still the hand of the master is seen, and although Beethoven comes down and freely holds conversation with the people, yet he always preserves his dignity, and never dishonors his profession in this pleasing composition.

A very good singer followed; Frau Leopoldine Tuczek-Herrenburg, from Berlin, in a Recitative and Arie from the opera of "Sylvana," by C. Maria von Weber.

This was followed by a grand Concerto for the Piano Forte, with orchestral accompaniment (G moll), composed by J. Moschelles, and played by Clara Schumann. I have already spoken of Madame Schumann's playing; her performance of this Concerto was perfect, and received the warmest approbation from the audience.

An air of *De Beriot* followed, by Frau Tuczek-Herrenburg; after which Madame Schumann played most charmingly a Notturno (B. major) for piano forte, by F. Chopin. In this she was encored, and played in answer to the call another piece unknown to the writer.

The second part of the concert was that in which the musical ones were most deeply interested, for it consisted of *Robert Schumann's new Symphonie*. This has not been published, and was played from manuscript, conducted by the author, who was cordially greeted on his appearance at the head of the orchestra. It is undoubtedly a work of great merit; but it is truly a *great work*, and can only be performed by a very thoroughly trained band. Its analogies and correspondencies are deeper and more hidden than in Mozart or Beethoven, but nevertheless they are there, and can be discovered to some extent even at a first hearing. The Symphonie consists of five movements, there being in addition to the usual movements a short adagio (fourth) introduced. In the second movement (scherzo), there is playfulness and relief, but throughout the whole the idea of *greatness* prevails ; so much so as almost to oppress one with a feeling of grandeur and sublimity. The fourth movement especially seems to partake in the highest degree of this character, and stirs up the deep feelings to awe and reverence. But vain is any attempt at description, especially by one who has heard it but at a single performance. It was played with great energy ; every member of the orchestra had enough to do. The captain inspired confidence, and the result was most satisfactory. There was but a momentary pause between the parts, and in this respect the learned conductor's example is well worthy of imitation. The Symphonie occupied *thirty-three* minutes in its performance, and at half-past eight the concert closed.

LETTER XVII.

Dedication of the Music Hall of the "Thomas School"—M. Hauptmann—Chorus Singing.

LEIPZIG, March 22, 1852.

THE "Thomas School" is connected with the Thomas Church ; and the choir of the latter is obtained from it. JOHN SEBASTIAN BACH was formerly Music Director here ; and he has been succeeded by several distinguisned men. The present incumbent is M. HAUPTMANN, who is also Professor of Harmony in the Conservatory. The place was procured for him by MENDELSSOHN, with whom it was a favorite object to gather around him men of science, and Hauptmann most deservedly ranks among these. He is now everywhere known as one of the most profound theorists living. He has also published Motets, and other pieces of Church Music, which are held in high estimation by musicians. But there is something more attractive about Hauptmann than either genius or learning; it is amiability. He seems to be filled with kindness, gentleness, and courtesy; and I have met no German, nor indeed any one, in whose presence one is made more perfectly at home, and by whom one is treated with more affability and attention than by him. Although standing at the very head of musical science, he has, as yet, published no work of importance on harmony; he says that he waits for more experience, so that when he publishes a book, *it may be of some value.* A good hint is this to some of us, who write and publish works on the theory of music in the United States, without knowledge and without experience. How often we see verified the old saying (and frequently in musical productions), that "a little knowledge is a dangerous thing." Hauptmann is now, however, engaged in the preparation of a philosophical treatise, which he intends to give to the public in a few years. His health is not firm; he is a diligent student, and bodily infirmity is probably the result of severe and long-continued mental labor. He is very popular, and is, perhaps, equally respected for his knowledge, and beloved for his goodness. He called yesterday, bringing tickets to a musical performance, on the occasion of the dedication of the Music Hall of the School. It is not indeed a new hall, but an old one repaired, painted, and ornamented; it is in the same house where BACH lived, and is the very room where BACH, HILLER and others labored and conducted musical performances. Hauptmann now occupies the same apartments which were formerly occupied by the great Fuguist. The exercises, with the exception of a short address by one of the pupils, were exclusively musical, as follows :

I. Prayer. "Kommt, lasset uns anbeten.". . . . .*Hauptmann.*
II. Motette. "Der Geist hilft unserer Schwachheit.". . . . . . .*J. S. Bach.*
III. Four part-songs :—
      1. "O Thaeler weit, o Hoehen.". . . . .*Mendelssohn.*
      2. "O sanfter, suesser Hauch". . . . .*Mendelssohn.*
      [The above may be found in the "Social Glee Book," and have
      been sung in the Boston Musical Conventions.]
      3. "Waldeinsamkeit.". . . . .*Hauptmann.*
      4. "Ich stand auf Berges Hoehen.". . . . .*Hauptmann.*
IV. Motette. "Jauchzet dem Herrn.". . . . .*Schicht.*

The singing was by the choir of the school and church, which consisted of about fifty voices; Soprano and Alto by boys. It was entirely without accompaniment. A grand Pianoforte in the room was only used to announce the pitch before each piece. This singing most difficult music without accompaniment is something wholly unknown with us in America. I know full well that there are choirs and Quartet clubs who sing comparatively easy music in public without accompaniment; but even in this, what is often the result? Bach's music is exceedingly difficult. Handel, in comparison to Bach, may be said to be easy; and yet our choirs could but few of them sing Handel and sustain themselves well without instrumental aid. But here is a chorus who stand up and sing Bach's and other most difficult motets, the most difficult vocal music perhaps ever written, by voices alone, with as much certainty as the sure aim of an experienced marksman.

I think I have never before witnessed such devotion to the work as in these singers. Here is indeed entire self-committal. Every one throws all the powers he has, physical and spiritual, into the performance of the music. Every tone is attacked with a conscious certainty of success; no matter how complicated the rhythm, it is given with an energy and truthfulness that a first-rate violinist can hardly excel. The singers seem to have a perfect command of their vocal organs, and are no less certain of results than is the accomplished pianist when he strikes the keys, or the violinist when he draws the bow. There is an entire absence of that sleepiness, drowsiness, inattention, and foolish levity too often witnessed in our choirs. No looking about, or whispering, or laughing, or silliness; but close attention is ever manifested. I wish I had words to point out that consecration to the work, that deep, heartfelt interest which these choir members seem to possess; so that it might be sought for by our American singers. But we cannot obtain it unless we use the appropriate means; education only will do it; musical training, such as we have but little idea of, must go before; and as we plant, so we shall reap in these things. This choir is *drilled* daily; five o'clock is the hour when they come together every day for their lesson, or rather their *training* and *practice*. For so far as I have had opportunity to observe, the *teaching* here consists mostly in *training*. But I must not enlarge. I have never before heard a vocal chorus so prompt, so energetic, and perfect in time and tune, as on this occasion. The place, too, was holy ground, for all the great musicians have visited that saloon; BACH lived there as his home, and HANDEL, and HAYDN, and MOZART, and BEETHOVEN have been there. A new portrait of Bach (or rather an old one put in perfect order) has been placed at the head of the hall, and opposite to it is a fine bust of SCHICHT, who, though less known, was a very profound musician, as his works testify. On the whole, I have not attended a more interesting musical performance in Germany.

LETTER XVIII.

Distinct Articulation in Singing—Congregational Singing, with reference to the utterance of the words.

LEIPZIG, March 29, 1852.

THE importance of a clear, distinct, tasteful, and appropriate delivery of the words in vocal music cannot be too strongly urged. A good utterance of words is one of the elementary technicals in singing ; as much so as is tone, intonation or time. Singing combines both the elements of speech and of song, and no one can claim to be a vocalist who has not cultivated as well his articulating as his vocal powers. Teachers of singing should urge this point as one of the greatest importance ; for, whatever other qualifications one may possess, he cannot be even a *tolerable* singer who does not utter his words with distinctness and propriety ; and no one sings well who does not go further than this, and deliver his words with taste and elegance.

But, strange as it may seem, while this is a point of so much importance, it is one which is much neglected, and one would sometimes think, when listening to an untaught choir, that the very elementary sounds, or powers of the letters, had not been learned. Instead of the clear, open, full *vowels* of the language, we often hear strange and distorted sounds, which seem to belong to mere animals rather than to men, and which give to a chorus a feline or canine character, a mewing or a howling altogether unworthy of the human voice. And the *consonants*, too, are not less absurdly misplaced or omitted. One principal reason of this neglect or abuse of language in singing is that but little careful instruction has been given in the common schools, until within a few years, in elementary reading. But even where this instruction has been given, a separate and distinct attention to the subject, in connection with singing sounds, is necessary; for we have sometimes known professors of elocution (and most worthy ones) who made sad work of the language in their attempts to utter it in song. We rejoice to know that teachers of music are giving this subject more attention than formerly. At the Teachers' Institutes held in Boston, teachers of elocution have been employed to lecture, and in the musical conventions held in different parts of the country instructions are given, which, if followed up with a suitable practice or training, must lead to improvement. But all the lectures and all the preaching in the world will not do without careful and continued *training ;* and this must be done under the direction and superintendence of one who is capable of doing the work. If ministers or school teachers could be induced to exercise our choirs in *reading* and *declamation,* we should soon witness improvement. Chanting and reading simultaneously by choirs, are recommended as valuable exercises in acquiring a good articulation of words. Than this, there is no more important subject connected with singing-schools and choral performance.

Is it possible to articulate words with as great distinctness in song as in speech ? Much depends upon the character of the song. In plain chanting we think it can be done, and with equal ease. In tunes of very simple rhythmic form, of a melodic compass that is quite within the range of the singer's voice, strictly syllabic, and favorable as to movement, or length of tones, we think, too, that the question may be answered in the affirmative. If it be asked whether it is as easy for a choir of thirty or forty persons to articulate their words as they may be articulated by a good speaker, then we may answer the question by asking whether it is easy for twenty or thirty persons to read a hymn simultaneously, so that the words can be heard as distinctly as when read by an individual ? Undoubtedly it is much more difficult for a *choir* so to deliver their words as that they shall be clearly understood, than it is for a single person to do so. When we use the speaking voice, we adjust it in all respects to our immediate wants, or use it in that way in which a clear utterance of the words is best promoted ; but in *song* we are not at liberty always thus to use the voice, for here a melody or tune has been prescribed, and it may be so high or so low as to make it exceedingly difficult to connect words distinctly with tones ; or it may be too soft or too loud in power, or too quick or too slow in movement for this end; or all may be combined, and length and pitch and power present an insuperable obstacle to the singer's success.

In the application of this question to choir-singing, and taking into view the nature or different characteristics of the *speaking* and the *singing* tones, we should reply in the negative.

Two inferences follow :

I. Much careful practice and thorough training are necessary to enable a choir to sing well. The St. Thomas' choir in this place, meet for practice *every day at five o'clock* ; the English cathedral choirs sing together the service once in the forenoon and once in the afternoon of each day. We cannot expect then that any choir can do well with less than one or two thorough, close, protracted drillings in a week. Choirs must meet for practice, and really practice too, if they would speak their words well in song, or sing well with respect to any of the essential elements of vocal music.

II. Such tunes should generally be chosen for public worship as are well adapted to the articulation of words ; and choirs should not be willing to sacrifice the words to musical effect. It is not uncommon for congregations to desire the singing of tunes in which the parts are so mixed up as to render the hearing of the words impossible, and then blame the singers for not speaking the words plainly.

Singers should strive to speak the words plainly, and strive to do this without violating the laws either of musical or elocutionary taste.

We do not believe that congregational singing can ever prevail unless the essential elements of a good musical performance are given up. That is, we cannot have a good musical performance (or what is usually understood to be a good musical performance) in connection with congregational singing. History, and the actual state of things now existing, tell us that such a general state of musical improvement as would be necessary for this, is merely *ideal*, something imaginative only, and not to be realized. We have heard congregational singing in many places in the United States—south, and west, and east —and also in different European countries, but (to say nothing about taste) we have never heard it where the musical laws of *time* or *tune* were observed; nor have we ever heard it where to a listener all would not be confused with respect to the words. No two persons speak the words alike, or precisely at the same time, both latitude and longitude are unknown, and although the tide of rhythmic form forces obedience so far as to cause the arrival of each one at the end of the stanza within hailing distance of the others, yet the effect is almost always quite *Babelian*.

From this view of the subject, or looking at congregational singing as it *has been*, *is now*, and probably *will be*, it follows that *where it prevails*, no one will be able to hear the words with any degree of certainty. But we must also consider that where it prevails there is no one to hear the words. Every one is engaged in singing for himself, and has nothing apparently to do with those around him. To be sure he is influenced by the mass of tone, but of this he is at the time unconscious, and worships as an individual. As there is no one to listen to the words then, so their clear enunciation is comparatively unimportant.

This is also equally true of the other elements of good singing as it is with respect to the words. Everything that belongs to taste in music must be given up as we enter the very threshold of the congregational chorus; and even time, and tune, and the articulation of tones and of words, cannot be expected.

But if such be the fact, is congregational singing desirable? Go with me to the Nicolai Church in Leipzig, and look down from the upper gallery upon a congregation of fifteen hundred or two thousand persons; see them with hymn books open, apparently unconscious of those around, listen to their rough and uncultivated voices, *in* time and tune, or *out* of time and tune, joining with the loud pealings of the deep diapasons, rolling through the arches of the great building, and filling the whole with a mighty chorus of sound; mark the movings of your own spirit, and you will not need an answer to the question from another.

LETTER XIX.

St. Peter's Church—Richter, the Organist—the Tomb of Bach—Chorals sung at St. Peter's.

LEIPZIG, March 24, 1852.

THIS is said to be the oldest church in Leipzig. The present edifice which stands close to the eastern gate of the city, was erected in 1507. It is, I should judge, about 120 or 140 feet in

length, and only about fifty feet in width. There are double galleries on each side of the house, with a space of only about
twenty feet between them ; besides which there are about
twenty private boxes or apartments, belonging, as I suppose, to
distinguished familes, who keep them locked, opening them
only for their own use. After the reformation the building
was for a long time unoccupied, and was not used for the purposes of worship until 1710. When Napoleon was here, and
during the war of 1812 and 1813 it was used for barracks, and
afterwards as an hospital. In 1816 public worship was again
resumed, and has been continued to the present time. It is a
Lutheran church, and the service is the same or nearly the same
as in all the other churches. The musical director, Richter,
Professor in the Conservatorium, is the Organist. I attended
service there this afternoon. At the precise hour the organ
prelude commenced ; it continued two minutes, and the first
Lied immediately followed. There was no introit, or introductory motette as in the Nicolai and Thomas churches. The
choir consisted of *three boys* and *two men ;* and beside these,
the organist, another person walking about in the organ loft,
and myself, there was but *one* person present—a goodly old
lady ; so that when the service commenced, the congregation
in fact consisted of but one woman. It reminded me of the
clergyman who, when he had no one present but the clerk, took
the liberty to alter the prescribed form of the service, reading
not " Dearly beloved *brethren*," but " Dearly beloved *Roger*."
Here was an occasion then, when the singing was indeed *congregational*. The members of the choir were all singing, the old
lady appeared to sing, and I joined the general chorus. The
organ was full and made up for any deficiency of vocal power.
I observed that in some stanzas the voices commenced without
the organ, and sung three or four syllables, when they were

joined by the full organ ; though in some other stanzas the
voices and organ were simultaneous in their commencement.
This, however, can have nothing to do with that which *we* sometimes call *expression* or the *adaptation of the tune to the different stanzas of the hymn,* for no attention whatever is paid to this
subject here ; there is no variation of soft and loud, but every
stanza is loud, and is apparently sung and played without the
slightest reference to the principle above mentioned.   Indeed
the principle of adaptation (as generally understood by us in
the United States), seems not to belong to the Congregational style of singing.   The minister, who was not present
at the commencement of the service, came in during the
singing of the last stanza, faced the cross upon the altar for
a few moments, and then turning towards the people (by this
time numbering perhaps between twenty or thirty), he commenced the responsive chanting service.   His first sentence
is confined to about half a dozen words, which are given in the
tones *three* and *five* of the scale ; this being responded to by
the choir, the minister chants quite a long sentence, after which
the choir respond Amen.   The response closed upon *five* of the
scale, ascending to it by the *sharp four*—thus *five, three, sharp
four, five.*   After this the minister read about two minutes—
the people rising.   This was followed by the organ, and another hymn.   The minister retired the moment he had finished
reading (prayer) and was not present during the singing that
followed ; but at the close of the hymn, as before, he came in
and read a scriptural lesson ; again he retired, and again the
organ announced another choral.   By this time some fifty or
sixty persons had assembled, and they succeeded in raising
quite a chorus.   At the close of the last stanza the minister appeared, not at the altar, but in the pulpit, and after half a dozen
words of prayer, commenced his sermon.   And now the choir,

three boys and *two men*, took their turn in going out; as the minister seemed to have nothing to do with their part of the service, so, I suppose, they were alike relieved when he began to preach. Considering myself by profession and long habit as more nearly allied to choristers than preachers, and especially as I could not understand what was said, and as I could retire without being noticed, and without disturbing others, I followed their example.

Last Sabbath I attended church at St. John's, an old building a little way out of the city; but the service was the same. Around this church are many old monuments, and in the cemetery was buried JOHN SEBASTIAN BACH. The exact place of his interment is not known.

That your readers may have a more exact idea of what the tunes are which are sung here, (and they are all of the same character,) I send you a copy of two which I heard at St. Peter's this day. They are sung in slow time, pausing on the last note of each line.

WIE SCHÖN LEUCHTUNS DER MORGENSTERN.

SCHATZE UBER ALLE SCHATZE.

LETTER XX.

Concert by the Pupils of the Conservatory—Original Overtures by the Pupils.

LEIPZIG, April 2, 1852.

LAST evening the saloon of the Gewandhaus was crowded to listen to the pupils of the Conservatory. Concerts are occasionally given, perhaps once a quarter, or once in six months, under the direction of the Professors, in which the pupils give specimens of their proficiency in the composition and in the performance of music, vocal and instrumental. The weather was very unfavorable; but notwithstanding the rain, the house was crowded : indeed some persons could not find admission. Tickets are not sold, but are given away by the teachers and pupils to their friends. The orchestra at such times is in part made up of the pupils, deficiencies being supplied by professors employed for the occasion; of course they have an efficient band. DAVID and DREYSCHOCK were at the head of the violins. MOSCHELES conducted the pianoforte pieces; DAVID conducted the violin concertos; REITZ conducted the songs; RICHTER conducted the chorus music, and the respective authors themselves conducted the overtures. There were two original overtures performed :

I. Overture for Orchestra, composed by W. FREDERIC NICOLAI, of Leyden, Holland.

II. Overture for Orchestra, composed by HEINRICH VON SAHR, of Dresden, Saxony.

Both of these overtures were highly creditable to the young men, and were well received ; the last, perhaps, being the most meritorious production. The other music consisted of selections from various authors, as follows :

PIANO FORTE MUSIC.

I. Concerto for Piano Forte with Orchestra, by BEETHOVEN, (C Minor, first part,) performed by Wilhelm Gerbig, of Almelo, Holland.

II. Trio for Piano Forte, Violin, and Violoncello, by Mendelssohn, (No. 2, C Minor,) performed by three pupils, Fraulein Laura Boerngen, of Verden, Hanover ; Herr F. George Haubold, of Leipzig ; and Herr Gruetzmacher.

III. Grand Sonata for Piano Forte, (F Minor, op. 54,) by Beethoven, performed by Fraulein Rosalie Hirschfield, of Danzig.

VIOLIN MUSIC.

I. Concerto for Violin with Orchestra, by Molique, (A Minor, No. 5, first part,) performed by Herr George Japha, of Koenigsberg, Prussia.

II. Military Concerto for Violin, with Orchestra, by Lipinski, (first part,) performed by Herr Carl Hahn, Nuremberg.

III. Introduction and Variations for Violin, with Orchestra, by David, performed by Herr Wilhelm Langhanns, Hamburg.

VOCAL MUSIC.

I. Aria, from Stradella, sung by Fraulein Anna Masius, Leipzig.

II. Aria, by Rossini, (Barber of Seville,) sung by Fraulein Marie Kuehne, Magdeburg.

III. Recitative and Aria, from Figaro, by Mozart, sung by Fraulein Marie Grohmann, Magdeburg.

CHOIR MUSIC.

The 137th Psalm for Soprano Solo, Choir and Orchestra, by E. F. Richter.

Such was the music of the school exhibition, and it was in all respects highly creditable to the institution. The students are from various parts of Germany and England; and for the last few years America has also been represented. Such an institution is much needed in our country. A Conservatory of Music upon a proper basis, and under suitable regulations, would do much for the advancement of a pure style, and correct taste. It would be to music what the Normal Schools are to education generally; would raise the standard of musical education, and the qualification of music teachers; and put forth an influence in many ways to promote the cause of secular and sacred, vocal and instrumental music in the land.

LETTER XXI.

Mendelssohn and Robert Schumann.

BERLIN, April 5, 1852.

In a recent number of one of the musical papers in New York, *Robert Schumann* is said to be an imitator of *Mendelssohn*. A strange charge, indeed, and one that could not be made by any who had heard some of the principal productions of the two writers.

These two original composers have both established schools of their own; quite unlike each other, or any one else. Robert Schumann is a little the older of the two, though they were contemporaneous for many years, or during the whole of Mendelssohn's professional life.

It is said they were always intimate and friendly, although each one had his friends; and these friends of the parties of course differed with respect to the merits of the two composers; but we believe that neither was ever charged before with being an imitator of the other. If there has been any original composer of music in latter times; one who has penetrated farther into the unexplored region of harmony than any other, that man is, we suppose, Robert Schumann. At least he has this reputation among some of the most learned musicians of Germany. He is quite unlike all other composers, and while he has imitators and Mendelssohn has imitators, it cannot be said in truth of either of these distinguished men, that he is an imitator of the other. As well might it be said of Shakspeare that he is an imitator, or of Milton, as of Schumann. Both as it respects *form* and *harmony*, these authors differ widely. Who that has ever listened to a symphony by Schumann would compare it to a like composition of any other writer? Surely, no one.

The difference between Schumann and Mendelssohn has been the subject of no few criticisms and discussions; but all truly learned musicians acknowledge that they not only walk in a new path, but that they both are truly original—investigators of nature—searchers-out of things not before discovered—advancers of scientific knowledge. Robert Schumann is generally regarded as the more deep, and difficult of interpretation. Mendelssohn, indeed, was not understood at first; but he is now well known. So too of Beethoven, some of whose works are mysterious even to this day. It also requires such a well trained and talented orchestra to represent Robert Schumann as is not everywhere found; and even when he is interpreted by an orchestra fully competent to the task, with all the hints that he himself can give as conductor, the best musicians cannot fully comprehend him at a single hearing. Since Mendelssohn's death, Robert Schumann seems to stand at the head of the German school. It is not wonderful that a disciple of Donizetti or Verdi should not like Schumann, or that a child should not receive pleasure from the reading of a profound and learned work; it is not surprising indeed that Schumann is not favorably received by many good musicians, for even Beethoven was rejected for many years. How long was the Philharmonic of London in decyphering his ninth? Several years, to say the least. One should be careful, and be certain that he knows what Robert Schumann is, before he ventures to charge him with being an imitator of the highly gifted and talented Mendelssohn, or of any one else. That Robert Schumann is an original composer, a musician will not deny; that his compositions are not designed to please the unlearned in music, is also true; but that he will be admired whenever he is *truly interpreted*, cannot be doubted.

LETTER XXII.

Berlin—Wilhelm Bach—Symphonie Concerts and Orchestral Music—Military Music—
The "Tod Jesu" by Graun, the "Passion Music" by Bach, and the "Seven Words" by
Haydn.

BERLIN, April 9, 1852.

THIS is one of the finest cities of Europe, and is said to be
one of the four most splendid cities in the world. Its palaces,
statues, and monuments, including those of Charlottenburg and
Potsdam, are magnificent; and with its museums, library, and
paintings, are full of historic interest. Frederick the Great is
everywhere to be seen. He is to Prussia what Napoleon is to
France; his name is on the tongue of every child, and his memory seems to be even more sacred here than is that of Washington in America. His monument, lately erected, at an expense of about a hundred thousand dollars, is regarded as the
greatest work of the kind of modern times. Would that a
similar monument to the memory of Washington stood in each
of our large cities in America; its moral power would be great
and good. Drawings of it are everywhere to be seen; I will,
therefore, only remark concerning it, that in one of its group
of statues, among the literary and scientific men of the age and
country, as Lessing, Kant and others, is seen that of GRAUN,
well known to the musical world. GRAUN is honored here, as
BACH in Saxony, or HANDEL in England; though among all the
names of German musicians, that of BACH takes rank, perhaps,
the highest. That he was a most profound writer, and that his
Fugues especially have never been equalled, is, we believe, universally admitted. His *passion music* is performed at this season of the year in the principal cities. Having been in Berlin
but a little more than a week, and at a time when there is less
music than usual (passion week), we cannot report very fully;

but we must not omit to tell our musical friends of some of
the things we have heard or seen.

WILHELM BACH, now probably nearly seventy years of age,
is of the family of the famous JOHN SEBASTIAN, of whom he
has several interesting relics.   He has long been a music-direc-
tor in Berlin, and one of the finest organists in Germany.   He
is a professor in a school for church-music here, which is under
the patronage of the government.   The school has a good number of students, although other institutions which have more recently arisen have drawn considerably upon it.   We called upon
Mr. Bach in 1837, accompanied him to the school, and also to
the church, where we had the pleasure of hearing him play the
organ for nearly an hour.   We remember a fine compliment
paid to Mr. Bach by the celebrated organist, JOHN SCHNEIDER,
whom we afterwards met in Dresden.   When on the way from
Mr. Schneider's house to the church where he was about to
play, he said, "I will play for you some of Bach's fugues."
"Thank you, sir," we replied; "we are always delighted to
hear these charming organ pieces, and had the pleasure a few
days since of listening to several of them as performed by Wm.
Bach, of Berlin."   "*So ?*" said Schneider ; "if you have heard
Wilhelm Bach play Bach's fugues, I will play something else,
for I do not like to play the same music which you have heard
by so excellent a performer as he is."   Mr. Bach is not
only a very thorough and scientific musician, but also a very
gentlemanly man.   He had a perfect recollection of our former
call, and was as ready now as then to exhibit his old manuscripts
and musical curiosities, and his conversation was filled with anecdotes and historic recollections and instruction.   It was painful to part with one so cheerful, pleasant, learned, and accomplished, after an interview of one hour, feeling almost certain
that we should not meet again on earth.

We had an opportunity of attending only one Symphonie Concert, or " *Grand Concert Serieux*." The orchestra was not large (three contra-Basses with other instruments in proportion), yet they played well, and gave fine character to the Overtures to Don Juan by Mozart, Egmont by Beethoven, Ruy Blass by Mendelssohn, Jessonda by Spohr, and also Haydn's Symphonie, G major No. 3. The orchestra of the Royal Opera House is of course excellent, and ranks with the best in Europe. Yet we did not see that it was much superior to that of the Leipzig Gewandhaus. It is somewhat larger, and its *pianos* are, perhaps, more *piano*, and its *fortes* more *forte*. The great points of excellence, as quality of tone, blending of the different instruments, Piano, Forte, Crescendo, Diminuendo, Sfortzando, Syncopation, &c., are most perfectly brought out, and the most fastidious hearer seems to be compelled to say, *enough*.

An excellent military band plays daily at eleven o'clock. It contains about sixty instruments, and we were truly glad to see that the use of the old-fashioned military band instruments is continued. Here were *Oboi, Faggotti, Clarinetti, Corni*, as well as all the modern brass instruments. The band usually play an overture and one or two smaller pieces daily, at the hour above mentioned ; and in its performances, it is sufficient to say, that the characteristics of good orchestral playing are carefully observed.

Throughout Germany three great compositions are performed at this season of the year. Thus, the present season the " Passion Music" and the " Last Seven Words" have been given in Leipzig. The " Passion Music" and the " Tod Jesu" have been performed in Berlin, and one or both in Dresden. We were so unfortunate as to lose both the " Seven Words" and the " Passion Music," but have had the satisfaction of hearing the

" Tod Jesu" twice in Berlin. It is a learned work, not designed for amusement merely, but rather to paint with a deep coloring, the death scene of the Saviour of the world. It is, in general, too serious for a popular audience. "It is quite tedious,"
said a German lady to me, " but yet it is very grand." It does
not afford sufficient immediate musical gratification for many ;
indeed it appeals to a higher principle than that of the mere
sensuous,—even to the *religious ;* and to appreciate it, one must
be both *musically* and *religiously* educated and inclined. Modern musical taste, especially in our country, is of too light a
character for Graun or Bach, and for the great religious works
which we have mentioned ; and then again, religious emotion
has been too much separated by our educational habits from a
musical form of utterance or expression ; indeed, the *nasal
twang* of an uncultivated voice has sometimes been regarded
as more natural and appropriate to the expression of religious
feeling than the most pure and musical tones.

The "Tod Jesu" was performed on Wednesday by a choir
and orchestra under the direction of Julius Schneider, in the
Garnisonkirche ; and on the Friday following by the "Sing
Academie" of Berlin, in their beautiful Hall. It was well done
on both occasions, but was much the most effective in the "Sing
Academie." The choir was in excellent order, and consisted
of about two hundred vocalists ; the solo singing, though not
by great artists, was all in good style and keeping, and the orchestra were fully adequate to the work they had to do. The
recitatives were accompanied by the pianoforte, and the songs
and choruses by the orchestra. There was no organ on either
occasion, and I find that it is not common to unite the organ
with a *choir* performance. If an orchestra play an overture,
they are not supposed to need the support of an organ, and if
a choir sing a vocal motette, they are supposed to be able to

sing it independent of instrumental aid; so that the organ is seldom heard, except when it is telling its own story, or sustaining and leading along the great congregation in the choral songs.

Every seat was occupied; indeed it was necessary to secure tickets a day or two previous to the performance. The king was there, and both the sovereign and the people seemed to enter into the spirit of the music. The house was perfectly still, and there was not the slightest indication of applause; not because the music was not well executed, but because the usual method of manifesting approbation seemed to be inappropriate to the solemn state of feeling existing. It seemed indeed to be an occasion of deep solemnity; all the members of the choir, male and female, were dressed in black, so that an appeal was made, through the *eye* as well as the *ear*, to the religious sympathies in view of the sufferings of the Son of God. I shall not attempt any analysis of the "Tod Jesu." With the exception of one chorus, and Luther's chorale, it is, I believe, quite unknown in America; the chorus to which I refer may be found in the "Boston Academy's Collection of Choruses;" I do not remember the words, but it has been very popular and much sung, and is the only piece by Graun in the volume. More of Berlin in my next.

LETTER XXIII.

Easter Sunday—Music in the Catholic and Protestant Churches—The Picture Gallery—
John Schneider, the Organist.

DRESDEN, April 12, 1852.

YESTERDAY being Easter Sunday, we were awakened at early day-light by the ringing of bells, and the discharge of cannon. The day was ushered in, much in the same manner as is the

4th of July in America. I liked the music of the bells, but the cannon seemed to be less adapted to the occasion. At 8 o'clock I attended the Frauen Church, a very large circular building, having four galleries all around, and in some five and even six. The Organ, which is powerful, stands very high over the altar; perhaps thirty feet from the floor. A fine introductory voluntary, full of joy, was played, closing with a very lively fugue; after which the people sang a *chorale*. At 9 o'clock we went to the *Kreuz-Kirche*, where we heard an *ostercantate* with full orchestra, composed by Theodor Weinlig. It was brilliant and joyful as can be imagined; the trumpets and the drums being fully employed throughout. At 11 o'clock we attended the Catholic Church, where Grand Mass was performed; the music, by *Hesse*, was sung by a very good choir, accompanied with an efficient orchestra. It was brilliant and exciting, and occupied a little more than an hour. Both the cantate at the Kreuz-Kirche, and the Mass at the Cathedral were well done, though far inferior to the performance of the *Dom-Chor*, Berlin. Indeed, the two were so different in style as not to admit of comparison. The music of the Berlin choir was churchlike in its composition, and it was exclusively vocal; whereas, here the music was of the modern secular character, and was rather orchestral than vocal. The trumpets and drums (with other brass instruments) were in constant requisition; and more brilliant and animating flourishes of these instruments I have never heard. The whole musical performance made its appeal to lower principles of taste, than did the singing of the *Dom-Chor*. That was, intellectually and tastefully considered, music of a high order; whereas, in this the strains were more common, adapted to the popular ear, and had much the appearance of mere show or exhibition. *That* was ecclesiastical, religious music; *this* was was secular, like that of most of the productions of modern composers of *Masses*, *Te Deums*, and other vocal music with orchestral accompaniment.

The congregational singing in the *Kreuz-Kirche* was excellent, that is, excellent *congregational* singing; but the organ was played with mighty power, and without variation of *Piano* and *Forte*. It seemed to support, bind together, and lead the people, who bore a somewhat similar relation to the organ, to that which a large factory wheel does to the water power by which it is moved. It seemed almost to take away from the people voluntariness or free agency, and to compel them onward in their song. It was certainly impossible for any one to commit any overt act of sin against the laws of *time* and *tune*, during such a torrent of sound as that which the organ poured forth. In the afternoon we heard, in the Kreuz-Kirche, an *ostercantate* by Berg, and a fine *Te Deum* by Naumann, both in the modern orchestral style, brilliant and dazzling. It was a day of pleasure, and the Concert-Gardens, Opera, and other places of amusement, were well patronized in the evening.

We must leave our readers to imagine whether feelings religious—of gratitude to a risen Saviour, or those of a more worldly or sensuous character, were called forth by the scenes of the day. It seemed to us somewhat different from the manner in which Paul would have rejoiced in the contemplation of the resurrection.

The Picture Gallery is regarded as one of the best in Europe, and contains choice specimens of the old masters. The grand picture of the collection is, the *Madonna di san Sisto*, by RAPHAEL; but there are many fine pieces by *Correggio*, *Titian*, *Guido*, *Reubens*, and others of different schools. It is most interesting to stand and gaze on the works of those great masters of which one has always heard and read; but instead of the day or two which a traveler has to bestow, months and years could be devoted to this one collection, and indeed are necessary to any proper appreciation of such works of art as are here exhibited.

Many things in this beautiful city are well worthy of attention, some of which we visited; but it is of musical things only which we design to write.

The Opera in Dresden is good, though inferior to that of Berlin; the conductor is *Carl Krebs*, who is regarded as very able, and a very thorough musician. One of the best German Tenors resides here, and is a member of the regular opera company, viz.: Herr Tichatscheck.

No lover of the organ should pass through Dresden without hearing the celebrated John Schneider. He is an organist of the old school, and probably no one ever lived who had a greater command of the instrument. We made up a little party, and having previously called on Herr Schneider, went by appointment to the Sophrine-Kirche, (the church of which he is the organist,) where we had the pleasure of hearing him for a little more than an hour. He played five of the fugues of John Sebastian Bach—he cares not to play other music. Bach is his musical Bible, and he has read him so much that he has ceased to take pleasure in inferior or uninspired writers. Bach is musical truth, unmixed with error; it is really interesting to see with what enthusiasm his works are spoken of, played, and heard by the German Musicians. Herr Schneider used no fancy stops, made no see-sawings with the swell, no contrasts of reeds and dulcianas, no high-diddle-diddles in his playing. His appeal is always to the intellectual musician. His great point of excellence, we suppose, is his *legato* touch, by which the chords are bound together, or melted into one continuous flow of harmony. Would that our young organists could hear such playing, even from childhood upward, so that they might be "trained up in the way in which they should go."

LETTER XXIV.

The Dom-Kirche, or Cathedral—The Exercises.

BERLIN, April, 1852.

THERE is no choir of music in Berlin, and perhaps none in the world equal to that of the Dom-Kirche, or Cathedral. This choir is very celebrated; it is the same choir, a part of which gave concerts in London in the summer of 1851. It is said to be even better than the far-famed choir at Rome. We attended three distinct services at the cathedral, and heard the choir each time. It consists of about fifty singers; the treble and the alto parts are sung by boys. It is arranged in double chorus, and the music of the old composers, in eight parts, is often performed; so that one may hear Palestrina, Lotti, Durante and others of the Italian school; Bach, Graun and others of the German school, together with the best modern authors. We infer from their collections of music, however, that they confine themselves almost exclusively to the *ecclesiastical style*, for we find their books contain nothing in the manner of Haydn's or Mozart's hymns, motets, or masses, or like other modern orchestral vocal music. The choir is entirely professional—that is, the singers are such by profession; they have learned to sing, and that is their business or calling. The boys who sing the upper parts are trained daily, and are preparing in their turn to be professors, teachers and composers of music, vocalists or instrumentalists, here or elsewhere. The parts are, of course, well balanced as to power, and the chorus of men's voices (tenors and basses) singing in unison, as they often do, is peculiarly grand and effective. In addition to the regular choir, there is a preparatory department, consisting of some twenty or thirty fine-looking little boys, of from eight to ten years of age. These are candidates for future membership, and form a juvenile choir; 'they stand on one side of the choir, and lead in the congregational singing, thus affording relief to the regular choir, and giving them time to breathe and recruit. We have said that these boys *stand;* this is equally true of others, for there are no seats in the organ-loft, and the members of the choir all stand during the whole service. The various exercises are distributed between the choir, the people, and the minister, so as to hold the attention and keep all employed. Those parts of the service which are performed by the choir, or by the people, are *sung*, and the part belonging to the minister is *read*. In this respect, the service is unlike that of the Lutheran churches in Saxony, where the minister's part is chanted, or uttered in singing tones. The *musical* forms of the choir performance are motets, (anthems they would be called, perhaps, with us,) short responsive sentences, in harmony parts, or unison, or a plain syllabic chant, with Hallelujahs, Hosannas and Amens. The *poetic* forms are mostly from Scripture, though sometimes metrical hymns are sung by the choir, but these are usually sung by the congregation. The *musical* form of the congregation is, of course, that of the *chorale*, and is Old Hundredth, St. Ann's, or York-like. The congregational tunes are sung much slower than we heard them in England, and about the time similar tunes have been generally sung in America. There is not an instant during the service that is unoccupied, one exercise following another without the least pause, so that the minister's voice seems to be joined on to the choir performance, or to the organ, or *vice versâ*. There is no interruption of the devotional exercises, by rubrical directions— " Let us sing," " Please to sing," " Omitting such and such stanzas," or by reading over a hymn before it is sung, as with us ; the hymns to be sung are known the moment one enters the church, their numbers being suspended on tablets in various parts of the house, so that they may be seen by all; and the particular hymn that is about to be sung, or that is being sung, is known by the tablet in front of the organ-loft, which contains the number of that only, so that any one coming in after the service has been commenced, has only to turn his eyes towards the choir-tablet, and he knows immediately where to find his place. The organ is not played when the choir sing, but is used only for voluntaries, intermediate responses, interludes or trans-ludes, and for accompanying the congregation when all unite in the song. There are no interludes either between the lines of a stanza, as in Saxony, or between the stanzas, as with us. The fashion of organ-interludes in hymn-tunes, seems to be passing away; and I observed, when in England, that they were but seldom introduced there.

The service is entirely liturgic, or is pre-composed, no pro-vision being made, that I could perceive, for extemporary per-formances. Yet the same liturgy is not always used, but there are different liturgies for different occasions. The most inter-esting service I attended was one for Passion Week, and which was used twice during the week. There was no sermon, or anything in homiletic form, but only devotional exercises, in connection with Scriptural readings. The time occupied was an hour and twenty minutes; and of this I should judge that an hour at least was occupied by the singing exercises of the choir, or congregation, and only about twenty minutes by the read-ings (prayers and lessons) of the minister; yet the minister stood during the whole service in front of the altar; and the whole congregation stood also during most of the service, the king himself, who was present, setting the example. The organ-loft is in a gallery immediately back of the altar; so that the congregation, when they face the minister, face the choir also. As I think a more definite idea of the service will be acceptable to those who are interested in such things, I will give a detail of the order of exercises on the occasion of which I speak :

1. A very short organ prelude, of perhaps two minutes.

2. Choir—Psalm xliii. (as it is found in the Bible) "Judge me O God, and plead my cause," &c. This beautiful psalm has been set to music in the motette form, by Mendelssohn, expressly for the *Dom-Chor*, and it was admirably sung without accompaniment.

3. Congregation—Hymn. The instant the anthem was concluded, or rather on the chord with which it closed, the organ commenced, in its loud diapasons, a *chorale*, in which all the people (some two thousand in number) without waiting for the organ to play over the tune as with us, immediately joined. One double stanza only was sung, during which the minister came in and took his stand in front of the altar.

4. Minister—Reading a single verse only : "Behold the Lamb of God, which taketh away the sin of the world." (John, i. 29.)

5. Choir—"He was wounded for our transgressions, he was bruised for our iniquities, the chastisement of our peace was upon him, and with his stripes we are healed." (Isa. liii. 5.) This was sung to most beautiful music, in eight vocal parts, composed by Otto Nicolai, of the old Italian school.

6. Minister—"The Lord be with you."

7. Congregation and Choir—"And with thy spirit."

8. Minister—Prayer.

9. Congregation and Choir—"Amen."

10. Minister—Lesson selected from the Gospels, entitled, "Jesus in Gethsemane."

11. Choir—"He hath borne our sins and carried our iniquities." Music by Graun.

12. Congregation—Metrical Hymn.

13. Minister—Lesson selected as before, entitled, "the trial of Jesus."

14. Choir—Micah, vi. 3, 4 ; music in four parts by Palestrina.

15. Congregation—"Holy Lord God," &c., and "Kyrie eleison."

16. Choir—Sentence or short Motette, in a chanting style, having relation to the indignities offered to Christ on his trial.

17. Congregation—Same as 15.

18. Minister—Lesson selected as before, entitled "the crucifixion of Jesus."

19. Choir—Metrical Hymn, beginning "O Lamb of God;" music by Johann Eccard. Most touching, tender, and effective was the pianissimo, yet crescendo and diminuendo performance of this single stanza.

20. Congregation—Metrical hymn, single stanza, sung to the famous old German chorale with which Graun commences his "Tod Jesu."

21. Minister—"And Pilate gave sentence that it should be as they required."

22. Choir—"Father, forgive them, for they know not what they do;" music by A. Neithardt.

23. Congregation—"Lord have mercy (or have pity) upon us."

24. Minister—Luke, xxiii. 39–43, being an account of the malefactors crucified with Jesus.

25. Choir—"To-day shalt thou be with me in Paradise." Music unknown.

26. Congregation—Same as 23.

27. Minister—John, xix. 25–27. The mother of Jesus standing by the cross.

28. Choir—"Woman, behold thy son," and to the disciples, "Behold thy mother!"

29. Congregation—Same as 23.

30. Minister—"Now from the sixth hour there was darkness over all the land until the ninth hour ; and about the ninth hour Jesus cried with a loud voice, saying, "Eli, Eli, lama sabacthani !"

31. Choir—"My God, my God, why hast thou forsaken me?" This was sung very softly and tenderly, with appropriate expression, and apparently with deep emotion.

32. Congregation—"Christ, thou Lamb of God, who takest away the sins of the world, have mercy upon us!" The music slow, and in the style of a chorale.

33. Minister—"After this, Jesus knowing that all things were now accomplished, that the Scripture might be fulfilled, saith, I thirst." (John. xix. 23.)

34. Choir—"Mich durstet," (I thirst,) most effectively sung, in the most simple manner possible, to the music—

Mich dur - - - - stet.

The alto and tenor may be easily supplied.

35. Congregation—Same as 32.

36. Minister—John, xix. 29, 30, concluding with "he bowed his head and gave up the ghost."

37. Choir—"It is finished!" Music simple, soft, and touching, as before:

Es ist voll - bracht!

38. Congregation—Same as 32.

39. Minister—Luke, xxiii. 45, 46.

40. Choir—"Father, into thy hand I commit my spirit."

41. Minister—"And when he had said this, he bowed his head and died."

42. Choir—A single stanza of a metrical hymn, the subject of which was prayer for Christ's presence in the hour of death.

43. Congregation—A stanza in continuation of the previous one by the choir.

44. Minister—Prayer for the king and country.

45. Choir and Congregation—"Amen, Amen, Amen."

46. Minister—The usual benediction. (Minister left.)

47. Choir and Congregation sang a closing stanza.

Thus there were in this service *forty-seven* exercises. If any one should think the detail dull or uninteresting, let him take the Bible, turn to the passages, and also from his Hymn Book select similar hymns, read them, sing them, and meditate upon them for an hour and twenty minutes, until his sympathies are awakened and his feelings moved, and he will change his mind, and say, "It is good to be here."

But to the choir again. It is hardly necessary to say, that its members seem to be perfect with respect to all the technicals of singing, such as the formation of the voice, utterance of words, and of tone, time, tune, pitch, &c. To all these things they have been *trained;* they have formed correct habits with regard to them, so that singing out of time or tune, falling from the pitch, bad tone, or inarticulate delivery of words or of tones, are never expected, thought of, or heard, and certainly would not be tolerated for a moment. They have a regular conductor, who stands in view of all the members, directs the time, and indicates such other things as are usual with the baton. But it is not only with these preliminary pre-requisites that the members of this choir are familiar; they seem to know what belongs to the higher departments of taste and expression, and in their performances they make such a practical application of the dynamic degrees and tones, as to bring out in a much more satisfactory manner than is often heard, the signs of a deep internal feeling; and all the externals seem to say that the spirit of worship may be there. We do not mean to say that all the people, or all the members of the choir, or the minister, *are* or *are not* true spiritual worshipers; this we do not know, but we think that such a *form* is presented, both as respects the matter and the manner in song and in speech, as is well adapted to the spirit of worship, and to aid the true worshiper in his sincere attempts to worship "in spirit and in truth."

We do not suppose it to be possible to train a choir of boys of twelve or fourteen years of age, to sing independently with any high degree of expression, (except so far as it may be done by imitation,) not even if the true spirit and worship is in the heart; the immaturity of taste and judgment belonging to their age must prevent this; but yet, something may be done, as is proved by the boys of the Dom-Chor; and certainly a much higher degree of excellence may be attained anywhere by *trained boys' voices*, than by *untrained female voices*, or such female voices as may sometimes be heard in our choirs. I presume there is no choir to be found in which a higher degree of excellence exists than in that of the Dom-Kirche; it is certainly much in advance of such of the English cathedral choirs as we have heard. That union or blending of the voices by which true chorus effect is produced, and without which it cannot exist, is realized in a high degree. Some exception must however be made here, and especially with respect to the union of *boys'* with *men's* voices; but this blending of the voices of the *Dom-Chor* is admirable, and when the tenors and basses are singing by themselves, or even when the altos unite, it is almost perfect; but the soprano of the boys, especially if it be above the twice marked small *c*, is so different in quality or character, that *that* close union by which many voices become *one*, is not attainable. In the English choirs there is indeed none of this blending, and the soprano of the boys stands out quite disconnected from the other parts. The choirs are so small, too, that this of itself is sufficient to prevent the effect of which we speak; for it is a well-known fact, that it cannot be easily attained with a less number of voices than about six on a part; but it seems not to be sought after in these choirs, so that in respect to this point, a choral performance in one of the English cathedrals, reminds one of Nebuchadnezzar's image, partly of brass and partly of clay. Not so, however, in the great musical festival choirs of England, or in those societies where a female soprano is employed, for in both these we have heard such a perfect union of fully-developed male and female voices, as to leave nothing more on this point to be desired.

The points which struck us the most forcibly with respect to the *external* of the singing of this choir, are *first*, the *decision* and *firmness* with which the tones are taken or delivered, and this is equally applicable to piano and to forte passages; and *second*, the *perfect truthfulness with which the pitch is held* by the mere voices alone, for the organ, as we have already remarked, is not played when the choir sing, but is only brought in to aid the congregational chorus; then indeed its pipes are not spared; but the greater part of the musical exercises are by the choir, *senza stromenti.* The choir seem no more to need the accompaniment of an organ, than does a well-organized and perfect orchestra; and the use of the vocal organs of the one seems to be as *firm, decided,* and *true to the pitch,* as are the *bows, strings,* and *mouth-pieces* of the other. A *third* point in which this choir excels—the *great* point—has already been spoken of, but yet we wish to add a few words on the *appropriate expression* which marks their singing. It is *tasteful,* or it conforms to the generally-received laws of taste in choir or orchestral performances. It is easy and natural, without any approach to coarseness, roughness, or crudeness, on the one hand, or affectation of beauty, or elegance, or feeling on the other. There is an absence of that stiffness or formality too often witnessed, and especially of that mechanical straining for effect which is apt to characterize the performance of such choirs as depend upon a marked hymn book, and endeavor to obtain expression from noted directions. True expression can only proceed from a well-educated taste, an instantaneous appreciation of beauty, a quick sensibility, and a warm and sympathizing heart; and this is equally true, both in elocution and in song.

That the choir of the Dom-Kirche is the best in the world, (as we have heard it called,) we do not know, but that it is, on the whole, the best we have heard, we are willing to admit; and the performances of the choir and congregation, separately and together, present us with as fine a form of church music as we may ever expect to witness in this world.

We cannot close these very imperfect remarks on the music of the Dom-Kirche, without contrasting for a moment, the form of church music which it presents, with one which prevails to a considerable degree with us. What would the quartet clubs of our churches do, if they should become familiar with such choir singing as we have attempted to describe? If governed by correct musical taste, or by religious propriety, and if uninfluenced by *that*, the love of which is the root of all evil, we think they would, at least, draw the curtains in front of the organ-loft closer than ever, or perhaps hang their four-stringed harps on the willows, and let the people sing their own songs, until a choir, properly so called, could be formed. What worshipping assembly, *knowing* the power of a good choir, would be satisfied for a single Sabbath with the drawing-room effects of a single voice on a part? The substitution of a piano forte for an organ in church worship, would not be in worse taste than the substitution of a quartet for a choir. A quartet is beautiful in its place, and in connection and in contrast with a choir, may be truly effective in church music, but save us from that form of song in the house of God, which consists in the monotony of a four-voiced performance, without the light and shade afforded by a chorus.

Again, the true form of church music can only be found in the union of a choir, (including solo and quartet,) with a congregational performance. And while these two combined present us with a most perfect form of church song, each must be kept in its own proper place; they must be related and de-pendent, and yet preserve their own independence.   Choir singing must be one thing, and congregational singing another, both with respect to the character of the music and the style of the performance.   Congregational singing can never be good, until such tunes as are now attempted are laid aside, and a plainer and easier class are alone encouraged.   No German congregation could sing such tunes as St. Martin's, Abridge, Devizes, and a host of others, old and new, now supposed to be appropriate to congregational performance in America; but let a plain and simple style of tunes be sung, such as are sung here, and let the more difficult and more tasteful pieces be reserved for a well-trained choir, and then both may flourish, strength-ening in each other's strength.   It is a grand mistake, but one that has extensively prevailed, to suppose that these two forms of church music are antagonistic, so that if one is encouraged, the other must be discouraged.   They are friendly, and should ever go hand in hand.

Once more—the account given of the Dome Choir should not discourage such choirs in our country, as can never expect to equal, or indeed to come near to that, in the excellency of their performances.   *That* is a professional choir, sustained at a great expense, and of course, the circumstances under which it prospers are quite unlike anything existing in our country. *Ours* must be voluntary choirs of amateurs, supporting them-selves, and in most cases paying their own expenses.   But yet, if those who have good voices will but apply themselves accord-ing to their opportunity, as much may be done by our choirs, to promote the cause of a spiritual and sincere worship in America, as is done by the more skilful, better trained, and better paid choirs in Germany.

LETTER XXV.

The Service at St. Nicolai—Mad. de La Grange.

LEIPZIG, Sunday, May 2d, 1852.

I HAVE just returned from the morning service. Since Easter, the Motets with Orchestra have been resumed; and to-day, the musical exercises were somewhat different from what they usually are. A *Chorale* was first sung; but there were not many people to join in. The exercises commence precisely at eight o'clock; whether anybody is there or not; and sometimes I have attended *public* worship, when there was no one present at the commencement, except the singers. After the *chorale* to-day, the first two movements of a mass by Cherubini were sung, " Kyrie," and " Gloria in excelsis;" sung, too, not in the vernacular language of the land, but in the original Greek and Latin. The " Kyrie " commenced with a short Violoncello solo; this is followed by a vocal solo for a Bass voice; after which the other parts join. There is much solo throughout the movement. The music, although very fine, did not appear to me to be very supplicating in its character, nor did it seem to urge the cry for mercy as one might suppose David urged it in the fifty-first psalm. At the close of the " Kyrie," the minister, at the altar, chanted a few words of prayer, and then followed a brilliant " Gloria in excelsis," mostly in chorus. A fugue is introduced, and the closing movement, to the word Amen, is very animating and triumphant. At the close of the " Gloria," the minister chanted the collect for the day with response by the choir; afterwards followed prayer, and then came a very fine Motet or Hymn with Orchestra, composed by Spohr. The moment this closed, choir and orchestra scattered, and were seen no more. The organ instantly announced a *chorale*, and the loud congregational chorus arose, most cheering, most refreshing, Sabbath-like, a song of worship, solemn, grand, majestic, " fit for an angel to play, or a martyr to hear ;" raising one's feelings, and bringing home thoughts of God, heaven, holiness, redemption, and eternity.

I am a great lover of music, I delight to listen to an orchestral performance, and never intend to omit an opportunity of hearing a good concert. But on the Sabbath-day, when one wishes to turn his thoughts upward, and bring himself into converse with his Father above, I love the great vocal chorus, plain and unpretending though it be ; it lays no claim to either science or art, yet it grapples with the spirit of worship, draws it out. and bears it with certainty and rapidity towards the object of its search, and penitence, and thanksgiving, and adoration fill the soul. Oh, that those who love the worship of God in our happy land, knew the power of song, to their aid ; and knew, too, that form of song, so well adapted to their end. I love the choir ; I would spend days and nights in its trainings, and labor without being weary in attempts to bring it to perfection ; I would listen to it on the Sabbath, be made sorrowful by its tones of penitence, strong in faith and confidence by its full, and scientific-wrought harmonies, jubilant by its Hosannas and Hallelujahs ; but even this is not enough. In addition to all that a choir can do, I want the *plain song of all the people*, above science, above art, above everything save Him into whose presence it hastens one, and before whose throne it fills one with the spirit of them who sing without ceasing : " *Worthy is the Lamb that was slain to receive power, and riches, and wisdom, and strength, and honor, and glory, and blessing.*"

I heard the congregation singing hymns of praise to-day ; the loud organ led them on, binding all together, so that the voices were as the voice of one man ; the grand chorus filled the house of the Lord; it seemed to say *Holy, holy, holy is the Lord of hosts! let the whole earth be filled with his glory;* and I came away wishing that the people of America could hear it too, hear it until they should know what we mean when we speak of congregational singing, become sensible of its immense importance to their worshiping assemblies, and hasten to take the appropriate preparatory measures for its introduction.

We have been favored with an opportunity to hear another very excellent singer, in MAD. DE LA GRANGE. She is a French lady, and a true artist. When Jenny Lind was here, some years ago, she was regarded as the best singer who was ever heard in Leipzig; save that now and then one remembered Catalani, and were, of course, unwilling to give up their earlier impressions with respect to that lady. Afterwards came the Countess Rossi-Sontag, who seemed to bear away the palm, and, indeed, she cannot be excelled; but now we have truly an artist of the first class here in the lady above named. Of her a very competent critic has said, in one of the papers, "She has never been equaled by any of her predecessors." While we might be willing to admit the truth of this remark in regard to some particular points of excellence, we do not acknowledge it as a general truth; and it must be credited to the favorable disposition of the newspaper critic. She has a voice rich in tone, extensive in compass, and of great flexibility. Her lower register is very fine, having more power than that of Sontag; indeed this is true of her whole compass, and in this particular she may be compared to Jenny Lind. With respect to quality and purity of tone, we think the latter lady may have the preference in the higher register, but elsewhere the voice of De la Grange is superior. In her lesson in the "Barber," of Rossini, she ran up with apparent ease to the thrice-marked small

g; and in her songs in the Zauberflöte she touched the thrice-marked small f with the ease and accuracy of a pianoforte. She sings with a freedom, openness, frankness of voice (so to speak) that we have scarcely ever heard equaled, and never excelled. She is, perhaps, thirty years of age, and of most interesting personal appearance, good figure, large and bewitching eyes, easy, graceful, and elegant in every movement and gesticulation. We have been delighted with her singing; but yet not more so than with that of Sontag or of Jenny Lind. Either of these singers will awaken the most perfect ideas of beauty, and fill one with delight; but to a singer like the Wagner, of Berlin, alone it belongs to move the deeper fountains within.

We have lately seen in a Boston paper a notice of Mad. Sontag, in which she was compared to *a marble statue, with a music-box in her throat.* While this in one respect is an excellent comparison, it is very unjust in another; in regard to the power of execution (technical) it does really give one a very correct idea of her wonderful performance; but with respect to the expression of appropriate feeling, entering fully into the character she represents, or of the song she sings, it is false, wholly false; for if ever woman excelled in the latter named points, that woman is Mad. Sontag. She has a music-box, indeed, but in addition to its exquisite mechanism, this box has a soul, a spirit of life and love within, manifesting itself in every tone, inflection, and cadence.

Mad. de la Grange sung in Rossini's "Barber," Bellini's "Lucia," Meyerbeer's "Robert" and "Prophet," and also Mozart's "Magic Flute." It hardly need be added that she met with a warm reception, and, at the increased prices, drew a crowded house.

LETTER XXVI.

The Leipzig Fair.

LEIPZIG, May 3, 1852.

WE are now in the midst of the Fair. This changes the whole aspect of the town. The ways are crowded, and the people move in solid columns through the centre of many of the principal streets. Every hotel is two or three times full ; and it is not easy to procure even a seat at a *table d'hote* for a dinner. It is highly interesting for one who is not a business man (and perhaps more so for one that is) to walk through the principal places of business, and see the great variety of articles exposed for sale. The more one sees, the more there seems to be seen. Many of the stores on the principal streets seem to be vacated during the Fair, and given up to the manufacturer or others who come from afar, to exhibit and sell their productions. The market women are driven from the usual market place with their butter, cheese, eggs, &c., and temporary or locomotive shops, stalls, or tents have appeared in their place, filled with all manner of fancy articles. Many goods are exposed on tables in the open streets, and where they are kept in shops, they are brought out in large quantities and exhibited at the doors. One street is filled with cloths, cassimeres, and various woollen fabrics ; the display of fine cloths of every possible shade of color, is full of interest. There is no extra display of books : though much book-business is done ; and the congregation of book-manufacturers and sellers is very great. They meet in their own exchange, or appropriate building. Starting at a convenient point, and walking round the city on the promenade, we first come to the potters' ground, where we see all manner of earthen vessels, pitchers, pans, plates, bowls, mugs, &c., &c., black, and white, and red, and yellow, and green, and especially brown. The stone-ware is adjoining this, and then comes a large space devoted to wooden-ware, especial such as belong to household affairs. We next come to the sell ers of flaxen goods; and here is a fine display of the coarse linens, as Diaper, Crash, and the like. Passing onward, we shall find ourselves in the midst of farming utensils, and from thence among the willow-weavers, and all sorts of baskets, wooden boxes, trunks, chests, packing-cases; glass and porce-lain are in the vicinity, of which there is a large collection; ready-made clothing, hosiery, and gloves; bonnets, and all sorts of ladies' muslin preparations (names unknown); with men's hats, day-caps and night-caps, and worked slippers, &c. But we have now come to Augustus platz, the open space between the Post-office and the Pauline Church, and this is crowded with everything; it is, as to the variety of goods exposed, much like the market place, although the latter is somewhat more in the fancy line. I will mention a few of the classes of wares and merchandize contained in different stalls, as I noted them down when I walked through the place :—Looking-glasses and picture-frames; umbrellas and parasols; wooden over-shoes (much worn); bird cages; bonnets, ribbons, and laces; oil cloths; ginger bread, honey cake, and confectionary; extensive dry-goods establishments, somewhat classified; copper kettles and all sorts of boilers and household vessels; flannels, a large assortment of white and colored; pins and needles; buttons; musical instruments; soap and perfumery; cigars; walking-canes; engravings and colored paints; jewelry; pipes (there are many shops confined to this article, porcelain pipes in all sorts of forms, with painted bowls and various ornamental works); whips, sadlery, &c.; tin-ware; brass-ware; hard-ware generally, and cutlery; blank-books and stationery; busts and plaster work; combs—ivory, wood, tin, copper, iron and horn;

upholstery ; brushes ; powder-flasks and various dishes made
of horn ; woollen yarns; but the idea of enumerating is absurd ; the oftener one walks through the narrow passage-ways
the more things he sees, and at every time discovers many articles which had escaped his notice before. Toy shops and pipe
shops are among the most frequent of any, and the display in
this way is very great. A very large majority of these shops
are in the charge of females ; as we walk along, they very mo-
destly offer their wares for sale, but one is not annoyed by constant appeals to purchase, and is rather permitted to pass quiet-
ly along and gaze. At about a quarter of a mile out of the
city, around the St. John's church, there is a shoe and boot
mart; and so there are various places in and around the city
where everything that any one ever thought of, and many
things that no one ever did think of, are for sale. The general
complaint is, this season, that business is dull ; the Austrians,
the Russians, the Prussians, and foreigners generally, have not
come in so great numbers as they sometimes do. The places
of which I have spoken are places for retail; the great whole-
sale business is mostly done, as I am informed, the week before
the Fair.

As we proceed to Rossplatz, we come to a multitude of eating and drinking " Restauration" places. As you pass by them
you hear music ; look in, and you will see women harping upon
their harps, and men sitting at tables with beer-glasses before
them, some drinking, some eating, and all talking and smoking.
The show-places, theatres, menageries, panoramas, circuses, and
houses or sheds for various games, sports, &c., come next.
There are about twenty of these within sight of our window
in Rossplatz ; and as almost every one of them employs a band
of music, and as many of these bands are playing on the piaz-
zas or balconies outside of the buildings, at the same time, in

different keys and movements, we are not at a loss for instrumental exhibitions daily from three to ten o'clock. But at ten everything ceases, and within half an hour all is hushed to stillness.

The Fair brings together many musicians. All the little bands from the surrounding country come to town to reap a little something during the harvest time. These bands are from four to eight or ten, perhaps, in number, and are variously composed as to instruments. Some of brass, some of strings, and some curiously mixed; as a horn, a clarionet, a violin, and a bassoon; or a double-bass, oboe, flute, and trumpet, &c. As early as six o'clock in the morning they are out, and are seen and heard playing in passage-ways, entrances to hotels, or wherever many people may be supposed to be within hearing; depending for remuneration upon the voluntary contributions of those to whose edification they play. They are almost all of them apparently very poor, and are contented with small gains; indeed, one would suppose that even *without* "food and raiment" they are content. They seem to enjoy it right well, and to take it for granted that others will like their music as well as they do themselves. Many females are seen with a very ordinary kind of harp in their hands; these unite into bands, and three or four are seen performing in chorus. Female violinists too, are often seen, and a harp and a violin are regarded as helps meet.

Prices of living are high in Fair time, and it costs one about the same here as in London or New York.

LETTER XXVII.

The Reformed Church—Singing—Preaching.

LEIPZIG, May 10, 1852.

THERE is a small church here distinguished by the above title. In what respects it differs from the prevailing Lutheran church, I do not know; but one of the principal points of doctrine, I believe, is that which relates to the Lord's Supper, or consubstantiation. The society have no entire building for the purpose of worship, and meet in an "upper chamber," in a large building near the St. Thomas church. They have here a very commodious chapel, neatly finished, capable of seating, perhaps, five hundred persons. The whole congregation yesterday did not number more than one hundred and fifty persons. The form of worship does not differ essentially from the Lutheran church; yet there is a space in the service left for extemporary prayer. There is no choir, but the singing is lead by five or six boys, who sing at the top of their voices the principal melody; tune or pitch being as true as the organ-pipe. The organ was played quite loud throughout all the hymns; so that the boys and the organ together quite filled the small place with sound, and constituted a ground or foundation upon which any one of the congregation might rest his voice with perfect security. One might sing under such circumstances without the danger of deviation from pitch or tune, or of being frightened, or of fearing he might frighten others by the sound of his own voice. The fact is, that in these German congregations such a current or tide of sound is put in motion by the organ and the leading boys that one has no fear of joining his own voice, however harsh or unpleasant it may be ; and this for two reasons : *First*, it is hardly possible that in such a loud chorus he can sing wrong; and *Second*, no other person will be likely to hear him, even if he should be able to hear his own voice. But it is very evident that, in this congregational singing, every one is attending to his own song, and not to that of others; every one is singing the hymn for himself, and no one listening to others' voices. It is as evident, too, that no one is thinking of good music, or of bad music, as is sometimes the case with us; and I do not think that the thought of music at all, (according to the common acceptation of the word,) comes into the mind. Music is regarded as one thing, and the singing of hymns quite another. For good music the people go to a concert or to the opera; or perhaps to a choir and orchestral performance in the church; but in the singing of the *chorale* by the people, good music is not looked for or expected. So it must be everywhere, unless such an attention is given to the subject in the way of cultivation, as can hardly ever be expected.

In this church everything was plain, almost as much so as in the churches of New England. There were no pictures, statues or carved images; no representation of the Saviour upon the cross, no altar or burning candles, but a simple reading-desk or pulpit, from whence proceed the prayers and the preaching. Prayers were read by a young man, a curate or assistant minister, and the preaching was by a fine-looking man of perhaps sixty years of age. His sermon I could not understand, but his *tones of voice, inflections* and *gesticulations* indicated a high degree of cultivation, excellent taste, and an ardent spirit. There was nothing severe, no harshness or scolding, but the winning tones of love were so mingled with the solemn declarations of truth, as to captivate one's feelings and make effectual the message of salvation. His manner was excellent indeed; and where this is the case, or where the preacher's whole external appearance seems to receive its general form and impress from a warm heart—a spirit glowing with love to God and man; and where this manifests itself in the most simple and unaffected way, yet always according to the laws of good taste and judgment,—the *matter* will be good too.

We wish our preachers could give more attention to the cultivation of the voice (not in song, but in speech), or to elocution, including gesticulation and all that belongs to a perfectly simple, easy and natural, yet elegant vocal delivery. There is a mighty power in the human voice; it is more irresistible than arguments; it takes possession of the heart, after which it is not difficult to control the head. To what, for example, was Whitefield's success to be attributed, (and many similar instances might be quoted,) but to his captivating voice and general pulpit manner? A sermon may be sound, logical, doctrinal, practical, experimental, and be lost because of an artificial, awkward, or forbidding manner. Harsh and severe tones of voice, and a scolding manner, will drive to antagonism, or to the defensive, when those of gentleness will draw with a power not to be resisted; and in the pulpit as well as in the choir, we need " apples of gold in pictures of silver."

LETTER XXVIII.

Churches—Royal Library—Military Bands—Church Music.

MUNICH, May 18, 1852.

THIS is a most interesting city, second only to Berlin, and in some respects before it. It has a population of about one hundred and ten thousand persons, almost all of whom are Roman Catholics. Its streets are wide and well paved, and its buildings are large, and not crowded thickly together. Its galleries of sculpture and paintings are among the best in Europe ; its public buildings are magnificent, and are embellished with statues, frescoes, painting upon glass, and whatever is ornamental ; with regard to *music*, although it may be second in some things, it is first in others. The Orchestra of the Royal Opera is admirable, and is under the direction of Kappelmeister Lachner, well known as one of Germany's distinguished composers ; some of his symphonies and overtures having been often played in Boston and New York.

The churches are large, and filled with altars, monuments, statues, &c., interesting to the *eye*, and often with music not less attractive to the *ear*. A new church, finished only a year or two since, is very elegant. In its interior are sixty-four beautiful columns, of rich Tyrolese marble, each twenty feet in length. The church is two hundred and eighty-five feet long, and one hundred and twelve feet wide. It is richly decorated with frescoes illustrative of the life of St. Boniface, to whom it is dedicated. To preserve the architectural view of the church unbroken, the pulpits are placed upon railroads, so as to be trundled out of sight when not in use.

The Royal Library is contained in a large and splendid building capable of containing two millions of volumes. The library now consists of about eight hundred thousand volumes. The collection of music books is large, and many of the works and manuscripts of old masters are found there ; especially those of ORLANDO DI LASSO, whose residence for many years was in Munich. In front of the building of the Conservatory of Music, Odeon-Platz, are statues in bronze of ORLANDO DI LASSO and GLUCK. There are many bronze statues about the city, but one in particular is attractive on account of its size. It is a statue of a female figure, emblematical of Bavaria, and stands in front of a building called the Bavarian Temple of Fame, a little out of town. The statue is upwards of sixty feet high, and stands upon a pedestal of twenty-eight feet. A lion of proportionate dimensions is by its side. Crawford's statue of Washington is about to be cast here, in bronze. One of the figures (Henry) is now in the foundry, and the others will be sent on, from time to time, as they come from the hands of the artist in Rome.

Among the most interesting features of these German cities, are the parks, gardens, &c., in which they abound. We have but to step outside of the gate of Munich, for example, and we find ourselves at once in a park of *four miles long ;* the whole being filled with trees, shrubbery, and flowers ; with roads, smooth as a floor, for carriages; and foot-paths winding in every possible direction. One may ride for hours in this park with ever-varying and ever-new prospects before him. The river Isar, a small but rapid stream, winds its way through these woods, adding much to the beauty of the place. It is a good ten-days' work to take a mere superficial look at the various works of art brought together in the Bavarian capital.

Military music abounds here, and is very fine. One of the best bands I have heard (but not better than the one in Berlin), consisting of about forty instruments, including oboes, clarionets, bassoons, &c., plays daily at eleven o'clock ; say an overture first, and then one or two pieces of lighter music. We have had this day an excellent opportunity of hearing military music, and at the same time, of seeing a military parade. The Prince Saxe, a brother of the Queen, died a few days since, at his residence in this city ; and to-day the body was removed from the house to the railroad depot, from thence to be taken to Altenberg, to the family vault. About three thousand cavalry, artillery, and infantry were called out to perform escort duty. There were seven fine military bands, a part of them being composed of mixed instruments, and a part of brass only. They played in admirable style.

This is a Roman Catholic place, and the music is, of course, such as belongs to that Church. There is but one place where a good choir is sustained, namely, the "Chapel of All Saints." This a beautiful building, about one hundred and fifty feet in length, ninety in width, and seventy in height. There are a number of fine carvings ; and the whole interior is finely covered with fresco paintings, on a gold ground ; so that the appearance, as one enters the building, is very splendid. We attended at this chapel on two occasions, on each of which high mass was performed, viz., Ascension-day and the Sabbath morning following. The music on the first day was by the director, AIBLINGER, well known as a composer of Masses, Motets, &c. The choristers numbered about twenty-four, or six voices on a part, being composed of the best professional vocalists, or opera singers, in Munich. The organ was well played, but never as an accompaniment, as the vocal music was without any accompaniment whatever. There was, in the performance of this choir, all the full, clear, and certain delivery and union of vocal tones that the most fastidious critic could desire ; though less of the *crescendo* and *diminuendo* than in the Dom choir at Berlin ; but in one respect, the Munich choir had a great advantage,—*the Soprano and Alto parts were sustained by female voices*. Consequently, there was a fulness, richness, and maturity of voice, and a blending in the chorus ; neither of which can be obtained in choirs where boys sing the Soprano. There is a disagreeable effect always resulting from the predominance of boys' voices in a choir. The attempt to unite them with adult voices, is like the attempt to mix oil with water ; they will not coalesce. I have not, in a single instance, heard boys' voices in a choir in which they did not stand out by themselves, as a separate thing, without sympathy, resemblance, or congeniality. There can be no perfect chorus where the Soprano, or even the Alto, is principally sustained by boys. Twelve or twenty boys, with good voices, trained to sing together, will form an excellent chorus of one part to lead in the singing of a large assembly of people ; but they fail not, usually, to spoil a complete choir or chorus of each of the four parts in one.

Mr. Aiblinger is an able musician, and a fine composer; and his vocal music seems to be a very happy medium between the old and the new. " A little too modern," said one of the best musicians in Munich to me, as we left the chapel. " A little too modern," I suppose the best musicians would almost all of them say ; but, while I admire the old, and regret that in America it should be entirely unknown, I cannot agree with those who for conscience sake would confine us to the old ecclesiastical tones. Mendelssohn has given us a happy medium in some of his vocal music, (written without accompaniment,) as the Berlin Psalms, and some other things.

I did not learn by whom the music performed on the second occasion was composed; but, on both occasions, most beautiful indeed was the performance of the choir. I never expect to hear it surpassed.

The music in the other churches, so far as I had an opportunity of hearing, consists of the old chant, the performance of which was, in some cases, very full and satisfactory.

The Protestants are but few in number, and their singing is congregational.

LETTER XXIX.

Henrietta Sontag.

MUNICH, May, 1852.

OF this inimitable artiste and mistress of song, we have already reported at length; but we have had the unexpected pleasure of hearing her again in the Bavarian capital, and cannot forbear saying a few words more. Since being in Leipzig, in February last, she has been singing in some of the most important German cities with the greatest success. In *Dresden, Breslau, Hamburg, Bremen,* and other places, she has met with the warmest reception; and now, in Munich, she is receiving the highest approbation that can be bestowed. Increased prices, crowded houses, wreaths, bouquets and showers of flowers, greeting her whenever she appears, all testify to the high stand which she takes as an artist. I have repeatedly seen her recalled after singing, three times, and even then the delighted multitude were hardly satisfied. It is indeed next to impossible that, in purity of tone, and perfection of execution, she should be excelled.

The man who, in describing her singing, said " she is a statue with a music-box in her throat," said well, so far as a perfect execution, *touching* or *bowing,* is concerned; but he should have added that it is a statue of humanity, having a spirit from the divinity within; a heart manifesting itself in every tone, look, gesticulation and movement. So easy, so graceful, so elegant, so chaste, so artistic, and yet so simple and natural is Sontag; who has ever seen and heard the like? One would think her to be a mere child of nature—(as indeed she is in the best sense of this expression;)—for there is an absence of all stiffness, formality, pedantry, and affectation, and yet the highest degree of cultivation and artistic excellence which can be imagined. One cannot give attention to her singing without being delighted. To listen to her is like looking at the most beautifully variegated bouquet, or collection of flowers, that can be brought together ; it is like the glittering plumage of the most brilliant of the feathered race; like the appearance of a thousand charming little girls of six years of age, wreathed with freshest roses, and dressed in purest white.

But she is coming to America, and then every one can hear her for himself. She expects (we have it from her own lips) to sail the latter part of August for New York; and then we promise all the lovers of perfection in song, full satisfaction. We cannot forbear adding, that which we have heard from various sources in Germany, that in addition to her artistic excellence as a singer, she is a most excellent woman, wife and mother.

LETTER XXX.

"Conservatorium der Musik."

MUNICH, May 25th, 1852.

THERE is a Conservatory of Music here, which seems to be in a very flourishing condition. A letter of introduction from Hauptmann secured for us a warm reception from the Director, F. HAUSER, (pronounced How-zer.) There are now connected with the Conservatory, fifteen professors of music, and ninety students. Every student is required to attend to the theory of music, harmony, fugue, and instrumentation, and also to either the Piano Forte or Violin ; in addition to which, such as desire it can attend to wind instruments, and to vocal music. Much attention is given to vocal music; the Director himself, being first teacher in this department. Many of the eminent singers now popular in Germany, were educated here. It is an excellent place for one who wishes to study the voice under the best advantages; and also for one who wishes to become acquainted with chorus effects, and the manner of drilling, training, and conducting a choir. Above one-half of the students constitute a choir, and meet regularly once a week for a two-hours' exercise, under the vigilant watch and care of Director Hauser. They practice the very best music, from Lasso and Palestrina all the way down to Mendelssohn; and on the afternoon when we were permitted to be present, the Oratorio of Elijah was performed, with Piano Forte accompaniment. The recitatives, songs, and concerted pieces were all given by pupils, and both these and the choruses were highly creditable to the institution. It was not a public performance, and was without rehearsal. Mr. Hauser was so kind as to allow us to choose what Oratorio should be sung, mentioning Elijah, St. Paul, the Creation, Seasons, and others; we chose Elijah, and it was put down before the choir accordingly, and, by them, quite satisfactorily rendered. It was a drilling, or training exercise, and the Director did not hesitate to stop the song whenever anything appeared to him to require it. Solo singers were in several instances stopped and corrected. The Director has full authority, and fears not to use it. After the performance was over, we spoke to him of the great advantage he had over an American Conductor in this respect; for surely no choir with which we are acquainted, would bear such close bringing up to the mark of perfection; and we said to him, that were he in America, and thus corrected faults, especially in a Solo singer, the vocalist would very probably take his hat, bid him " good evening," and be off. Mr. H. smiled, and said: " I am a tyrant here."

This, however, was his own saying, and not that of his pupils, who seemed to regard him with great respect and confidence. He is apparently a very able Conductor, instantaneous in ear and in speech, ever watchful and vigilant, detecting the smallest errors, and commanding respect and obedience. Where there is such a Conductor, there will be a good chorus, provided he has good materials at his disposal. Some of the pupils manifested much talent, especially a young girl, not more than fifteen or sixteen, who sang with an openness of voice, and fulness and purity of tone, charming in the hearing, and pleasant in the remembrance. A voice of such perfection is of more value than gold ; and (although there may be exceptions) indicates a good disposition. Happy are they in whom both are united.

We regret that we failed to obtain a printed plan or prospectus of the Conservatory at Munich, but we came away deeply impressed in its favor. The Library contains a good collection of the works of the best musical writers, and writers on music. Munich is a place where one can live as cheap as at any place in Germany—rents and tuition are very low, and food and raiment can be obtained for as small a sum as anywhere, except, perhaps, in some parts of Italy. Were I an American youth, wishing to obtain a thorough musical education, I should make careful inquiry as to the advantages of the Conservatory of Munich, before making engagements elsewhere.

LETTER XXXI.

Orlando di Lasso and Gluck—Prof. Dehn, of Berlin.

Munich, May 26, 1852.

Of all the old writers of vocal music, Palestrina seems to stand at the head. He seems to be held in the highest estimation by every truly learned musician. After Palestrina, perhaps there is no one for whom superiority may be claimed to Orlando li Lasso. He is the boast of the Germans, and passed the best part of his life in this city. In the Odeon Platz, in front of the building occupied by the Conservatory of Music, is a fine bronze statue of Orlando di Lasso, and also of Gluck. They stand there together; the former, the head of the German writers of the old school of church music; and the latter, at the head of modern dramatic musical composers. Gluck's opera of "Ipheginia in Aulis," can only be considered as equaled by Mozart's "Don Juan" and Beethoven's "Fidelio." Indeed, there are not a few who give Gluck the highest place. His operas never fail to draw out the most intelligent musicians, and it is always regarded as a rich treat to listen to them. The one we have mentioned certainly holds the highest place, but the Iphigenia in Tauris, the Alceste, and Orpheon, may still be heard; and hardly a classic concert is given in which there is not something found on the programme from this popular writer. Mozart, no doubt, owed much of his success to the fact, that in the order of time he followed Gluck, who is still held up to the student as one of the very best models. His "De Profundis" (138th Psalm), and other things, show that he might have excelled in church music. His music seems to be but little known in America, but it will hereafter be studied by the musical pupils of our country, and " Iphigenia in Aulis," at least, will be found in the libraries of all those who wish to analyze the very best specimens of song, and of recitative. Extracts from several of Gluck's tasteful melodies are to be found in a late work (and most beautiful and effective pieces they are) ; but, besides these, we do not know that any of his works have been published with us ; and even his very popular overture, so often played here, we believe is unknown to the American concert-going public.

The fame of Orlando di Lasso rests very much on his connection with David (good company, truly !) ; and his psalms are studied as affording some of the finest examples of·counterpoint, or four-part voice-writing, that can be found. In this respect, these old masters have not been surpassed by any who have followed them ; indeed, some of the best theorists have told me that no one now can equal them. Haydn and his followers have made great advances in all that belongs to instrumental music, but the capacities of the voice, it would seem, were thoroughly understood by the old composers. As Bach carried the fugue to perfection, so Palestrina, Orlando di Lasso and others worked out the full problem of vocal four-part writing.

It is pleasant to the musician to see such monuments as those I have mentioned erected to the memory of the great composers; and the statues of Orlando di Lasso and of Gluck, side by side, seem happily to unite the different schools and ages represented by these two distinguished men..

An anecdote shall close this communication. When in Berlin, we had the pleasure of an interview with Professor Dehn, one of the most learned musicians in Germany. Prof. Dehn has charge of the musical department of the Royal Library, and, as he was showing us the valuable and scarce old books, he came to Orlando di Lasso's Psalms. Wishing to express a decided opinion, and not being able to speak much English, he took the volumes into his hand, and touching me, to call my attention, gave them a very intelligible and affectionate kiss! Professor Dehn has edited a new edition of some of Orlando di Lasso's best works.

LETTER XXXII.

Pestalozzi—Nägeli—Church Service—Sunday School—Sacred Concerts in America—Schnyder Von Wartensee.

ZURICH, June 7, 1852.

PESTALOZZI lived here, and so did Nägeli; and here the first efforts were made to apply the principle of inductive teaching to music. The work of Nägeli and Pfeiffer was excellent, and its influence has been felt far and wide. Other manuals, based on this, have been since published, better adapted, perhaps, to the common purposes of teaching; but the work of Nägeli and Pfeiffer is a text book which every teacher should study until he makes the principle his own. "The Boston Academy's Manual of Instruction in Vocal Music," is the only work of the kind in English, so far as we know, in which these principles are carried out. Nägeli died in December, 1836. A very handsome monument of black marble, surmounted by a bust, has been erected to his memory, dedicated by the Swiss Singing Societies to their "Vater Nägeli." He died at the age of sixty-three. His family, consisting of his wife, son and daughter, still live in the same house in which he died. The son and daughter are both well-educated musicians, teachers and composers.

The contrast between the Lutheran churches of Germany, and the Zwinglian churches of Zurich, is very great in the Sabbath-day service, in many respects. The great Cathedral, where we attended, and where ZWINGLI once preached, is as plain as plain can be. There are no carvings, paintings, crosses, statues, or anything ornamental; not even a leather cushion can be found, or the smallest piece of drapery about the pulpit or elsewhere. There is neither organ, choir nor any instrument of music. The seats in the centre of the main floor are of plain, hard boards, unpainted; this part of the house is occupied exclusively by women. The men are mostly in the gallery, which is divided into separate stalls, each for one person. Each stall has a seat swung on hinges, that turns back after the fashion of the old New England swinging seats of a hundred years ago. The men on going into the church did not sit down, but each one took his stand in one of the stalls, waiting for the commencement of the service. Some took off their hats, others continued to wear them. When the bell ceased, the minister stepped up to the railing near the pulpit, and gave out the pitch by sounding the four principal tones of the scale to the syllable la, (1, 3, 5, 8,) and immediately the large assembly began to sing. The singing was slow, very slow; I have never before heard a tune sung so slowly as on this occasion. In singing a tune—"The Old Hundredth," for example,—I am persuaded that the Rev. Mr. Havergal's congregation would get through the tune by the time this Zurich assembly would get through the first line. The hymn-book used here, includes, also, the tunes, printed in four parts, and, although the tenor and the alto were not to be heard, yet many of the men made a bold attack upon the bass, which they made to tremble with uncertainty, if not with fear. The trebles in one line sought to attain the pitch of E; they reached a little higher than

E♭, but yet fell short of their aim, and this caused the sinking of the pitch, so that at the end of two stanzas it was something like a tone below its starting point. It was well that but two stanzas were sung; for a new pitch would have been necessary if the number had been much greater. Here, then, is a specimen of congregational singing without a choir or organ.

After the hymn had been sung, a prayer was read, and a lesson from the Bible followed. At the close of this, there was a chorus of seats, reminding one of half a century ago in New England; a chorus, which has long been discontinued with us, and which, certainly, I never expected to hear again. Every man let his seat fall at its own discretion. It brought vividly to mind the time when the boys in adjoining pews used to vie with each other in the *slamming* of the seats at the close of the prayer.

At the dinner table at the hotel, I was much amused at a conversation between two persons who seemed to be German-Americans, and another whom I supposed to be an Englishman. The conversation was in English, and related to the improvement of Americans in things pertaining to the fine arts, music and amusements. The theatre, the opera and concerts, were alluded to. Sunday concerts were especially spoken of, and the fact was mentioned that concerts on the Sabbath-day were more frequent.

"But," said the Englishman, "they call them *Sacred* Concerts, do they not?"

"No, not now," was the reply; "they used to call them *Sacred* Concerts although they performed overtures, waltz and dance music; but the word is no longer needed; it is pretty generally dropped; and now they simply call them concerts."

This is the progress of which they told; and they told of facts. We have often been surprised at the virtue of that word

Sacred ; when thus applied, it has great power to control the actions of many, and serves often to relieve the mind, or to calm and quiet a disturbing conscience. If the word *Sacred* were taken away from many concerts to which it is attached, it would be favorable to truth; even although the words sung are from David, Watts or Wesley; since the words are too often a mere apology for the song.

While at Zurich we had the pleasure of meeting the distinguished theorist, X. SCHNYDER VON WARTENSEE. He resides at Frankfort-on-the-Main, but usually spends his summers in his native Switzerland. He is not only a scientific musician, but is also a learned man. He was the intimate friend of Nä-yeli, and we believe also of Pestalozzi. He is the author of symphonies, quartets, &c., and has written one opera, but is better known as a profound theorist than as a popular practical composer.

LETTER XXXIII.

University—Castle—Singing Conventions—Wine Casks—Duels—Jerome of Prague.

HEIDELBERG, June 12, 1852.

THERE are quite a number of things here which cannot fail to interest the traveler. The University is very celebrated. There are usually some seven or eight hundred students attending the various lectures. Once a year there is a grand musical festival, many hundreds of voices uniting in chorus in one of the large open spaces found amongst the ruins of the old castle, a mile above the town. It was omitted this year on account of the death of one of the royal family. On such an occasion all amusements are suspended, and as the singing convention was regarded in no higher view than these, it shared the fate of the theatres and the dance parties. We saw the place were the meetings are usually held, and could easily imagine that the effect of a multitude of voices, under such circumstances, amidst the old towers and walls, would have been very imposing. We wandered about amongst the ruins and apartments of the castle, one of the most interesting in Germany. It was built and destroyed several times before the year 1764, when it was struck by lightning. The fire burned for eight days, and consumed most of the interior of the vast building. The grounds around are owned by the University. They are well laid out, and are kept in a fine state of repair. One cannot turn in any direction without seeing the most beautiful flowers and shrubbery, and these shady groves afford most delightful promenades. Fine views of the surrounding country are obtained from different points on the castle. A cellar contains a famous *tun* or *wine cask*. It was made in 1751. It is thirty-six feet long, and twenty-four feet wide. It is capable of holding eight hundred hogsheads, or upwards of 280,000 bottles. It has only been filled three times; the last time in 1769; and if the Maine temperance law should be adopted here, there will probably never be occasion to fill it more.

In a valley not far distant, our guide pointed out the place where the students of the University fight their duels. It is not an uncommon thing to have five or six of these gentlemanly combats in a day. There is not often a death, for the sight of blood is usually regarded as satisfactory.

The old church of St. Peter is visited with some interest, for it was here that Jerome of Prague, who, with Huss, was burnt at Constance, proclaimed the doctrines of the Reformation, and on the door he posted the *thesis* which, together with his bold preaching, resulted in his martyr death. One does not fear the stake now, but the spirit of persecution has not yet been entirely subdued; and uncharitableness is not a rare thing in the churches, even in the nineteenth century, and in our own happy country.

We need more of music's influence in the family, in the school, in the social circle, and in the church; for a man cannot hate his brother whose heart is filled with the true spirit of sacred song.

LETTER XXXIV.

Abbe Vogler—Rinck—Music in Schools—The Kappelmeister's Wife and her Rose.

DARMSTADT, June 19, 1852.

To the scientific musician, and to the lover of church music, Darmstadt is a place of interest. Here the ABBE VOGLER—a name well known to every musician—lived, and produced some of his greatest works; and here, too, he died and was buried. A plain monument of black marble, erected to the memory of "the excellent, learned musician, and talented composer," by Ludwig, Grand Duke of Hesse Darmstadt, stands in the old cemetery. It attempts to tell his fame, but his various theoretical works, and compositions, known to all the musical world, do it much more effectually. He was born in Würtzburg, June 15, 1749, and died in Darmstadt, May 6, 1814.

The organist, too, must be interested in Darmstadt, for here lived RINCK, a name better known in England and America than any other organ composer. He was for many years the organist to the Grand Duke, and was universally esteemed as a learned and accomplished musician, an elegant and tasteful organist, a worthy citizen, and an excellent man. His only son, Rev. George Rinck, is now a clergyman in Darmstadt, and his only unmarried daughter occupies the dwelling where the parents formerly lived, and which during their lifetime was a happy home. The editor of the *Musical World* * can tell of the excellence of Rinck, and of the happy domestic circle that surrounded him, for he was intimate with the family, and is still remembered by the surviving members with great affection.

Rinck's works, or many of them, have been re-published in America; especially his Organ School, and much of his organ music. They have circulated in every part of the land; so that wherever there is an organist, Rinck is known in his works, and studied. Whoever studies his organ music, with a tolerable musical ability, cannot fail to form a good style. We have for many years been accustomed to say, in answer to the question, " How shall I acquire a good style of organ-playing, and especially of voluntary playing?" "Study Rinck, for he is a sure guide." He is not great, like Bach, but he is ever beautiful and elegant. It was said long ago, that one who desired to acquire an elegant style of writing the English language, must spend his days and nights with Addison; and it is equally true that he who would acquire the most tasteful style of organ-playing, must spend his days and nights with Rinck.

We visited Darmstadt with especial reference to the library of Rinck, which we knew was for sale. The lover of music and of its progress amongst us will be glad to know that it is already packed, and will be on its way to America in a few days. If it arrives safely, it must be useful to some of the young men who are looking forward to the musical profession. There are now many young men who are beginning to feel the necessity

* R. Storrs Willis, Esq.

of a more liberal education for the profession of music than has hitherto been supposed important. One of the essentials, undoubtedly, is a knowledge of the German language. A man may, indeed, make a singer or a player on an instrument without this, and without much intellectual effort or study ; but to one who aims to be a liberally educated and thorough musician, a knowledge of the German is indispensable ; for there are more valuable scientific and miscellaneous books on musical history, criticism, taste, and general musical literature, than in all other languages together. It is indeed true that some of these are being introduced to the English reader by translation. The recent publication of the valuable work of Marx on Musical Theory, in New York, is an example of this ; but notwithstanding all that may be done in this way, there is a vast amount of musical knowledge that must remain inaccessible to the mere English reader for ages to come. The library of Rinck contains the most approved musical treatises, and popular works on the literature of music, that are to be found in the German language ; with books of music, and especially of church music, in the greatest variety, from the sixteenth century down to the present day.

Music in the schools is better taught in Darmstadt, at the present time, than in most other places we have visited. This is probably to be attributed not so much to the school directors, as to the fact that there is in this generation a man living there, whom God has made *a teacher*, or rather one who, having in a high degree the natural qualifications for a teacher, has, by study, observation, and especially by experience in the strength of the Lord, made himself one. There are but very few *really good teachers ;* for the office of a teacher is one of the most difficult to fill among men. But we have seen one here ; one whose heart is filled with the love of children, of his fellow-men, and of communicating knowledge; one who, delighting to teach, gives himself wholly to the work. He cannot live long, for there is such a continued drawing upon his physical, intellectual, and moral being, (and the drafts are all honored, too,) that he must soon wear out. But such a man will live *more*, if not *longer*, in ten years, than many will in fifty. It is most interesting and cheering to see a really *good teacher* before his class. We were permitted to accompany the gentleman to whom we have alluded to several of his classes, and to witness the intercourse between teacher and pupils. He seemed to come up to our recollection of Mr. Mann's descriptions, in his famous report, when Secretary of the Board of Education of Massachusetts. Let the music teacher obtain that report, and read it, and learn what he ought to be. His method was eminently *Pestalozzian*, full of interest, always lively, never wearisome, filled with variety of illustration, and in all respects satisfactory. We have such teachers in America, but all are not so.

Rinck's grave is in the new cemetery. A monument of freestone, in the form of a cross, tells of his resting place. He died August 7, 1846.

As we entered the cemetery in search of the grave, we met an elderly lady, having in her hand a vase containing a rose-bush, in which was a beautiful fresh and fragrant flower. We happened to meet the keeper of the grounds, or sexton, at the same moment that she also came up, and as we inquired for Rinck's grave, she said—" Rinck! I, too, wish to find Rinck's grave!" So we went in company. When we had arrived at the spot, she handed the vase to the sexton, requesting him to plant it on the grave of the organist, which was carefully done. "So," said the lady; and after looking in silence for a moment at the flower and at the monument, she took her departure. On inquiry we found her to be the wife of a military Kappelmeister residing here; and she had come out on a rainy day to pay this tribute of respect and affection to the memory of one whom, while he lived, all Darmstadt loved, and whose works now following him, all the musical world admire, Dr. CHRISTIAN HEINRICH RINCK.

LETTER XXXV.

Military Music—Schnyder von Wartensee—Prof. Schindler—Schmidt, the Pianist—Church Music—Organ Playing—Congregational Singing.

FRANKFORT, June 21, 1852.

THIS is a free or independent city, of about 70,000 inhabitants; some 6,000 or 8,000 of whom are Jews. Frankfort is the seat of the German Diet; consequently a military force of 10,000 or 12,000 soldiers is stationed here. A part of the city is elegantly built in modern style, but the *old Town* is the more interesting to a stranger. The streets are often very narrow, and the high old houses have often gables or projections jutting out at each story, until they almost meet in the centre at the top.

The military music is very fine. There are many bands, as Prussian, Austrian, Bavarian, and others. One of them plays daily in the square in front of the guard house; and, as each one tries to surpass the others, their performances are often carried to a high degree of perfection.

Several distinguished musicians make Frankfort their home. The SCHNYDER VON WARTENSEE, so well known not only as a learned musician, but also as a man of general literary attainments, is one of these. The Editor of the New York Musical World (R. S. Willis), knows him well, as he was for several years his pupil. He is now absent, spending the summer months in his native Switzerland. SCHINDLER, the biographer of Beethoven, also makes Frankfort his residence. He has many relics of Beethoven which he values very highly. He conversed for nearly two hours, with great interest, on his favorite author and his works. He says that Beethoven is played in quicker time now than formerly, and especially the *allegros* in his Symphonies. These, he thinks, lose much of their true effect by the quickness of the time in which they are played. The first violin, or the leading melody, is heard, but the inner parts lose their efficiency. He thinks Mendelssohn has injured Beethoven, by giving his great influence in favor of the quicker movement. He illustrated and proved his remarks on the degree of quickness with which Beethoven himself directed his own compositions, by anecdotes of Hummel, Hiller, Czerny, and others, who all agreed as to the general fact. He makes the same remark, also, with reference to Mozart and Haydn. There can be no doubt that the time is now taken quicker, in the performance of the compositions of these masters, than it was when they themselves directed it; but it is doubtful whether it will be restored. Modern associations and habits seem to require the change; and, it is not improbable that, had Beethoven lived, he too might have changed with the times. Herr Schindler remarked, that in Paris he has heard Beethoven played with very great perfection, notwithstanding the quickness of the time. The inner parts were there distinctive and clear, but generally it is not so.

ALOYS SCHMIDT, a fine pianist of the old school, and the teacher of both the Messrs. *Lange* of Boston, also resides here. He still plays in public occasionally.

By a recent act of the Government all places of business are closed on the Sabbath; so that, on this day, Frankfort appears

much more like an English or American, than like a German
city. The act is said to have originated rather from some
political considerations, than from a religious regard to the
day.

All the churches have organs, but there is no choir in any
of them, so that the singing is, as in most other German places,
exclusively congregational. Of the several specimens we have
heard, the best, perhaps, was at the Reformed Church. The
building is in good taste and convenient, being in size and form
much like one of our larger city churches. It is quite free,
however, from all those appearances of finery, or attempts at
display or show, which we sometimes see in our American
churches, and which are always unbecoming; while, on the other
hand, there is nothing of the rudeness or coarseness which is to
be seen in some of the Swiss churches. It seats, probably, from
1,200 to 1,500 persons, and was, when we were present, quite
full. The centre of the house, below, was occupied by women;
and the outside or wall slips, by men. The galleries, on both
sides, were occupied exclusively by men. The organ is large,
extending nearly across the end of the house; one man (precentor) leads the singing, aided by some twenty girls and boys,
whose voices could hardly be heard. The organ was played in
fine church style, with dignity, elevation, and firmness. It is
certainly a great relief to hear these German organs (or many
of them) played without the least attempt at showing off stops,
or at that prettiness which seeks to please or tickle, without
elegance or grandeur; and also entirely free from an evercon-
tinued and sickening seesaw of the swell, thought to be so exquisitely fine by some organists in England and America.
That the swell may be tastefully used we do not doubt; but,
its abuse is so much more frequent than its judicious use, even
by some who are otherwise truly good organists, that it is al-

most doubtful whether it would not have been better if this *im-provement* had never been invented.

The service commenced with quite a long voluntary of ten minutes or more, consisting of an introduction and fugue. The subject of the fugue was, perhaps, a little too chromatic for the dignity of worship, but it was played slowly and with great precision and certainty. Fugue-playing is usually slower by the good organists in Germany, than it is in some other places. The fugue is often taken in so quick time as to produce a con-fused mixture of subject and answer, depriving the composition of meaning, and rendering it almost unintelligible, and quite embarrassing to the hearer. One reason of this is obvious; it is vastly easier to play a fugue upon the run, with constant ac-celeration, than it is to play it in moderately slow and strict time. At the close of the voluntary, the minister, followed by the session, entered; the former took his place in the pulpit; the latter took their places in seats appropriated to them, on each side, facing the congregation. The organ then gave out the tune Iosco (Cantica Laudis, p. 296)—the melody was made very prominent, the bass was played by the pedals, and an in-termediate figured accompaniment filled up the harmony, pro-ducing a fine effect. The hymn, the subject of which was *prayer to Jesus for his spirit*, was finely sung by the whole as-sembly, all singing the melody. At the end of the first line of the last stanza, which was doxological, the minister rose in the pulpit, *not to find his place in the Bible as if he was in a hurry to cut off the last act of praise*, but apparently as an act of rev-erence, as he kept standing, without any movement, and was soon followed in his example by all the male part of his con-gregation. A short prayer followed the hymn; then an address (extempore) of four or five minutes; after this the regular morning prayer was read; another hymn was sung as before, and the sermon followed. There were two hymns sung afterwards, making four times singing during the exercises. Here was a very simple, appropriate, devotional service for a Sabbath morning,—almost the same, indeed, as is the religious service in our Presbyterian, Baptist, or Congregational churches, and vastly superior to the Lutheran or English Cathedral repetitions and forms. But, if in addition to good choirs, we could have the Congregational singing exercise, it would be a vast improvement on our present forms of worship. The beauty of the singing exercise, or its adaptedness to worship, is to a great extent lost with us, and we need, in order to its recovery, the congregation in connection with the choir, in the singing of " Psalms, and Hymns, and Spiritual Songs."

We heard, also, a very excellent example of Congregational singing in the St. Catharine Church. The congregation consisted of at least some twelve hundred persons. The exercises commenced by an organ voluntary of about four or five minutes, at the close of which the whole congregation joined in the old choral everywhere heard in Germany, the first line of which is 1, 5 3, 1 5, 6 6, 5, &c., in the key of E flat major. Two stanzas were sung, each taking four minutes. At the close of the second stanza, the organist, continuing to play, changed gradually his key to A minor, closing an intermediate voluntary of about three minutes, diminishing to pianissimo so as to hush the house to perfect silence; then, after a moment's pause, the people joined again to the lead of the organ, in the fine old choral beginning as follows: e, a g, f e, d—, e—, &c. Four stanzas were sung of three minutes each. Here, then, were two hymns sung in connection; which, with the organ prelude and interlude occupied full half-an-hour in the performance. Men's voices predominated, marking in strength the bold outlines of the tune; while female voices were heard and seemed to come in echoing, enriching, beautifying, and rendering that charming and lovely which otherwise would have been too severely grand and majestic. The organ was firm and steady, leading along the whole combined chorus with the utmost certainty, and giving full confidence to all the voices.

LETTER XXXVI.

Matinée—Mozart—Bach—Elocution—Singing—Piano Forte—Bonn—Beethoven's
Monument—Cologne—Aix-la-Chapelle—Don Juan—Musical Conventions.

Aix-la-Chapelle, June 24, 1852.

Just before leaving Frankfort, we had an opportunity of attending a *matinée*, or very select morning concert, in the saloon of the Mozart House. Such morning concerts are quite common in the larger German cities. An individual, having the means to do it, employs at his own expense an orchestra, or more probably a quartet, or quintet, makes out his own programme, and invites his friends to spend a couple of hours in listening to fine music. On the present occasion, an audience of perhaps two hundred persons (the most musical people of Frankfort) were brought together. Schindler, the biographer of Beethoven, *Schmidt* the pianist, and other distinguished persons, were present. The concert consisted of both vocal and instrumental music; and Music's sister, Elocution, was also brought in, and lent her aid in the exercises of the occasion. The programme contained the following pieces (though not in the order in which they are here put down), viz. :—Quintet (G. minor), *Mozart*, charmingly—I suppose it may be said, perfectly played by Messrs. Wolff, Baldenecker, Posch, Drinnenberg, and Siedentopf. Quintet Movement, *Mozart*. This

very beautiful movement by Mozart has not before been played since the year 1783. It has been recently discovered in
Mozart's own hand-writing, among his manuscripts, which for
some twenty years have been in the family of André of Offen-
bach. It will shortly be published. RECITATIVE and AIR, with
violoncello and obligato accompaniment, composed by *John
Sebastian Bach.* This song is quite of a popular character, notwithstanding it is by Bach, reminding one somewhat of Han-
lel's most popular songs. It is a sacred song, from an unpublished cantate ; but the Recitative and Song will soon be published. PART-SONGS, for soprano, alto, tenor, and bass. Two
songs were sung by a well-trained double quartet. A POEM
on Mozart was well read by a lady, having a rich alto voice,
Fräulein Gräemann. The effect of introducing this elocutionary exercise was very pleasing, and the example is a good one
to be followed wherever a really excellent reader can be found
to sustain the part. Strangers are sometimes invited to play
in these concerts ; and on the present occasion two pianoforte
pieces, " *Amitie pour amitie,*" composed by the performer, and
Doneyschock's *Rhapsodie in C. Minor,* were played by Mr.
William Mason of Boston, U. S. A.

On our way down the Rhine, we made a stop at Bonn, just
long enough to see a little of the place where the great modern
composer, BEETHOVEN, was born, and to look upon the monument which art has here erected to the memory of one of the
greatest of artists. The monument stands upon a public square,
and consists of a fine bronze statue of the symphonist, holding
an open sheet of paper in the left, and a pencil in the right
hand. Our little company, together with a few strangers who
went to see it at the same time, stood under the deep shady
trees by which it is surrounded, and gazed upon it for a few
moments in perfect silence, and with intense interest. No mu-

sician who is able to bring up to his imagination the wonderful original, can look upon this statue without a deep feeling of reverence and admiration, amounting as nearly to worship and adoration as may be rendered to the highest manifestations of human genius.

The darkest, most uncleanly, and uninteresting city we have seen is Cologne. Farina himself, nor the whole company of Farinas, can keep it clean. Yet its cathedral, though unfinished, is grand ; and there we heard the priests, with organ aid, chanting their Gregorian mass.

At Aix-la-Chapelle, as we rode from the railroad station to the hotel, we found the streets filled with people ; a large band of music occupied a central position, and the whole town seemed to be awaiting some important event. On inquiry, when we reached our hotel, we ascertained that the occasion of the general turning out was the expected return of the singers of Aix-la-Chapelle from Lille, where they had been for a few days to attend a grand musical festival. Different choirs had contended for a prize which had been offered for the best vocal performance, and the news had already arrived that a choir from this place had been the winners ; and the multitude had assembled to give them due honors and a cordial reception on their return home. They came soon after, but unfortunately a violent shower of rain prevented the procession through the principal streets that had been intended. But it did not prevent the performance of Mozart's *Don Juan*, which was given in a very respectable manner in the evening.

Although we have been fortunate in occasionally coming unexpectedly upon musical performances, we have necessarily lost others, which we should have been delighted to attend ; for example, in addition to that already mentioned at Lille, there was, on the 22d and 23d June, a grand festival at Ballenstedt,

Hanover, where a very large choir and orchestra performed, under the direction of FRANZ LISTZ. The two most attractive pieces were " The Ninth (choral) *Symphonie*" of Beethoven and the " *Walpurgisnacht*" of Mendelssohn. There is also within a day or two from this date a large musical festival to take place in Brunswick, at which the great pieces are Mendelssohn's *Elijah* and Beethoven's *Ninth*.

But we have lost musical meetings which we value, on some accounts, even higher than we do these. We refer to the several conventions and anniversaries in our country which take place during this and the next month, to which we were honored with invitations, and some of which we have for many years been accustomed to attend. Success to their summer assemblies! We hope hereafter to be permitted to join them again in those exercises of teaching and training which we have reason to believe have heretofore been acceptable and useful.

LETTER XXXVII.

Church Music—Catholic—Protestant—Old Psalms—Hotel des Invalides—Concerts—Meyerbeer—Onslow—Adam—Henrietta Sontag—Americans—Etc., etc.

PARIS, July 7, 1852.

WHAT shall we say of Church music in this city ? Those who *know* what it is, will not expect much, and yet we must attempt to glean something.

The church of St. Roch is said to be one of the best with respect to the musical service; but, the singing in the mass was so indifferently performed, the day we were present, that it is difficult to find anything to say in favor of it. At the Church of Madeleine, it was about equally good, bad or indifferent. The fact is, the Roman Catholic service (musical) seems to receive but little attention, and to be very carelessly performed everywhere, with the exception of a few of the Cathedrals or Royal Chapels of the larger cities. The best choir-singing, (Roman Catholic,) without accompaniment, we have heard, was at Munich; and the best, with orchestra, perhaps, at Dresden.

We attended, last Sabbath, the Church " De l'oratoire," one of the old Calvinistic churches of France. The church contained a good-sized organ, which was indifferently played. There was no choir. The organ led, and was followed by a very nasal precentor's voice, with a few of the congregation joining in humming under tone ;—one of the worst specimens of Congregational singing we have heard, yet interesting by association, for it carried us in imagination to our home country (beloved) where we have sometimes heard similar attempts. At this, and the associate churches, the old psalms of Clement, Marot, and Theodore Beza, with the tunes originally set to them, are still sung. But the tunes have recently been much injured, nay spoiled, by a rythmical arrangement by Wilhelm. He has introduced dotted notes, which, with other things, makes them so difficult, that a congregation cannot keep together in singing them. Even the organist did not come very near to correct time in playing them. The Old Hundredth psalm tune (134th, in the book here used), is turned into triple measure, thus :

The second, third and fourth lines are exactly like the first in rythmic form. Other tunes are treated with as little judgment and knowledge of Congregational singing.

We cannot forbear mentioning in this place that we have been so fortunate as to obtain in Paris an old copy of the Bible, entitled " *Calendrier Historial*," published in 1567, containing the original " *Les Pseavmes mis en Rime Française par Clement Marot, and Theodore Beza.*" The word *Bible* is not used on the title-page or elsewhere. It was printed at a time when the Bible was not permitted, and the title " Calendrier Historial," was adopted, that the soldiers, who could not read, but had learnt the word " Bible," should not, when they came round to search, be able to identify the book, and thus it would be preserved. After the title-page, it contains a " *lectevr* on *Almanachs and Calendriers,*" and a " *Table dv cycle solaire, Lettre Dominicale, Bissexte, Pasque, Nombre d'or, and indiction Romaine.*"

We attended the service on Sunday at the " Hotel des Invalides," to witness the manner of worship provided for the old and disabled soldiers, who find their support here. They were formed in two single columns, one on each side of the centre aisle, each man bearing a flag-staff, which was " carried," " ordered," " presented," &c., at the word of command.

The *religious* exercises commenced by a grand voluntary, by the military band in attendance, which was nothing more or less than the overture of the *Caliph of Bagdad*, by Boieldieu. The grand military mass now followed, and it consisted of a succession of popular operatic airs, played by the band, with an occasional roll of the small drums, an " order," or a " present " by the old soldiers, and a pantomime by two or three ministers, bowing, kneeling, crossing, &c., &c., now here and now there. Words or thoughts are not necessary in such a worship as this, which seems to be designed for mere external sensuous impression—yet there were a few words chanted by the drummers, towards the close of the *solemnities*.

" It is a very solemn service," said a young man, whom we happened to fall in with as we came away, and whom, from his speech, we supposed to be an American or an Englishman. So may a theatrical exhibition, or other spectacle, or pageantry, be solemn, and yet be quite without that " spirit and truth " so essential to religious worship. To see these things is enough to make one long for the simple worship of a church of the Puritans; yet, there are young men who come from America, and see, first, perhaps, the Puseyite worship in England—then the more consistent Roman Catholic forms, and become decided Romanists, and, perhaps, take upon them Holy Orders.

There are a multitude of concerts here, and musical festivals; grand orchestras of many performers, under distinguished conductors; and they play grand " *Quadrilles, Valses, Polkas, Mazurkas, Redowas, Schottisches, les plus en vogue ;*" with " *Cloches, Grelots, Fonets, Vapeurs, Tam-tam, Coeur-infernal, Feu de Bengale, etc., etc.*" Our *Grand* Concerts " *every night in the week, Sunday excepted, as whites and Ethiopians,*" are not inferior to these Parisian daily *grand* performances. It is but justice, however, to say that the concerts of the " *Conservatoire de Musique* " have a very high reputation; so that even the Germans say that at them Beethoven is admirably performed. These are now closed for the season. Meyerbeer has been in Paris several days. He is out of health, and is soon going to the waters of Spa. Six representations of his opera " Struenzée " have been given lately in Hamburg.

Onslow, the composer, is suffering with a severe malady of the eyes, which causes him, for the present, to rest from his labors.

A new mass, by ADAM, was lately performed in the town of Avray. The composer, accompanied with a choir of singers, went from Paris for the purpose, taking with them one of Alexander's melodeons, and a harp, as a substitute for organ and orchestra. The accompaniment was so arranged and dis-

tributed between the reeds and the strings as to produce a fine
effect.   A Credo from Cherubini, and a Gloria by Dietsch, were
also well performed.

A late Munich paper contains an account of the last concert
of Henrietta Sontag in that city.   It was given for the poor of
Munich ; and, after its close, the artists and amateurs of the
city complimented Mad. Sontag in a manner " worthy of themselves and of her."   As they were bidding her farewell, in the
name of the Bavarian public, they formed a circle around her,
and sang a chorus composed many years since in her honor.
Madame Sontag was deeply affected at recognizing in the words,
an ode which was written for her by the present King of Bavaria, Maximilian II., when he was Crown Prince, at the University of Berlin, in the days of her first triumphs, upwards of
twenty years ago.   From Munich Madame Sontag went to
Ems, where she spends a few weeks for rest, and will then soon
proceed to New York.

Mr. C. C. Perkins, of Boston, is here, industriously pursuing a course of scientific study.   He has cultivated a taste
for the most classic compositions ; and his influence upon the
Art must be of the highest advantage to American music, and
to the progress of music generally in our country.   He intends
to continue his studies next season in Germany.

We have had the pleasure of meeting here, also, Dr. S. P.
Tuckerman.   Dr. T. has now been in England for several
years, studying the English church music.   He has received
the degree of Doctor of Music, from the Archbishop of Can-
terbury ; the first instance of the conferring of the honor on an
American.   Dr. T. has just returned from a musical tour
through Italy, and he intends to visit Germany the coming
winter.

Mr. Nathan Richardson, of Boston, left Paris a few days

since for London, whence, after a few months, he will return to his native country, to commence his musical professional career. Mr. R. commenced his studies, we believe, under Mr. Webb; after several years' study in Boston, he went to Germany, where he remained about four years; he then spent some six months in Paris. He has all this time been under the best masters that could be found, and he has turned his special attention to the art of teaching. We rejoice in this, for there may be those who play well, or sing well, or are good theorists, and understand all harmony, counterpoint, and fugue, but who are poorly qualified to teach. Indeed, to be a good teacher, one must have a *genius* for it, and *a delight in it;* and, when we see a young man devoting himself to this particular musical department, and pursuing it with steadiness and perseverance, we may conclude (if we may judge of one of his works), that he has the love of it in his heart. Success must follow. So may it be in the present case.

Mr. J. C. D. Parker still pursues his studies at Leipzig. Mr. S. P. Homer, and Mr. William Mason, are in Frankfort.

We daily meet Americans in Paris; some seeking for health, some for pleasure, and many for knowledge in some department of science or art.

LETTER XXXVIII.

Singing in the Jewish Synagogue; also in the Church St. Roch.

PARIS, July 12, 1852.

ON Friday evening last, we attended the regular service at the Jewish synagogue. There was a congregation of perhaps three hundred men occupying the lower part of the house, and a few scattering women were seen in the gallery. The men all sit or stand with heads covered; and although four of us Americans took off our hats when we entered, we were told to put them on again, and obeyed orders. There was very little appearance of reverence or solemnity; indeed, none that could be observed. The appearance of the assembly was somewhat like that of a New England town meeting, after having been called to order by the chairman. There was a choir of about twelve or fourteen boys, with men for tenor and bass, and the harmony parts were sung. All the service was chanted, in a responsive manner, by priest or priests, choir and people, with the exception of two airs and melodies, which were sung by the choir. These were both modern, and even the chants did not seem to come from David or Solomon, but were more like the common chant, somewhat modified by a kind of recitative or declamatory manner of utterance. On the whole, the Jewish service here was not one of much interest, considered either religiously or musically.

On Sabbath morning, we attended the Roman Catholic service at St. Roch. Music receives more attention here than at, perhaps, any of the other Paris churches; and the whole mass was, to-day, quite well done. The choir, including ministers, boys, and all, numbered about fifty persons. There are two organs; a large one at the end of the gallery, occupying about the place in the house that organs generally do with us; and a smaller one in the choir, near the altar. This latter was used exclusively for accompaniment, and the former, or large one, was played only when some flourish of overture or march triumphant was desired. Then it sent forth its tones loud and jubilant, so as to make the welkin ring again. The music was quite modern; as much so as if composed by the latest Dcnizetti or Verdi, and quite in the orchestral, anti-ecclesiastical style. It was indeed vocal,—words were sung; but, as they could not be understood, the effect of the whole was such as is the musical effect in a grand pantomime. Indeed, the worship in the Roman Catholic cathedrals seems to be little else than a mute, gesticulatory action of bowings, crossings, and kneelings, with grand processions, musical accompaniment, &c. Musically considered, however, the performance was good. It was prompt and energetic, and the pianos and fortes were well observed. The organs too, though far different from the German style, were played with all the power of execution that could be desired.

LETTER XXXIX.

Concert of the Musical Union—Church Music—London Sacred Harmonic Society—
Opera Singers—Henriette Sontag—Spohr.

LONDON, August 2, 1852.

WE did not arrive in London until after most of the musical season was over; consequently there is not much to be heard. On the very day of our arrival, however, we had the pleasure of attending a very fine performance of "The Musical Union." The following was the programme for the occasion:

1—QUINTET, G minor.................................*Mozart.*
Allegro, Adagio, Minuet, Finale.
MM. SIVORY, MELLON, VIEUXTEMPS, OURY, and PIATTI.
2—TRIO, E flat. Op. 70................. ....*Beethoven.*
Adagio and Allegro, Allegretto, Minuet, Finale.
MM. HALLé, SIVORY, and PIATTI.
3—LEIDER.,.......................................*Mendelssohn.*
4—QUINTET, Op. 20......................... ....*Beethoven.*
Allegro, Adagio, Minuet and Trio, Presto.
MM. VIEUXTEMPS, MELLON, OURY, WEBB, and PIATTI.

Here was a programme worth one's attention, whether the compositions, or the performers be considered. It was interesting to see such artists taking subordinate parts, that the compositions might be as perfectly rendered as possible. It is needless to add that the result did not disappoint expectation. This was the last concert of the Union for the season. Sixteen performances have been given; eight evening concerts, and eight subscription *matineés*. The Union have secured the very best artists; and *three* Italians, *two* Hungarians, *two* Bohemians, *two* Belgians, *one* Bavarian, *three* Prussians, *one* Austrian, *one* Frenchman, and *five* Englishmen, have been employed. So, it seems as many foreign artists are employed in London as in New York.

On Sabbath last we attended public worship at the Scotch Church, under the pastoral charge of Dr. John Cumming. Dr. Cumming is a very popular preacher; his house is generally crowded, and it is not easy always to obtain seats—which favor, however, we procured, through the politeness of the leader of the singing, Mr. Purday. The order of exercises observed in this church is an excellent one, and I therefore copy it.

I—Singing—a Hymn by the Congregation.

II—Prayer, half as long as the Prayer usually is in Presbyterian Churches.

III—Choir Singing. An Anthem.

IV—Reading Scriptures, with Exposition.

V—Hymn, sung by the Congregation.

VI—Prayer, about the length of the first.

VII—Sermon.

VIII—Singing by Congregation. Notices.

IX—Concluding Prayer, and Benediction.

The standing position was observed in the singing exercises, and the sitting posture in *all* others. I will not attempt to report the sermon, but will only observe that one more plain, faithful, and edifying can hardly be imagined. The text was

"It is good for me to draw near unto God."

It will be observed that the singing exercise occurs four times; thrice by the congregation, and once by the choir exclusively. The people generally united, although the tunes, (with the exception of the last, which was York,) were too difficult to justify the expectation of the best congregational singing. The old tune of Martyrdom was sung; but in singing it, the people could not keep together, on account of the triple measure, and the crotchets in the fourth line. The other tune (we do not know its name) was so high that many could not reach the pitch. A congregational tune should not go higher than D, or E flat.

At three o'clock we attended the Episcopal service, at Lincoln's Inn Fields. Mr. J. A. Novello is the principal bass in this choir. The service was quite well done, and the popular anthem by Purcell, " O give thanks," was highly interesting. In the sermon there was a great falling off, indeed, from that of the morning.

In the evening we attended the Baptist Church, Devonshire Square, Bishopgate street. A precentor, standing in front of the pulpit, led the singing. He first read a stanza, and then it was sung by all the people; and, thus, the whole hymn was alternately read and sung. The same obstacle to success in Congregational singing was observable here, as at the Scotch Church in the morning—*the tunes were too difficult*, and the effect of the singing was wretched. We are more and more satisfied that tunes must be made more simple in *time*, and *limited in compass of melody*, to insure success in this form of church song. The St. Nicholas Church in Worcester, England, has the true Congregational style, and when that, which we have heretofore described, shall universally prevail, Congregational singing will be excellent and effective.

We have recently attended a rehearsal of the London Sacred Harmonic Society, under the direction of Mr. J. Surman, There are two societies meeting in Exeter Hall; the Sacred Harmonic Society, under the direction of Mr. Costa, and the one before mentioned. There were about one hundred and fifty members of the choir present at the meeting of the *London Sacred Harmonic Society*, with an accompaniment of about twenty stringed instruments. A new Anthem, by Dr. Elvey, of Windsor, was sung, and also Mozart's Twelfth Mass. The performance was decidedly poor—vastly inferior to the German choruses which we have recently described. The *time* was tolerably well kept, but *tune* was far enough from accuracy. The same feeling about for the pitch, and uncertainty of tone, was observable in the more difficult modulations, which is so common with our untrained New England choirs; with this difference, however, that *we* occasionally stop to correct a badly-intoned passage, whereas *here* it was passed over as if unobserved, or as if such a dissonant performance had become a matter of habit. There was, too, an absence of all those things that go to make up a good choral performance, as *Forte* and *Piano*, *Sforzando*, *Syncopated accent, distinctness and clearness of vocal utterance, &c.* The leader would occasionally sing out at the top of his voice, " Piano," but he did not seem to expect that attention would be given to what he said, and kept on, *under a press of sail*, until another opportunity should occur for calling out with like result.

This was, indeed, a rehearsal ; but if a choir is permitted to sing *thus* in rehearsal, will they not form habits that will prevent improvement, and will not the public performances be of the same general character ?

The violins were badly played. One could hardly help coming to the conclusion that they were mostly *beginners*, assembled for practice. It would not be surprising to hear as bad, or even a worse, rehearsal, on the Western Continent; but, in Europe there should be, at least, a correct performance of the technicals of music, if not something belonging to the higher department of appropriate expression.

The contrast between the singing of this choir, and that of many of the choirs which we have heard, during the last six months, in Germany, is very striking indeed, and tells much to the praise of the latter with respect to progress in the performance of vocal music.

We have not spoken of the great singers; the fact is, they have been often described and criticized; and then, again, we have not had opportunities of hearing them often enough to come to a full appreciation of their various positive or comparative excellencies; and, besides, it is with respect to church music that we wish more particularly to make report. *Mad. De la Grange*, of whom we wrote from Leipzig, has been singing for some time past with good success. *Grisi, Mario, Formes, Lablache, Castellan, Favanti*, and others of less distinction, are singing as usual; and the papers tell us that the most charming artist, HENRIETTE SONTAG, is engaged for a short time in London, previous to her departure for America. There is no singer who seems to give more universal delight than Mad. Sontag; and we are truly glad that there will ere long be opportunities of hearing her on the western shores of the Atlantic.

The great composer and violinist, SPOHR, is now here, superintending the performance of his opera, *Faust*, in which he has been very successful. It has had several representations to full houses, and the·author has been much honored. But the opera is too good (musically considered) to be very popular. Musicians will delight to hear it; but it contains too much musical learning for the many. The lighter and more unmeaning compositions of the Italians are better appreciated.

"It is very good, it will do for the Germans," said a Frenchman, as he came away from hearing *Faust.*

Yes, it will do for the Germans, provided they be musically-educated Germans; but, whatever be the country to which one belongs, or in which he was born, he cannot understand or like Spohr, unless he has a cultivated musical taste. He is a great and a learned, but he can never be a popular, writer. He is too good for common use.

On Sabbath last we attended Rev. Mr. Binney's church, Fish Street Hill, Weigh House Chapel. Mr. Binney was in America a few years since, and is well known to many persons there. He is not only an excellent preacher; but, although not a musician, he is a lover of music, and has done much to promote psalmody among his own people. The order of the service in his church is most beautiful; I hardly know that it could be improved; it is as follows:

I—Invocation. The Lord's Prayer alone was used the Sabbath we were there.

II—Hymn.

III—Reading first lesson from Scriptures.

IV—Prayer—half as long as the *long prayer* in American churches.

V—Psalm, chanted.

VI—Reading second lesson from Scriptures—New Testament.

VII—Prayer, about the length of former.

VIII—Hymn.

IX—Sermon.

X—Anthem, a hymn.

XI—Very short prayer, and benediction.

There is no choir; the singing is congregational, and led by a precentor. It was quite good; one does not often hear a better performance of this part of the public worship, but yet it would be much improved if simple tunes, appropriate to Congregational singing, were substituted for the too difficult ones attempted on the Sabbath we were present. A peculiarity of the singing here, is, that the whole congregation engage in chanting. The 24th Psalm was chanted to one of the plain old English chants, with an effect far, very far better than one hears when he listens to the trained Cathedral choirs. We have heard it said that a congregation cannot chant together. It is not true: this congregation kept quite well together; nearer together than such Cathedral choirs keep, as we have heard. A very little practice of such a chant as *Tallis'* or *Dr. Turner's*, will prove the truth of this assertion. Another peculiarity of the singing here, is, that the congregation sing anthems. They have a little book containing a collection of *three anthems for congregational use.* Smile not at the number; it is sufficient for their purpose; and, when more are required, they can easily be obtained. Anthems, however, for Congregational use, must have a simplicity such as can hardly be imagined by one accustomed to the chants that commonly prevail in choirs. We are fully satisfied that not only Congregational hymn-tune singing, but Congregational anthem singing, and chanting, may be successfully introduced where there is a desire for it, and where there is a necessary knowledge to guide in the selection of appropriate pieces; and we should not be afraid to undertake to insure success to a congregation who would give us one or two hours preparatory practice. Mr. Binney's sermon, on Christian growth and development, was most able and satisfactory. The standing posture was observed in singing, and the sitting posture in prayer and the other exercises.

From Mr. Binney's we went directly to the Chapel Royal,

St. James, where we heard an excellent organist, a poor choir, and an uninteresting preacher.

Hence to Westminster Abbey, at three o'clock. Excellent organ playing, but all else very indifferent.

LETTER XL.

Church Music in the Chapel of Rev. Baptist W. Noel.

Mr. Noel has been, until recently, a clergyman of the Established Church; he left this a few years since, and is now the pastor of a large and flourishing Baptist congregation in John street. We have not often attended a public religious service more satisfactory than that in his chapel; and we know not that we have ever listened to a preacher with greater interest. His subject, the morning we heard him, was The Sabbath. His text, Isaiah lviii. 13, 14,—"If thou turn away thy foot from the Sabbath, from doing thy pleasure on my holy day; and call the Sabbath a delight, the holy of the Lord, honorable; and shalt honor him, not doing thine own ways, nor finding thine own pleasure, nor speaking thine own words: Then shalt thou delight thyself in the Lord; and I will cause thee to ride upon the high places of the earth, and feed thee with the heritage of Jacob thy father, for the mouth of the Lord hath spoken it." The heads of his discourse were—

1. The authority for the Sabbath.

2. The reasons for keeping the Sabbath.

3. The manner of keeping the Sabbath.

4. The blessings of keeping the Sabbath.

Such a clear and convincing argument for the Sabbath, and

yet so perfectly plain and easy to be understood, we know not that we ever heard before.

The *manner* of the preacher, whether it relates to general pulpit deportment or to style of delivery, is admirable. His appearance is very plain, being without the ornament of surplice, gown, or bands. He is dignified and solemn, without the least approach to formality or ceremoniousness. His voice is not remarkably good (it is strange that preachers do not try more to improve *quality* of voice), yet not disagreeable, and his speech is excellent. Every word and syllable is beautifully spoken, with a clear and distinct articulation, but yet so natural and easy as to be far removed from affectation of exactness or precision. He appears to be entirely free from the scolding style on the one hand, and the canting or whining on the other; nor does he assume the dictatorial, authoritative way that is sometimes seen, which seems to say, " Listen to me ; I am the Doctor !" Yet there is a clearness and thoroughness in his treatment of a subject which makes one feel that he is in the presence of a teacher who needeth not to be ashamed, and of a preacher who rightly divines the word of truth.

But I am forgetting the psalmody. There is neither organ nor choir in Mr. Noel's chapel. The singing is entirely Congregational, and is led by a precentor, who occupies a secondary pulpit in front of that of the minister, and who, in addition to his singing duties, reads the notices. He gives out the hymn, proclaiming its number, and also at the same time gives the name of the tune ; then he reads a stanza which is immediately sung by all the people, and in like manner the succeeding stanzas are read and sung. It is not easy to see why the stanza is read before it is sung, since all the people have hymn-books, and many of them also tune books. The singing of the psalms was as good as may be expected where *choir tunes* are used for *congregational purposes.* The tunes here were altogether too difficult for the people's use; difficult in rhythmics and difficult in melodics. The attempt too, to sing in parts, was not in all cases productive of the greatest good; for example: We stood by the side of a young man who was furnished with a tune book containing only the bass part. In the first tune we sung out the bass with as much voice as we could conveniently command, but with the second tune we were unacquainted, and could not therefore join in the exercise. This was observed by the young man, who drew near and held out his bass part, thus enabling us to sing. But he, while he was looking carefully first at his hymn book and then to his tune book, so as to be sure and be right, was, with his bass part before him, singing all the way the *treble part, two octaves below the pitch!* How a little knowledge may expose one's ignorance!

The general effect of the singing was, notwithstanding these drawbacks, very good, vastly better than some of the attempts at musical display which we have witnessed in churches in England and on the Continent; and if it was not *musically attractive*, it was *religiously edifying*, and served to revive the affections and lift them upwards.

The standing position was observed in singing, and the sitting position in prayer. The people generally had Bibles, and often referred to the texts which the preacher quoted.

LETTER XLI.

Great Musical Festival at Dusseldorf.

DUSSELDORF, Sept. 18, 1852.

WE had heard of this festival, but had given up all expectation of attending it, because of distance, time and expense, and supposed we had left Germany not to return, until we had the pleasure of meeting in London, the celebrated composer, SPOHR, who was there superintending and directing the performance of his "Faust." Upon the recommendation of so distinguished a man, we decided to retrace our steps, and make the journey back again to Germany, for the purpose of seeing and hearing what we could of the musical gathering at Dusseldorf, (in Prussia,) hoping that we might learn something from it, or that, at least, such an imperfect report of it as we might be able to give, would be interesting to our home musical friends, all of whom we suppose are, or certainly ought to be, readers of THE MUSICAL WORLD. Accordingly we left London on Thursday, 29th of July, at twelve o'clock, in the steamer for Antwerp, where we arrived at six the next morning. We stopped long enough to visit the Cathedral, and the Church of St. James, where we heard a part of a mass sung by the priests, with organ accompaniment. The effect was solemn at the early morning hour, but there was nothing in the performance peculiar, or differing from what one hears in all Roman Catholic places. Leaving Antwerp at half-past nine, A. M., we arrived at Cologne at six o'clock, P. M. Here, on the following morning, we had another opportunity of wandering about through the great unfinished Cathedral, and the unexpected pleasure of meeting two American friends, Rev. Dr. W. and son, from New York, with whom we spent several hours in visiting places of interest, and who accompanied us to Dusseldorf. The fine Church of St. Peter

was one of the places we visited. At this church is one of Ruben's great pictures, " *The Crucifixion of St. Peter.*" This celebrated picture was taken away from Cologne by Napoleon, and
was placed in the Gallery of the Louvre, at Paris, where it remained for many years. Its place was supplied by an artist at
Cologne, who painted the same subject from recollection. On
the return of Ruben's picture to Cologne, that which had been
furnished by the modern artist, and which had occupied the
place of the great picture, was retained in the church, and so
placed at the back of the Ruben's that the two may be seen in
immediate succession, by the turning of a pivot. The contrast
is most striking and instructive; for, although the modern
painter undoubtedly deserves much credit for his very successful
effort, one is most forcibly struck with the amazing power of the
great artist, by viewing the two pictures in such close connection. The church of St. Peter contains a very fine organ, one of
the best we have ever heard. In the clearness, firmness, decision, and stability of its tones, it is not excelled. Leaving
Cologne at eleven o'clock, A. M., we arrived at the end of our
journey in an hour and a half.

Dusseldorf is a pleasant German town, of nearly forty thousand inhabitants, a large majority of whom are Roman Catholics. The Festival was one of the " Grosses Männer gesang
feste," (great men-singing festivals,) common in some parts of
Germany, at which singing societies, consisting entirely of men,
in a certain district of country, assemble and spend three or
four days in musical and other festivities. The primary, or
professed object of these meetings is, to sing (strive or contend
by song) for certain prizes. Valuable pieces of plate are prepared and awarded to the most successful chorus performances.
In addition to this, premiums are given for the best original
vocal compositions. On the present occasion there were *three*

premiums given for compositions, and *seven* prizes awarded for the most approved performances. The most highly-valued prize was an elegantly-wrought vase of silver, presented by the government of the city of Dusseldorf; the others were vases or cups of silver of various forms, and beautiful workmanship, presented by individuals, or procured at the mutual expense of the societies. There were present on this occasion *twenty* singing societies, consisting of from twenty to sixty members each, besides delegations from *twenty-nine* other societies, who did not enter as competitors for the prizes. The competing societies were divided into three classes, according (as we were told) to the number of inhabitants of the town to which they belonged, though there may have been some other principle of classification with which we were not made acquainted. There were *two* prizes prepared for the first, *two* for the second, and *three* for the third class. The following named persons, all composers of high standing, constituted the two Committees, or Boards of Judicature, by whom the awards were made:

COMMITTEE ON COMPOSITIONS.

Herr Musik Director, ROBERT SCHUMANN, Dusseldorf.
Herr Musik Director, FERDINAND HILLER, Paris.
Herr Musik Director, L. SPOHR, Cassel.
Herr Musik Director, JULIUS TAUSCH, Dusseldorf.
Herr Musik Director, W. KNAPPE, Dusseldorf.

COMMITTEE ON PERFORMANCES.

Herr Musik Director, ROBERT SCHUMANN, Dusseldorf.
Herr Musik Director, BERTELSMANA, Amsterdam.
Herr Componist, BEYER, Mainz.
Herr Capellmeister, FISCHER, Mainz.
Herr Musik Director, FERDINAND HILLER, Paris.
Herr Componist, MESSER, Frankfurt.
Herr Capellmeister, REICHARDT, Berlin.
Herr Musik Director, TAUSCH, Dusseldorf.
Herr Musik Director, KNAPPE, Dusseldorf.

Here is an array of musical strength, surely; and it was no
small gratification to sit and look around upon the individuals,
and to observe the physiognomies of these distinguished men,
during the performances to which they were listening, and with
respect to the comparative merits of which they were soon to
express an official and public opinion. With some of these
gentlemen, thus assembled from various parts of Europe, we
had the pleasure of a *mediate* interview, conversing through an
interpreter, and especially with Herr Componist MESSER, of
Frankfurt, Director of the Orchestral Concerts there, whose
compositions for stringed instruments, and for full orchestra,
are so well known and much approved. Herr MESSER's lodgings were at our hotel, and we had, at least, a good long Ger-
man-dinner interview with him daily. He is a very thorough
musician, scientific and artistic, and is well acquainted with the
works of the most celebrated composers, from PALESTRINA down
to MENDELSSOHN. Like many of the Germans whom we have
met, he was polite and attentive, and always ready to communicate information to American visitors.

The performance commenced on Sunday, 1st August, at five
o'clock, P. M. The morning was much occupied (as the previous day had been) in making various preparatory arrangements, and in ornamenting the city, especially those streets and
squares through which processions were to pass. The streets
(many of them narrow and without sidewalks) were filled with
workmen and lookers-on. Branches and boughs of trees, as
pines, birches, maples and the like, were brought into town in
abundance, and planted on each side at short distances, so as to
give the idea of pleasant woods, thick groves, and cool, shady
parks. The fields and the gardens yielded up their flowery
treasures, and windows, doors, balconies, walls, corridors, and
aisles were decorated with garlands and festoons of Nature's

gayest colors. Flags and pendants were suspended from the windows, and waved from the roofs of the buildings; the Prussian eagle proudly spread her wings upon the walls of many houses; the colors of the German States were waving harmoniously together, and the banners of the Fine Arts, with appropriate inscriptions, particularly those of music, poetry and painting, were especially honored, and floated triumphant amidst the standards of electorates, dukedoms, and kingdoms. The dwellings of the inhabitants, which were very generally opened for the gratuitous lodgings of the singing guests, were, many of them, most beautifully ornamented, and various ensigns, armorial devices, or mottos in garland frames, were suspended from the walls, often crossing the streets from house to house, welcoming the sons of song, telling of music's praise, or proclaiming the divinity of art. Indeed, *art* seems to be the only God to whom many here pay their vows.

At six o'clock in the morning (Sunday) we attended a Roman Catholic service, consisting much in choral singing. At half-past eight we went to the " Kleine Kirche," Protestant. The house was crowded, and many were standing; the service was simple, without liturgy, and not differing much from the Congregational or Baptist form of worship in the United States. From this we went at ten o'clock to the " Grosser Kirche," also Protestant. Here the house was larger, but the congregation smaller. The order of service was nearly the same; the organist acted also as precentor, or leader of the singing; besides him there was no choir; he, both by his instrument and his voice, caused himself to be heard. As we left the church, we found the streets crowded with people; men, women and children, arrayed in gay attire, bearing flowret wreathes, or sprigs of woody green, all manifesting the highest degree of expectation, eagerness and joy; and, indeed, the whole population seemed to be full of animation, gaiety and gladness, joyfully welcoming this commencement day of festal mirth.

Some of the societies arrived on Saturday evening. " These were greeted in the most friendly manner," says a Dusseldorf paper, " and conducted by the Committee of Arrangements to the various families in the town who were expecting them, where they spent the happy evening midst the chink of wine-glasses, joke and song." At about eleven o'clock, (Sunday,) the singing societies of Dusseldorf, together with such of the visitors as had already arrived, assembled at the Hotel " Prince of Prussia," and at the railroad station near by, to receive the various societies as they came in by the different trains. When all had arrived, or at about twelve o'clock, a grand procession was formed, numbering over sixteen hundred singers, which, accompanied by two bands of music, one at the head and the other in the centre, amid the ringing of bells, the roaring of cannon, the waving of banners, and the shrill sound of trumpet and drum, moved triumphant through various streets, to the " Rath-haus." Beautiful faces were seen at the windows of the houses, and smiling and joyful countenances, and the waving of handkerchiefs, cheered the spirits of those who were already not a little excited. The square in which the " Rath-haus" is situated, was filled by the dense crowd, and presented a most brilliant appearance. It was everywhere decked with flowers and flags; and from its centre the statue of the Elector Johann Wilhelm, seemed to look on with approbation, participating in the general joy. When the societies had assembled in the large hall of the " Rath-haus," they were addressed by the " Burgermeister," (Mayor) who, in a short speech, bid the singers welcome to the town. He met an immediate response, in the three times " Hurrah for Dusseldorf," which the assembled singers immediately raised, and in which they were joined by the multitude without, in cheering loud and long. As soon as silence was restored, the President of the "Concordia" Society from Bonn, replied to the speech of the Mayor, in the name of the assembled multitude. This speech was also followed with the flourish of trumpets and drums, and the merry shoutings "Huzza for Dusseldorf," "Huzza for the Burgermeister," "Huzza for the singers," &c. From this the procession moved to another hall, where Herr Director W. Dietze recited, (over the wine of honor, contained in a splendid vase, which was a present from his royal highness Prince Frederick,) a beautiful poetic "Greeting to visitors;" at the close of this, when the vase had been well emptied, and the wine of honor had been sprinkled upon the banners of song, lots were drawn to decide the order of the singing of each society, and text-books, order of performance, and cards of admission, were distributed to the members. The company then adjourned to attend to the immediate wants of the physical man.

At four o'clock the societies assembled again in the court-yard of the "Gymnasium," where they were addressed by Mr. Achenbach, one of the most distinguished painters in the place, (for all the artists took a deep interest in the Festival,) and were welcomed in the name of the "Dusseldorf Society of Artists." The processsion was now again formed, and the persons appointed having received from the place were they were deposited for safe-keeping, the glittering prizes of gold and silver, moved in grand display towards the Geissler Gardens, where the performances were to take place; on passing through the Court Gardens three hearty cheers were given for the Prince of Hohenzöllern, (a patron of the festival,) and on their arrival at the Gardens, the multitude of singers took possession of the vast Music Hall, which had been erected for their accommodation. It was easy to see in the glowing countenances of the guests, in their general movements and gesticulations, that the splendid arrangements, which they now beheld for the first time, far surpassed their expectations. The hall is one hundred and eighty feet long, seventy-six wide, and forty feet high. It was most tastefully decorated with flags, busts, portraits, inscriptions, paintings, plants and flowers. Over the chief entrance were placed the arms of the royal house of Prussia, and of his highness the Prince of Hohenzöllern-Sigmaringen. The stage at the other end was decorated with the Prussian and Dusseldorf arms, and also the arms of the "Society of Men-singers," and the Society of painters "Malkasten." Emblems of music, painting, poetry and sculpture, and the portraits or names of distinguished composers, authors and artists, were suspended from the walls. There were also arrayed, in various places, the names of the different towns to which the societies joining in the competition belonged, and the names of such towns as sent deputations to the festival. The columns and rafters were gilded, or painted in gayest colors, and the whole presented a fairy-like appearance, and especially so in the evening when brilliantly lighted with gas; so that it seemed some Elysian or Paradisian abode, rather than a portion of this sin-blighted world.

At a little past five o'clock, when the house was filled with an anxious and deeply-interested audience, and the singers, somewhat over sixteen hundred in number, all men, filled the stage, leaving room only for the performing society in the centre— and in front, and in view of all the people, the brilliant prizes, vases and cups, were tastefully arranged—the performance began. A flourish of trumpets and drums came first, then an overture, and then a grand vocal and instrumental chorus of welcome greeting by the united Dusseldorf Societies. A most charming choral performance of power and grandeur it was in-

deed, such as to call forth loud applause from the visiting societies and from the large company of spectators. This was the
only performance of the Dusseldorf Societies, since, as a matter of etiquette, none of them engaged in the singing for prizes.
The competition-singing, harmonious, now began, and the different societies followed in quick succession. The name of the
society about to sing was announced by a placard so disposed
as to be seen by the whole assembly, and also by the standard
or banner of the society, which always preceded the members
as they came forward on the stage, and waved encouragement
over them while they contended for the prize. It may be remarked, that many of these banners were very elegant, being
made of the richest velvet or satin, with gold or silver embroi-
dery of mottos, or emblematic figures. Each society sang two
pieces, under its own director, entirely without accompaniment.
After *six* societies had sung, a recess of half an hour was proclaimed, when the vast multitude retired to the garden, where
greetings were given and friends welcomed, and refreshments
abundant were passed round, with "wine which maketh glad
the heart of man." It was interesting to move about among
the thronged avenues and crowded tables, see the eating and
drinking and smoking, and hear the mirthful laugh and lively
prattle of the busy people. It was fraught with instructive lessons, too; but we must not moralize now, but only attempt to
describe. The half-hour having been prolonged by one half or
more, the sound of the trumpet was heard, calling again to action, and soon the contest was resumed. *Five* more societies
sang, making eleven in all on this first day of performance, all
of which belonged to the *third class*. It will not be expected
that we should attempt to remark upon the singing of the different societies; there was quite a wide range from *tolerably
good* (there was no performance positively bad) up to that which

approached as near to perfection as is often found even in music's chosen land. It was not difficult, however, to decide to which society belonged the first prize for the performances of this day.

At the close of the performance the crowd gradually dispersed, moving slowly back into the town, which was now splendidly illuminated. The singing societies again formed in order, and each person bearing upon a rod six or eight feet in length a colored light the whole moved through the principal streets, in grand torch-light procession, brilliant and dazzling. This being ended, the singers retired to a large hall, where things good to the palate and quickening to the spirits had been bountifully provided, and which were (even in Germany) summarily disposed of. Toasts and speeches followed, which we cannot record here; except that we will merely mention that Herr Capellmeister G. Reichardt of Berlin, in reply to one of the toasts, gave a brief history of the origin and progress of the men-singing festivals in Germany. He said they were commenced in Berlin in 1809, when the great ZELTER first called them into life. After he had finished his remarks, the whole company sang one of Reichardt's patriotic songs. The evening's entertainment was continued until it was no longer evening; and not until the light of day had arisen upon these sons of song, did they disperse to seek for a few moments' rest before the duties of the day, already began, should call them again to contend for the prize.

Monday, 2d August. Commenced with a general breakfast. Singers, guests, strangers, and inhabitants assembled at the "Ananas Mountain" (a little eminence situated in a delightful park, a short distance from the town), to take coffee, listen to "harmonie," and engage in conversation, with pipes and "cigarren." This was not, however, at "table d'hote," as is a breakfast usually served with us, but little companies of two, or four, or ten sat down together, ordering from the card such things as they chose. Preparations had been made by the committee of arrangements for refreshments, which were furnished at fixed and reduced prices. The prices of the various articles were posted up on placards, so that every one might know the price of what he ordered, and thus imposition be prevented.

After the breakfast, the singers spent the forenoon in visiting the different picture-galleries and other collections of curiosities, all of which were opened gratuitously for their benefit. At one o'clock, the gardens were filled with dinner-parties; at three, there was a general gathering at the "Ananas mountain," and from thence, at about four, the grand procession moved to strains of joyful music, to the Hall of trial, in the Geissler gardens. The meeting to-day was attended by the Prince Hohenzöllern, who was formally received, and welcomed to the Hall by the Bürgermeister and the Committee of Arrangements, amidst animating strains of military music. After the Prince had taken his seat, the President of the Society of Artists (painters) made the announcement that the said Society had determined to add to the splendor of the festival by awarding a prize to that society which should, *extempore*, without preparation and without notes, perform in chorus the best comic song. The prize should consist of a painting, the subject of which should be that of the song of the winning society; and the awarding of it should be by a committee of persons, *not musicians*, but of such as should judge by the immediate impression made at the time of hearing. Any of the societies present, desiring to do so, might join in the competition. This announcement was received with much applause.

The competition now commenced between those societies which came from towns containing between three and ten thousand inhabitants, and which, therefore, belonged to the second class. There were five of these societies, each of which sang two songs. The performances were generally better than those of the third class (which sang on the first day), and more equal; but yet it was not difficult to decide which society in this second class would take the first prize. After a recess of about forty minutes, during which time there was a general retreat to the garden, to engage in the performances there, the societies from towns of ten thousand inhabitants or more, of which there were four in number, constituting the first class, resumed and completed the prize-contest-singing. Three of these societies (of the first class) sang exceedingly well; but the "Concordia" from Bonn was decidedly superior to all the others, and the loud, long applause that followed their performance seemed to be a decision by the audience in anticipation of that of the judges, awarding to them the first prize.

At the conclusion of the singing, Herr Burgermeister Hammers came forward to the front of the stage, and being surrounded by the banner-bearers, each bearing the banner of his respective society, announced to the audience, in clear and distinct tones, amidst the loud cheerings of the assembly, the flourish of trumpets, and the waving of banners, the names of the composers to whom premiums had been awarded by the committee on composition. The prizes were three in number; for the best competition the premium was Fifty Dollars, for the second best Forty Dollars, and for the third Twenty-five Dollars. The songs received from different parts of Germany were *one hundred and ninety-eight* in number. These had all been carefully examined, and the Committee unanimously awarded the premiums as follows:—the first to the song, "*Im Weinhaus*," by HERR BONICKE, Organist in Quedlinbourg; the second to the song, "*Lebe Wohl*," by Dr. IMMANNEL FAIST, Director of the "Society of classical music," Auttgart; and the third to the song, "*Der Käefer und die Blume*," by W. H. VEIT of Prague. These announcements were successively received with the loud applause of trumpets, drums, and voices; while banners waved and beauty smiled at art's success.

After a few minutes' recess, the competition in comic song followed. Eight societies had entered their names as candidates, and sang successively for the prize picture. Some of them produced roars of laughter, and every one of them was received with more or less merriment and glee. One song (they were all part-songs) was truly good and exceedingly well done, but the others were commonplace, or even low and frivolous; so much so, as to appear quite at variance with the idea that these festivals are designed for improvement in musical taste. It was somewhat sad too, to observe that those songs which seemed to bring down humanity the nearest to mere animal being were the most admired, so that one in which imitations of the bleating of sheep and the cries of the domestic animals were introduced, called forth the loudest laugh and the most violent clapping of hands. The Committee retired for a few moments, and justly awarded the prize to the "Maenner-Gesang-Verein" of Neuss. The evening's festivities were concluded (professedly) by a display of fire-works on the "Ananas mountain;" but the *songs* and *hurrahs* continued to be heard through the night, and rising early the next morning, between four and five o'clock, we saw from our window a part of the *finale* of the second day.

Third day, Tuesday. The breakfast with "Harmonie" was as on the day previous. At nine o'clock there was a rehearsal for a grand concert which was to be given in the evening. To this rehearsal tickets were sold at a small price, and the amount thus collected was to be given to the poor. The house was filled, and quite a considerable sum must have been received. The rehearsal having closed, the dinner hour, and the hours devoted to smoking, drinking, and the like—in the garden—having passed away, the company began to flock in at about four o'clock to attend the concert. At a little before five, when the building was well filled, one of the most severe showers of rain and hail arose that we ever witnessed. The rain poured down in torrents, the rattling hail beat upon the apparently frail building, in which thousands were assembled, the lightning flashed and blazed in one almost continuous stream of fire, and the deep thunder roared, loud and terrific. To add, if possible, to the sublime chorus of nature, at the moment when the storm was raging most violently, the powerful voices of two thousand men were heard in the loud " HURRAH !" " HURRAH !" " HURRAH !" The rain began to find its way through the roof, umbrellas were spread, cloaks and shawls were wrapped around the elegantly-dressed but trembling ladies, the chill cold quickly succeeded heat, while the rattling of glass broken by hail-stones, seemed to indicate the crash of the whole building in one common ruin. But all was safe ; and quickly the rain ceased, the winds were hushed, and amidst the retiring roll of the more distant thunder, violins, clarionets, and the various orchestral instruments, were heard, seeming, like the rainbow of promise, to proclaim that Music's welcome sun should soon shine brightly upon the waiting multitude.

A little before six o'clock the concert, having been delayed nearly an hour, began. There was an orchestra of about fifty instruments, and the programme was as follows :

FIRST PART.

1—OVERTURE (C dur. Op. 124)............................*Beethoven.*
2—RECITATION. Poetry in honor of the King of Prussia.
            Read by............................*Herr Herchenbach.*

3—PSALM für Männerchor mit Solo...................*C. Schanabel.*
4—SCENE and ARIE from "Faust." Sung by Frl. Sophie
    Schloss...*Spohr.*
5—CONCERTO (E flat major) for Piano Forte with Orchestra.
    Performed by Madame Clara Schumann..........*Beethoven.*
6—"MEERESTILLE," "Männerchor" with Orchestra. Composed
    by...............................*Capellmeister Fischer.*

SECOND PART.

7—OVERTURE to Shakspeare's "Julius Cæsar."............*R. Schumann.*
8—ARIE from "Fidelio." Sung by Frl. Mathilde Hartmann...*Beethoven.*
9—VARIATIONS on a theme from "Preciosa," with orchestra
    accompaniment. Performed by Mad'le Wieck and
    Mad. Clara Schumann........................... *Weber.*
10—"BACCHUSCHOR" for Männerchor, with orchestra, from
    "Antigone," by...............................*Mendelssohn.*
11—"SALTARELLO,"....... ⎫ ....*S. Heller.*
  "NOTTURNO,"........ ⎬ ..For the....................*F. Chopin.*
  "LIED OHNE WORTE," ⎭ Piano Forte................*Mendelssohn.*
    Performed by Mad. Clara Schumann.
12—FINALE. Full Chorus, Männerchor, with orchestra. By..*Julius Rietz.*

The performance was a very fine one, but the building was too large, and the people seemed to be too much fatigued to enjoy it fully. At the close of the concert, the most exciting scene perhaps of the whole four days was witnessed, namely, the announcement of the successful competitors in song, and the presentation of the prizes.

A half-circle was formed around the prize committee, who had taken seats around the stage just in the rear of the table on which were placed the shining vessels of gold and silver. Amidst the loudest shouts the Burgermeister Hammers ascended the tribune to announce the decision of the judges. The following is the result:

FIRST DAY'S SINGING—THIRD CLASS—ELEVEN SOCIETIES.

First prize to the " Gesangverein " of Lobberich.

Second prize to the " Männergesangverein," " Apollo," of Kaiersworth..

Third prize to the " Leidertafel " of Dulken.

At the recommendation of the Committee three " hurras " were given for the " Liederkranz " of B. Gladbach.

SECOND DAY'S SINGING—SECOND CLASS—FIVE SOCIETIES.

First prize to the " Männergesangverein " of Neuss.

Second prize to the " Liedertafel " of M. Gladbach.

And three " Hurras " for " Liedertafel " of Ersen.

FIRST CLASS—FOUR SOCIETIES.

First prize, being the prize of honor presented by the town of Düsseldorf, to the " Männergesangverein " " Concordia " of Bonn.

Second prize, to the " Männergesangverein " " Polyhymnia " of Cologne.

And three " hurras " for the " Gesangverein," " Orpheus," of Elberfeld.

Each of these announcements was received with the waving of banners, the blast of trumpets, the rolling of drums, and the loud cheering of the multitude, which continued while the Mayor took from the table the prize, as it was announced, and handed it to the President of the Society to which it had been awarded. As soon as the cheering would permit, the President of the Bonn " Concordia " jumped upon the tribune and called for three times " Hurrah, and long life and prosperity to the friends in Dusseldorf," to which a most enthusiastic response was given. These ceremonies were all over by about ten o'clock ; then followed a grand festival ball, and this closed the third day's performances, somewhat before the rising sun of Wednesday marked the commencement of the fourth and last day of the meeting.

The fore-part of the day (Wednesday) was spent in various congratulations, social gatherings, &c., which cannot easily be described. All was excitement, all was joy ; and music, instru-

mental and vocal, and shoutings and "hurras" were heard all
around. Some of the societies marched through the streets,
preceded by their banner, and perhaps by the prize they had
won, to the music of their own well-tuned and harmonious voices.
Others rode inside and outside of omnibuses, with like demon-
strations of gladness. The gardens were filled in the afternoon,
and wine flowed freely. At five o'clock was a grand festival
of artists, entitled the "Power of Song." It consisted in a succession of very splendid "*tableaux vivants*"—accompanied by
appropriate music and recitation. A full orchestra, and a large
mixed choir of perhaps one hundred and twenty voices, with
solo-singers, constituted the musical department for the occasion.
The best speakers were employed for the declamation ; and the
living pictures were under the immediate direction of a committee of the painters of Dusseldorf. The hour arrived, but
vain was the attempt to commence. Bacchus had been there,
and had obtained such a sway over the sons of Apollo, that
music's voice could not be heard. The orchestra did indeed
play, or appeared to play an overture, but not even the loudest
passages could be heard, for the vocal shoutings quite overpowered trumpets, trombones, and drums. The speakers, in
appropriate costume, came on the stage, but their voices were
lost in loud shoutings, and they quickly gave up the contest and
retreated. Various attempts were made for nearly an hour to
command silence, and obtain a hearing, but in vain. The roar
of voices, and the loud "Hurrah," overpowered all the efforts
of the Mayor, the artists, and the orchestra. Even the presence of the Prince, the patron of the Festival, could not restrain
the tremendous cheerings. At length a *lady*, a beautifully-
dressed *lady*, appeared on the stage—and as the orchestra commenced, her arm was gently extended, and the song began.
Though faintly heard at first, she gradually prevailed, until, at

last, music gained the victory; the power of the god of wine was exhausted; reason resumed her sway, and she hesitated not quickly to restore music and the arts to the throne of universal dominion and admiration.

The "Tableaux Vivants" were now exhibited. Each tableaux was exhibited three times; they were all magnificently prepared, and the whole exhibition was exceedingiy interesting and beautiful. The order was as follows:

1—" *Orpheus liberates Eurydice from the under world.*" After P. Cornelius. Accompanied by extracts from the text and the music of Gluck's opera.

2--" *The Singer's Curse.*" After M. Tolz. Accompanied by music from Robert Schumaun's third Symphonie.

3—" *A Landscape.*" A group of young men accompany a comrade on his way out of town, and they all sing "Must I leave thee, Native Town." His beloved watches from a bower, and after all have disappeared sings a sad song of parting.

4—" *Ave Maria.*" After Rubens. Accompanied by a " *Salve Regina,*" composed by M. Hauptmann.

5—" *Grand Battle Piece.*" " Frederick the Great at the Battle of Prague." A most splendid tableaux with many figures. Accompanied by a military movement by the orchestra.

6—" *Landscape. Review.*" The muses appear on an eminence; on one side in the foreground is a group of Orpheus; next, the young and old singers from the second picture; then, the young man, and his beloved from the third, the monks from the fourth, and Frederick from the fifth. The muses, *Thalia, Euterpe,* and *Erato,* advance to the front of the stage, bearing crowns of evergreen in their hands. Euterpe sings a verse of greeting to the assembled singers, and the curtain falls.

The fourth and last day's exercises closed by a grand festive ball, of singers, visitors, and citizens.

NAMES OF THE SOCIETIES, IN THE ORDER IN WHICH THEY SANG, AND ALSO A LIST OF ALL THE SONGS THAT WERE SUNG.

THIRD CLASS—FIRST DAY.

1—MAENNERGESANGVEREIN, Kaiserswerth.
"Was wir lieben.".............................*C. F. Adam.*
"Still and schauerlich.".......................—— ——

2—MAENNERGESANGVEREIN, Volmerswerth.
"Das Kirchlein.".............................*V. E. Becker.*
"Sängermarsch.".............................*F. Abt.*

3—MAENNERGESANGVEREIN, Lobberick.
"Mein.".............................*Härtel.*
"Wer ist unser Mann.".............................*C. Zöllner.*

4—MAENNERGESANGVEREIN, Ratingen.
"Die Riesengletscher.".............................*Kreutzer.*
"Was ist das Beste.".............................——

5—MAENNERGESANGVEREIN, Wupperhofen.
"Frohlockt und jauchet.".............................*Roeder.*
"Patriotisches Soldatenleid.".............................*Kücken.*

6—APOLLO, Kaiserswerth.
"Am Neckar, am Rhein.".............................*Kücken.*
"Schlummerst du schon.".............................*Wilhelm.*

7—LIEDERKRANZ, B— Gladbach.
"Woner nur das linde Säuseln.".............................*Kreutzer.*
"Rund ist alles auf der Welt.".............................*Kücken.*

8—LIEDERTAFEL, Graefrath.
"Mein.".............................*Härtel.*
"Der Jager.".............................*Kücken.*

9—LIEDERTAFEL, Sonnborn.
"Am Neckar, am Rhein.".............................*Kücken.*
"Leib und Wein.".............................*Mendelssohn.*

10—HARMONIE, Dültgensthal.
"Aus der Jugendzeit.".............................*Stöppler.*
"Das Regenwetter.".............................*Reissiger.*

11—LIEDERTAFEL, Dülken.
"Die jungen Musikanten.".............................*Kücken.*
"Die Gunst des Augenblickes.".............................——

SECOND CLASS—SECOND DAY.

1—LIEDERTAFEL, Essen.
    "Jünglings Abschied.".................................. ——
    "Der Müllerbursche."....................................*Zöllner.*

2—LIEDERTAFEL, Viersen.
    "Den Schönen."....................................*Neithardt.*
    "Am Neckar, am Rhein."............................*Kücken.*

3—LIEDERTAFEL, M— Gladbach.
    "Gebet von See."..................................*Zöllner.*
    "Nächtliche."......................................*F. Abt.*

4—CONCORDIA, Dortmund.
    Chor und quartet aus der "Weissen Dame.".......*Boieldieu.*
    "Die Jungen Musikanten."..........................*Kücken.*

5—MAENNERGESANGVEREIN, Neuss.
    "Frühlingslandschaft."................................*Otto.*
    "Das Lied vom Rhein."............................*Reichardt.*

FIRST CLASS—SECOND DAY.

1—CONCORDIA, Bonn.
    "Trallerliedchen."....................................*F. Ries.*
    "Abschiedstafel."................................*Mendelssohn.*

2—ORPHEUS, Elberfeld.
    "Mein."..*Härtel.*
    "Am Neckar, am Rhein."............................*Kücken.*

3—BUERGER-UND HANDWERKER-GESANGVEREIN, Cologne.
    "Frisch ein Hoch."..................................*Herx.*
    "Gegrüsst seid All Ihr Sänger-Brüder.".................*Herx.*

4—POLYHYMNIA, Cologne.
    "Der Wald."..*Häser.*
    "Was uns eint als deutsche Brüder."..............*Mendelssohn.*

There were deputations of from one to upwards of fifty persons each, from *twenty-nine* other towns; hence, the deputed members numbered nearly as many persons as belonged to the Societies that entered into competition for the prizes.

EXHIBITIONS GRATUITOUSLY OPENED TO THE SINGERS DURING THE FOUR DAYS.

1—The Provincial Industrial Exhibition.

2—The Exhibition of the Society of Art of Rheinland and Westphalen.

3—The Exhibition of the Artists' Mutual Aid Society.

4—The Permanent Art Exhibition of Dusseldorf.

5—The Exhibition of three large paintings, by Herr Shadow, Director of the Academy of Fine Arts, Dusseldorf, viz.: HEAVEN, PURGATORY, and HELL.

During the performance on the first day, many of the members of the societies wore their hats on the stage, directly in front of the audience, and some were seen standing gazing about not only with hats on, but with cigars in their mouths and actually smoking. This positively took place (we repeat it, for it will hardly be credited) during the public performance at the Dusseldorf festival. The second day a notice was posted up to the following effect: "Smoking will not be allowed in the hall during the public performances." An advance in civilization, surely! Hats were worn on succeeding days, but the smoking disappeared.

PRICES OF REFRESHMENTS.

One plate of soup...6 cents.

One beef-steak, or other portion of meat.....................12 cents.

One buttered-bread, with cheese, or meat....................12½ cents.

One cup of coffee..5 cents.

One ice-cream...10 cents.

One glass lemonade, or grog, with ice.......................12½ cents.

Wine (a leading article) varied in price from 25 to 60 cents per bottle.

The price of beer was so well understood as not to require placarding.

There were other articles of refreshments offered, but the prices were not published.

The performance of the *Concordia* of Bonn was decidedly the best of the whole; this society was represented by *fifty-two* of its members; many of them are students in the University;

and the appearance of the society seemed to indicate a general cultivation to which all could not lay claim. The songs chosen by the *Concordia* were both very excellent and popular, a circumstance of much importance to their success. Very near to this, in point of merit, was the *Polyhymnia* of Cologne. It may be mentioned here that there is a society in Cologne which is very celebrated for the perfection of its performances. This society has taken the first prize for several years, but voluntarily gave way this year, or retired from the contest, so that others might have the opportunity of winning. One of the poorest societies, and yet one of the largest, was also from Cologne, the *Bürger-und Handwerker gesangverein.* What rendered their performance the less pleasing, though in itself poor, was the fact, that two inferior compositions, both by the director of the society (W. Herx), were sung.

The performance of many of the societies was much injured by those who attempted to sing solo parts, but who were not competent to do the work. Out of tune, and sinking the pitch, were faults common to quite a number of the solo singers. The chorus was, in the poorest instances, *tolerable ;* but it was not so with the solo singers, who were not, in all cases, better than we have heard heretofore, under circumstances where little was expected, and nothing realized. It is comparatively easy to have a chorus well done, but there are very few singers who have carried vocal cultivation so far as to be able to sing a solo part, or a part in a trio or quartet, well enough to save the hearer from absolute pain.

A "sperrsitz" (reserved seat) to all the four days' performances, cost three dollars and a half; other tickets cost much less. Tickets for a single performance were also sold.

The whole amount received for tickets could not have been less than several thousand dollars.

From what we saw of comic singing, it seemed to be very evident that the Germans, or, at least, those assembled on this occasion, with all their musical culture, are more pleased with a really silly or foolish song, which includes a little monkey-like acting or gesticulation, than with a " Lied ohne Worte" by Mendelssohn, or a quartet or a symphonie by Beethoven. Good music is undoubtedly appreciated by a greater part, comparatively, of the people here, than in America ; but if one may judge from appearances at this festival, the majority still prefer a good laugh to good music, and mere comic acting to classic song. We spoke to a German gentleman sitting near, and expressed our disappointment that such rapturous applause should be given to music so unworthy. " Ah !" said he, " that is German way."

It should be understood, especially by those persons who labor to promote church-singing with us, that these festivals have nothing whatever to do with this subject. Indeed, the idea of *music* seems to be disunited, in many minds, from any thoughts of public worship. The singing of psalms or hymns by the people on a religious occasion, is not regarded as *music*, but as a devotional exercise, as far removed from a musical performance, at least, as is the intonation of the Cathedral service of the English Church.

" In which church shall we hear the best music ?" is an inquiry we have made, when in a German town, on the Sabbath ; and to which we have received the reply :

" Oh, there is no music in any of the churches, except perhaps once or twice a year, on the occasion of some great festival."

" But, don't the people sing ?"

" Yes, they sing the hymns, but there is no music."

Thus the distinction is practically made (as it ought to be) between the people's psalm-singing or worship and musical performance. The festivals here are musical performances, and have nothing to do with the people's songs of worship.

At one of the churches we attended on the Sunday morning of the commencement of the festival, we received a tract, containing the protest of the minister of the parish. It is principally based upon the fact that the festival had its commencement upon the Sabbath. The following is a translation of a part of it :

" The opening of a large worldly festival on the Lord's day, like that in contemplation in our town, must awaken a deep sadness in the heart of every Christian man. For such a thing stands in direct opposition to the positive command of God. 'Remember the Sabbath-day to keep it holy,' is understood by the Christian Church in a sense that, the Lord's day is separate from other days, and that it should be honored and revered by public and private service to God, and also by resting from all labors and worldly pleasures. No one can contend that the opening of a festival, which is to be continued several days, must of necessity take place on Sunday. It could just as well have commenced on a week-day. A 'competition of song' is just as little to be reckoned among the works of love and mercy, as any other worldly festival. The evident and doubtless fact that the whole town will participate in these worldly pleasures, in open disobedience to the command of the Heavenly Father, must make sad the heart of every godly man.

" Far from giving approbation to a joy which thus manifests itself in illuminations, wreaths, garlands, or flags, on this holy day, we have felt it to be our duty to protest, even though our voice have little or no effect, against this shameful and sinful breaking of the sacred Sabbath."

Various other things more or less connected with the festival might be said, but we fear we may have already too much extended our report, and therefore forbear.

LETTER XLII.

Birmingham Festival—Powers of the Musical World—The Market Place—Service at Rev. Mr. James' Church—Sermon—Choir—Organ—Tunes—Church of St. Martin's—New kind of Chanting—Bread for the Poor—Wesleyan Chapel—Rehearsal—Money Matters.

BIRMINGHAM, September 2d, 1852.

ALTHOUGH we had decided, even before we left home, to attend the musical meetings in this place, yet, as the time drew near, we found ourselves so pleasantly employed in two simultaneous courses of lectures to music and school teachers,* that we had well nigh come to the conclusion to remain in London, relinquish the long anticipated performances at the Grand Birmingham Festival, and work on. But, a number of the *Musical World* came to hand, and it was no longer optional with us to come or stay away; for, the editor (without our permission) had pledged us to his readers for a report. We say *without permission*, but yet we are certainly ready to acknowledge that he had a kind of professional, social, or moral right to do as he pleased with us, in this matter, arising out of a relationship that has long existed,—which commenced, indeed, when he, a lad wearing a jacket and a cap, was brought to us, with a beloved sister—now no more—by an affectionate parent, to commence his musical education in lessons of Do, Re, Mi. Little did we think at that time, that in about a score of years he was to occupy the editorial chair of an American Musical paper! No mandate is so quickly or so cheerfully obeyed, as that which proceeds from love and good will; the way was now plain;—classes must be adjourned, lectures and other engagements postponed, and to Birmingham we must go.

It was Saturday night. The ride on the hard boards of the

* One in connection with the Home and Colonial Normal School, and the other to Teachers of the Birkbeck Schools.

second class, had been tedious, for we had been detained nearly an hour by the circumstance of a luggage train ahead of us running off the line. As soon as we could get a little refreshment, we went out into the crowded streets. On Saturday (as we understand) the manual laborers, or operatives, are released from their weary toil at an earlier hour than usual, and they then crowd the streets in search of fresh air, and to see or hear, or buy such things as they need for the coming day. The streets, and especially those in the vicinity of the market, were literally jammed full of people of all ages, from the child at the breast, to worn-out, feeble and tottering old age. It was difficult for one to press along, through the dense mass of human beings who thronged the ways. How different the appearance, from that of the multitude at Dusseldorf, where we were a few weeks since, on a similar errand to that which brought us here. The circumstances, indeed, were very different ; *there*, was the commencement of a gay holiday-time for the people, and men, and women, and children, with clean faces, combed hair, shining shoes and " go-to-meeting " clothes, were thick on every side. They were more like the people of our own happy land ; there being scarcely any evidence of deep poverty and degradation. It was otherwise here, for little children and old men and women were seen clothed in filthy rags, and it was enough to put to the test the olfactory nerves of the stoutest man to crowd his way through the motley groups. The people, too, in Dusseldorf, were interested in the festival,—indeed it was the *people's festival*, and if there were some who could not hear, all took delight in seeing. But *here*, the common people are entirely cut off from the music ; it is intended only for the rich, and only they can go to the expense of purchasing admittance. *There*, the people make their own music ; *here*, the greatest performers, vocal and instrumental, the world affords, are brought together, at an enormous expense, to give an exhibition of the triumph of art.

We followed the multitude into the market-place, and it was an alleviation to the circumstance of their apparent poverty, to see for how little money they could buy bacon, shoes, cheese, hats, potatoes, trowsers, sausages, cabbages, flutes, candles and other like things necessary and convenient. Very cheap are such commodities on a Saturday night in and about the market houses of the large manufacturing towns in England. There was a great plenty, too, of good fruit,—as pears, plums, and apples. A pint of ripe sweet plums could be had for one or two pence. Many of them were eaten upon the spot, and every now and then, one and another treading on the slippery skins, would slide and fall, not upon the floor, for there was not room enough for that, but against others by whom he was surrounded. The only music we heard here was the busy hum of voices, the cries of the sellers, " this is the cheapest stall in the market," " a pint for a penny," the whistling of boys, the crying of children, and now and then the distressed howlings of a poor suffering member of the canine society, who had been cruelly trodden under foot by some heedless passenger. We stopped at a Bible-stall and bought a very excellent copy of the New Testament, well bound, for four pence. Thanks to that noble institution, " the British and Foreign Bible Society," for such a provision as this, in the market.

We left the market-place and the crowd at half-past nine, and made our way to our lodgings ; thinking of our happy country, and the better condition of the laboring poor there, than even in the best-regulated manufacturing towns here.

Sunday came, and we attended, first, the church of Rev. Mr. James. How could we do otherwise ? What American, spending the Sabbath in Birmingham, would fail to hear this

distinguished man, since there is no better preacher anywhere
to be found, and since there is no living English divine so well
known, by his writings, across the Atlantic ?   We well remember his influence in the early history of Sabbath schools in the
United States; for, when they were yet in their infancy, his
" Sunday School Teachers' Guide " did more to mould them and
give them a right direction, than any other work ; and during
the score of years that have since passed away, many of his
books, of great practical worth, have been republished and
widely circulated.   Mr. James preached from the text, " If any
man will come after me, let him deny himself, and take up his
cross and follow me."   I wish I could give a detailed account
of his sermon, for I am persuaded it would be a report as interesting to many as any that can be made of the progress of
song, and it would do musical as well as other readers good to
contemplate the subject in the light he presented it.   Suffice it
to say, he represented it very clearly as *something to do ;* he
made it out also to be an extensive thing, reaching the whole
man, entering into his whole life ; moreover, he gave to it great
power sufficient for any emergency, and leading, if necessary,
even to martyrdom.   Any *self-denial* not reaching thus far, is
not that which the text calls for.   But I must not enlarge.   Mr.
James' delivery is not very good, and he often allows his
voice to sink so low in power as not to be heard in the latter
part of a sentence.   He is, as to his manner, a son of consola-
tion, and the kind, the gentle and tender prevail.   Indeed, his
whole manner, as well as the spirit which he manifests, seems
to say, " thy gentleness hath made me great."   There are little
things about his delivery that should not, we think, be imitated
by young men ; for example, the frequent abbreviations of can't,
won't, shan't, &c. ; however they may be tolerated in conver-

sation or familiar address, they do not become serious discourse, and pulpit dignity.

But we must not forget the part of the service that comes more immediately within our province. There is an organ in Mr. James' church, and also a choir; two things indispensable to the best results in church music. The organ was well played, yet not always with sufficient strength to support and guide the congregation. It is a great fault for the organist *in Congregational singing*, to play so soft for the sake of some fancied musical expression, as to leave the people unsustained, and even to ground in shoal water. The organ should ever maintain a fullness and depth sufficient to keep the voice from sinking, or to bear up the vocal song. In *choir singing* (that is when the congregation do not join), the case is different; expression should now receive attention, and the organ which in its mighty power held up, and bore onward, the chorus of the whole people, in a *choir performance*, becomes a mere accompaniment, often " unheard, unseen." We have known a congregation suddenly checked in their song, and thrown all into *pie* —as the printers say—by some sudden freak of an inexperienced organist, who, because he saw the word *peace* ahead, supposed he must instantly pass from forte to piano. This same fault was observable in the organ-playing here. There was also a painful pause at the end of each stanza, in which all rhythmic feeling was lost, and it became necessary to begin anew with the divisions of time at the beginning of every stanza. Surely there can be no reason for a full (apparently final) pause at the end of a stanza, any more than at the end of a line ; but if it be desirable for the *voices* to stop for a moment, then let the organ fill up the space by a few chords of transition (where interludes are not desired), keep up the rhythmic form or structure, and thus prevent a mental collision, or an apparent final close at the end of each stanza. An organ voluntary at the commencement of the service was in good style, appropriate and religious ; and we think it was in equally good taste that there was no voluntary at the close of worship. The principal effect of a closing voluntary is to endanger the vocal organs of the people, who are often obliged to speak louder to their friends and neighbors, in order to be heard, than is consistent with prudence and safety. The closing voluntary instead of covering or shading the voices of the retiring congregation, is not unfrequently a mere signal, which, when reduced to language, says " Now talk as loud as you can."

The choir in Mr. James' church did not seem to be much in advance of the people in the manner of their performance ; they tried to *help the organ to lead*, but no choir piece, either tune or anthem, was attempted by them. There was no chanting, as there is in many of the London churches, and metrical psalmody was the only form of song. Extempore parts were sung near to me, and especially by a gentleman who *knew* enough of music to sing always a third below the treble ; this *knowledge* he took care to bring into practical use, and so, of course, was often producing fifths as much at variance with music's laws as are nouns in the plural in connection with verbs in the singular number with the requirements of grammar. The first tune was St. Ann's, with the good old-fashioned cadence on the mediant at the end of the third line—grand and effective ; the second was St. Paul's ; the third we did not know, but while it was a *pretty*, " *all's well*" kind of tune, it was unfit for Congregational singing, and an *affected*, fainting away, or " oh dear" result was the consequence. As in other places in England, so here, the hymn is just named, the organist then gives out the tune on his instrument, playing it through, then follows the reading of the hymn, after which it is sung.

At half past 3 o'clock we attended the church of St. Martin's (Episcopal). The congregation was small, and was (as we supposed from the application of almost every one who came in to the Beadleship for a seat) composed mostly of strangers. The service was dull and monotonous, no one appearing to manifest any other interest than a desire to get through. The chanting, however, was an exception, and was of a character somewhat new. It was almost exclusively instrumental, being performed on the organ. Of course, we could find no fault with the articulation of words, or the rapidity of utterance, since the pipes appeared to do their best. But voices could not be heard in this part of the service with the exception of "Gloria Patri," in which there was a feeble attempt at vocal effect. It may be well for congregations who do not wish to be at the trouble of opening their mouths and speaking forth God's praises in the "Venite," "Jubilate Deo," and other canticles, to confide the matter wholly to a faithful instrument; for, under a master's hand, it is always sure.

We were pleased with one thing which we saw in this church : as we entered, we observed near the door a stall capable of holding twenty or thirty loaves, filled with nice-looking bread. Over it was painted on a sign : "Mr. John Billingsley's gift, 1629." I ascertained, on inquiry, that the good man had left a fund by which a weekly supply of bread for the poor was provided. I asked if there was applicants enough to receive the bread. "Enough, yes, and forty times as many more," was the answer. "The works of the righteous shall be held in everlasting remembrance."

In the evening, at half past six o'clock, we attended a religious service in the "Cherry street Chapel" (Wesleyan), where a sermon was preached and a collection taken in aid of Sunday schools. The singing was mostly by a chorus of about two hundred children, who sang in two parts, girls singing first, boys second. They sang in tolerably good time and tune, but in no better taste than we have heard some of the children's choruses in America. There was a kind of nasal, or feline quality of tone, which was anything but pleasant. One would think that here, as in America, the great thing sought for is to get as many children together as possible, make them exert their tender vocal organs to the utmost, strive for a loud noise, and perhaps the execution of something that seems very diffi-cult, while all that relates to taste, or to a truthful musical edu-cation, is neglected. It is immensely important that a child should be taught by one who has, at least, some practical phy-siological knowledge of the voice, and who has also a cultivated taste; otherwise the poor child suffers severely, forming habits which probably will follow him to his sorrow through all after life. The singing, by children, of music unfit for them, or un-adapted to their capacities, is a very common fault; on the pre-sent occasion a glee by Callcott was attempted, to sacred words, which had better been omitted; and at the close of the services, after the benediction, the poor children, not knowing what they were about, but led on by those who ought to have known bet-ter, made a bold attack on Handel's Hallelujah. It hardly need be added that the performance came as near to the ridiculous as need be; there was nothing good about it except the *inten-tions of the children;* they were innocent through ignorance; but not so with the teachers, for ignorance cannot, in a teacher, excuse such error in judgment and carelessness in execution.

It is no unimportant lesson for a teacher or conductor of music to learn *what music is appropriate to the occasion, what comes fairly within the capacities of the performers and the under-standing of the hearers, what is suitable for children,—what for congregations,—what for choirs without orchestra, and for choirs with orchestra, &c.* And how shall one learn these things and a thousand others? Answer. By the study of music under the direction of those who are competent to teach. How long will it take and what will it cost? Answer. Go to the members of other professions and ask them these questions, in relation to their own preparatory studies, multiply their answer by two, and the product will not deceive you.

Monday came. It was a great day of preparation. The streets were full of carriages, and strangers were constantly arriving. We went early to procure our tickets, but found a crowd already in the office. The office is a wooden building, erected on a vacant lot, for the express purpose of ticket-selling during the Festival. Some fifteen or eighteen clerks were employed in attending to the calls of purchasers. There was one clerk for selling reserved seats for each morning, and one also for each evening performance; two clerks for unreserved seats, one for morning and one for evening tickets; two for the sale of programmes, or books of words; besides which, several other officers were employed, giving the whole an air of business almost equal to the stock exchange, Paris. It was interesting to see the rush for tickets, a great part of which had been already taken by previous application. In order to prevent a preference being given to any one person, the names of all applicants are registered; the books are closed on a certain day, say three or four days before the performances begin, and then the places are disposed of, not in the order of applicants, but by lot. But here I must close.

LETTER XLIII.

The Birmingham Festival—Continued.

September, 1852.

THE Birmingham Musical Festival for 1852 is past, and its success has been most triumphant. The highest anticipations of its warmest friends have been fully realized, and they are satisfied both with the musical and pecuniary results. This Festival is triennial. We well remember the gratification an attendance in 1837 afforded us. At that time Mendelssohn's *St. Paul* was performed under the direction of the talented composer himself. He also gave, during an evening performance, an example of his wonderful power in extemporaneous organ-playing, which we can never forget. At the same Festival, the Chevalier Neukomm brought out an oratorio, *The Ascension.*

The Birmingham Festival has existed for almost a century. It had but a small beginning, but has been gradually increasing until now its occurrence may be said to move the whole musical kingdom. Its profits are devoted to the support of the Birmingham Hospital ; and, notwithstanding the great expenses, it never fails to pay over a large sum to the charity. It brings together the very best musical talent that can be found, and the works of the greatest masters are performed under circumstances more advantageous than are elsewhere afforded in the world. In looking over the list of performers, we find the names of Catalina, Malibran, Grisi, Sontag, Jenny Lind, Lablache, Tamburini, Mario, Staudigl, and all the first vocalists that have lived within the last fifty years. Several oratorios have been written expressly for this occasion, the greatest of which is, undoubtedly, *Elijah.* This masterly production of Mendelssohn was first produced here in 1846. "I feel," said

Mendelssohn, "much more interest in this work than for my others, and I only wish it may last so with me." It was his last great work, and it will carry down the name of the gifted author to many succeeding generations. It is remarkable that, in making alterations in this oratorio after the first copy had been given out, Mendelssohn gave directions to omit the very popular song " *O rest in the Lord.*" To this Mr. Bartholomew, the English translator, so strongly objected that it was allowed to remain. After the first performance of the oratorio in 1846, Mendelssohn made many alterations, and yet more when the German copy was finally published at Leipzig.

Great preparations were made for the Festival this year, and it is believed that a better band and chorus were brought together than on any previous occasion. The instrumental department was as follows :

First Violins...... 26	Oboes............ 4	Ophicleide......... 1
Second Violins.... 26	Clarionets 4	Serpents 2
Tenors........... 18	Bassoons.......... 4	Double Drum,
Violoncellos...... 18	Trumpets 4	Side Drum,
Double Basses.... 18	Horns 4	Triangle,
Flutes........ ... 4	Trombones........ 3	Bass Drum.

In all, one hundred and forty instruments ; to which must be added the great organ, one of the most powerful in the world. The vocal chorus consisted of eighty to ninety voices on each part, as soprano, alto, tenor, and bass ; in all, about three hundred and thirty or forty voices. It must be understood that these were all real (not merely nominal) singers, capable of sustaining their respective parts. The parts were well balanced, and the *chorus blending* was admirable, no individual voices being heard. The alto consisted of both female and male voices ; yet the men's voices were kept in good subjection, and only once or twice during the four days' performance, did they appear severe or hard. The solo singers were the best that could be obtained in Europe; they did not include some of the best artists, because they could not be obtained; for example, great efforts were made to procure the assistance of Henriette Sontag, but the Americans had drawn her away, and no inducement that was held out, could prevail upon her to remain. Madame Goldschmidt was also applied to in vain; nor could Lablache or Mario be obtained. But still, such an amount of vocal talent as was procured is not often brought together, as will appear by the following catalogue of names, all of whom were present:

Madame VIARDOT GARCIA,	Mdlle. ANNA ZERR,
Madame CASTELLAN,	Mdlle. BERTRANDI,
Miss DOLBY,	Miss M. WILLIAMS,
Madame CLARA NOVELLO,	Signor TAMBELIK,
Mr. LOCKEY,	Herr FORMES,
Mr. T. WILLIAMS,	Mr. WEISS,
Mr. SIMS REEVES,	Signor POLININI,

Signor BELLETTI.

Besides the above, there were solo instrumentalists as follows:—

Violin, M. SAINTON,	Double Bass, Sig. BOTTESINI,
Violoncello, Sig. PIATTI,	Pianoforte, Herr KUHE,
Organist, Mr. STIMPSON,	Conductor, Mr. COSTA.

The general rehearsal was on the day previous to the commencement of the Festival, at which the band, the chorus, and the solo singers were brought together. The former took their places in the orchestra, but the solo singers came into the body of the Hall. This gave us a fine opportunity of seeing them all, and of shaking hands with some of them. Belletti seemed glad to meet an American, and his countenance brightened as he spoke of Castle Garden and other concert places. He remembers his tour and his American friends with gratitude, and expressed a hope yet again to sing in the United States. Madame Clara Novello looks almost as young as in 1837, and is as social and pleasant as before she became a countess. Herr Formes is a noble specimen of a man; he is full of pleasantry and good humor; his voice in conversation is rich, full, sonorous, and, as a gentleman near us observed, "seems to come from a thirty-two foot diapason." Madame Viardot Garcia is a most interesting person; perhaps she appeared the more so to us, since we knew her to be one of the greatest singers living. She seems to be perfectly easy and unaffected in her deportment, and simple as a little child. Frankness, honesty, and firmness of purpose are strongly indicated by her open and intelligent countenance. She is not handsome: she may be called plain in her personal appearance; but, nevertheless, one cannot look at her with indifference, or hear her voice without a drawing out of the heart towards her. Miss Dolby, the greatest of English alto singers, has a noble countenance; generous, open, honest, and intelligent. Madame Castellan is always smiling and apparently happy; she turns her head one side, and looks as if nothing troubled her,—save, perhaps, Time; who is evidently making inroads upon a fair and blooming countenance, and a brilliant, sparkling eye. It was interesting to study the physiognomy of the fine company of artists, and to mark their cordial greetings as they first met. The rehearsal commenced at 11 o'clock, and (with the exception of the necessary intermission for refreshments) continued until nearly 12 at night. Such pieces only were taken up as were new, or not generally known. A part of Samson, a new posthumous motette by Mendelssohn, his fragment of an oratorio, *Christus*, and also of

Lorelie. Beethoven's great 9th, and various other pieces belonging to the evening performances, were more or less rehearsed. Beethoven's Choral Symphony occupied about two hours. It was evidently the piece for the success of which Mr. Costa felt the greatest anxiety—since it is the most difficult composition on the programme; and he spared no effort to make its performance perfect. It was originally written for the London Philharmonic Society; but it was not performed with any success until long after its production.

This rehearsal-day was full of interest and instruction, and afforded us an opportunity of standing a little behind the curtain, and of seeing something more of the principal vocalists than we otherwise could have done. Though tedious, the result was satisfactory; and when it was nearly 12 o'clock, and the company parted, there seemed to be a general assurance of a successful performance on the morrow.

FIRST DAY—TUESDAY. " ELIJAH."—The morning was inauspicious. The clouds, dark and heavy, at once shut out the cheerful light of the sun, and poured out a cold, continuous rain, which was anything but musical in its appearance and influence. We left our lodgings about an hour before the time appointed for the commencement of the performance, and as we came to the street leading directly to the Hall, we found the sidewalks filled with people of all ages and descriptions, who, notwithstanding the mud and wet, had taken their stand to look into the carriages as they passed. The row of carriages at this time extended full a quarter of a mile from the Hall. The police regulations were excellent, and officers were stationed all around to see that they were observed. As the carriages were not permitted to break the line, and moved very slowly, a fine opportunity was afforded to those on the sidewalks to get a glimpse of the beautiful ladies and their elegant dresses,—and this was about all that the common people could get of the Festival;—the eye was gratified with a passing view of elegance and splendor without, although the ear might not be permitted to hear the wonderful combinations and successions of sounds within.

On arriving at the Hall we took a stand so as to have a view of the carriages as they came up, and of the ladies and gentlemen as they alighted, under cover, and walked up to the entrance. No person was allowed to come within about two hundred feet of the outer door, where the carriages stopped, unless he was going to attend the concerts; so there was no crowding or pressing together at any of the places of entrance. At a quarter past 10, the unreserved places were all occupied, and those who had taken reserved seats were fast coming in and filling them.

The great Hall now presented a most splendid appearance. It seemed as if all the beauty and fashion of the kingdom, all the colors of the rainbow, and all the resources of embellishment, had been called in to enliven and give effect to the brilliant spectacle. Not the least interesting was the organ gallery, choir, or orchestra; its towering seats being so arranged as to bring within the view of almost every spectator the whole number (nearly five hundred) of instrumental and vocal performers. As the time for beginning approached, the organ poured forth its full and prolonged chords in the majestic and solemn key of D minor, setting the whole atmosphere in motion, and filling the space with a torrent of sound. This continued for three or five minutes, and afforded an opportunity for the instrumentalists to tune and prepare for action. At half past 11, Lord Leigh, the President of the Festival, took his seat in the front gallery opposite the conductor; at the same moment, the solo singers came in and took their seats. These were followed by Costa, who was received on this as on *every other occasion on his entrance into the Hall during the four days*, with warm applause by the performers as well as by the audience. After bowing repeatedly to both parties, he lifted the *bâton ;* when, in an instant, all was hushed ; and Madame Castellan led off (in the key of B flat) with *God save the Queen..* The whole audience instantly rose, and remained standing during the three stanzas, the second of which was by the solo voices in F, and the third by the whole band and chorus in the original key.

As soon as this was closed, Herr Formes (For-mez), as Elijah, arose, and in his deep, solemn voice, announced the curse : *As God, the Lord God of Israel liveth, before whom I stand ; there shall not be dew nor rain these years, but according to my word.* The effect was fearful ; and a sense of awe or dread seemed to rest upon the people. The gloom and desolation of the famine thus brought up to the imagination, was immediately and most effectively presented by the soft and plaintive strains of the overture, which was without a fault in its performance, and which prepared the way for the cry of the people, *Help, Lord ! wilt thou quite destroy us ?* This chorus, and especially the movement, *The harvest now is over*, was wonderfully effective. Thus the *Elijah* had begun in good earnest. The solo singers were Madame Castellan, Madame Clara Novello, Madame Viardot, Miss Dolby, Miss Williams, Mrs. Bull, Herr Formes, Mr. Lockey, Mr. Sims Reeves, Mr. Weiss, and Mr. T. Williams.

We have already alluded to the introductory prologue, (the announcement of the curse,) by Herr Formes ; great, very great was his rendering, throughout, of the extremely difficult part of Elijah ; and he fully met, in his after-performance, all the expectations he awakened by the splendid delivery of this opening recitative.

Mr. Lockey, who has a very pure tenor voice, and a chaste style, though not much power, sang with great acceptance, the charming air, *If with all your hearts ye truly seek me*, as also the preceding recitative. The double quartet (a very popular piece) was well given; and we thought that if those churches which perfer quartet singing could always have as good a double quartet as this, less offence would be given to true taste. There were time, tune, and equality of voices, three things not *always* found in our church quartets. It is comparatively easy to train a chorus to sing well, but a quartet requires artists. It is not easy to obtain a good one.

Miss Williams sang the recitative, *Now Cherith's brook is dried up*, as well as one could desire to hear it. A charming voice, and a most perfect delivery of every tone and of every word. The succeeding recitatives and duet between The Widow, and Elijah, were by Madame Castellan and Herr Formes. Mad. Castellan's manner was altogether too light and careless. She appeared indifferent, and manifested none of the deep feeling so necessary to the circumstances. Indeed, she did not seem to care whether her son was restored or not. Besides this, we cannot help thinking our author himself somewhat in fault here. The scene appeared to us to be a failure; that is, it wanted the appearance of appropriate emotion. Not so the scene between Elijah, Ahab and the People, *As God the Lord of Sabaoth liveth*, &c., in which the performers seemed to be in good earnest, and in which the composer appears to have furnished a musical form well adapted to express the sentiments of the text.

The recitative by Elijah, (Herr Formes,) *O thou who makest thy angels spirits*, &c., hushed the multitudinous audience to a perfect stillness. Softly, gently, yet most distinctly and solemnly, were the words uttered ; and the effect was most thrilling. The following air, or rather the latter part of it, *For God is angry with the wicked every day,* however well done by Herr Formes, was a failure. It is the fault of the composer ; Mendelssohn's music may well paint the anger of some earthly tyrant, or the rage and passion of some disappointed and jealous lover, but to attempt, in this way, to paint the anger of the great Jehovah, is absurd. His anger is terrible; so says his word ; but any human impersonation or representation of it must fail. A simple announcement of these words, in slow recitative, or in a plain, solemn melody, without any attempt at imitation, would be in much better taste. Indeed, the effect of the air is not to bring up to one's mind the fearful anger of God, but rather the power of the singer's execution.

But what shall be said of the 'following air, *Woe unto them who forsake him !* Here the composer has done justice to the text ; but we doubt whether it ever entered into his mind to conceive the wonderful effect produced by Mad. Viardot's rendering of the passage. Her whole external manner and appearance were most beautifully appropriate, and the very first tone she uttered seemed to tell of deepest compassion and strongest desire. Description here is impossible ; it was the gem, the strongest point in the whole oratorio. It touched the heart, and tears flowed forth. The audience were still as death ; every one was compelled to give breathless attention. We wish we could give some idea of the agony expressed by the words, *Destruction shall fall upon them, for they have transgressed against him.* And then came the contrast of that which had been done for them, with the return they had rendered. *By him redeemed*—that word "redeemed," especially, was given with wonderful power. It brought up to our minds most vividly, the passage, " How often would I have gathered, and ye would not." [See Matthew xxiii. 37.] Tenderness, deep compassion, strong desire for the deliverance of the guilty and the wretched, were perfectly expressed by Madame Viardot. Although Mr. Costa paused a little, after this wonderful effective air, as if he was unwilling to disturb the tender and deep feelings excited, yet too soon came the following scene. We were almost angry with Madame Castellan—*Hearest thou the sound of rain? Seest thou nothing arise from the deep?* " No; there is nothing:" said the youth. Quite descriptive of your performance, thought we; indeed " there is nothing"—or at least no appropriate feeling manifested in the singing. Here, again, we think our author somewhat in fault; it is a mistake thus to try to prevail on God by blasts of trombones;—more gentle language seems better adapted to him who cries for mercy in the words, " *unto thee will I cry, O Lord, my rock; be not silent to me; and in great mercies remember, Lord.*

The chorus that concludes the first part of the oratorio, " Thanks be to God," was most magnificently done. The second part, especially, *The stormy billows are high; their fury is mighty:* BUT THE LORD IS ABOVE THEM, ALMIGHTY, was given in a manner not easily to be surpassed by human power. A recess of twenty minutes gave one an opportunity to breathe again, to look around upon the splendid scene, and to recover strength for the remainder of the oratorio.

Again the loud organ poured forth its minor chords, the instruments were tuned, and in a few moments the clear, transparent, enchanting voice of Madame Clara Novello, singing most delightfully, *Hear, ye Israel; hear what the Lord speaketh,* was heard. Madame Clara Novello has indeed a most charming voice, than which nothing in the region of tones can be more perfect. Her use of it, too, is artistic and beautiful in the highest degree, and in her singing of this song, not a fault could be detected. She cannot execute a passage like SONTAG, (nor can any one else,) but in a different way, we had *almost said*, she is equally as good. To say this, however, or. to say that any one is as good as Sontag, is a bold thing; and we are glad we did not *quite say it.* But Madame Viardot is again heard in the splendid scene in which Jezebel denounces Elijah. The recitatives were delivered with great dramatic power; we have seldom, if ever before, heard such powerful declamation in recitative. Madame Viardot Garcia excels in this particular department of song; she belongs to the great, the tragic, or to whatever calls forth the deep passions of the soul. Mr. Sims Reeves made fine use of his beautiful voice, in the Recitative, *Man of God*; yet with still better effect did he give the fine song afterwards, " Then shall the righteous shine forth." The trio, " Lift up thine eyes," (originally written as a duet, and afterwards changed to a trio,) was sung by three perfect voices, viz. : Madame Clara Novello, Miss M. Williams, and Miss Dolby ; and we doubt whether it ever was or ever will be done better. Notwithstanding applause was strictly prohibited, the audience could not be restrained ; there was a gentle moving and slight clapping of the hands, which caused the President, Lord Leigh, to make a sign for its repetition. " He watches over Israel," the succeeding chorus, may be regarded as a part of the trio, and its performance was equally good. Most charming, too, was the air, " O rest in the Lord." Miss Dolby, who sang this song, has as fine an alto voice as any one in the world, not excepting even Alboni herself; she is also an accomplished singer, being one of the best English vocalists living. Herr Formes, always good, seemed to rise as he drew near to the end of his part ; his magnificent voice, his perfect declamation, his dignified manner, his pathos and expression, left nothing to be desired in the part of Elijah ; and that most beautiful air,

" For the mountains shall depart, and the hills be removed," with its rich vein of melody, was not only one of the finest exhibitions of the artist's wonderful vocal power, but a most appropriate *finale* to the fine reading of the music, and general representation of the character which had been given. We have heard it remarked that the close of the oratorio is heavy and uninteresting ; this, however, cannot be, if it is well done.

There was, on this occasion, but one feature to the pieces following Elijah's last song, and that was *unvaried excellence ;* while the closing chorus was truly magnificent. The choruses throughout the whole oratorio were well done, (though we think the English chorus singers less firm and sure than the German,) and the orchestra could have hardly been better. The oratorio closed at half-past two, and many were heard to exclaim, " We never heard Elijah so well done before ;" Costa himself is said to have made the remark : "I have no wish ever to conduct Elijah again, for I can never expect to have such a band under my control."

We cannot now enter into any review of the excellencies of the oratorio, but must assume that our readers have heard it, or have so examined and studied the score as to know something of this great production of Mendelssohn ; which has certainly taken stronger hold of the English, than any other oratorio since the days of Handel. It seems to be the opinion of musical men, that *Elijah* ranks with the greatest productions of human genius, and is destined to live with the *Messiah, Israel* and *Samson.* Indeed, not a few are found who even give to Elijah, considered as a *perfect whole*, the first place ; who say that it is free from those weaknesses that are found in all similar productions, and that in every piece, the music worthy of the subject is faultless. While we are clearly of the opinion that it ranks very high, coming next, perhaps, to Handel, and while we may be disposed to admit that in a mere scientific or technical view it may be more finished than the Messiah, still we cannot, as yet, believe that it comes near to that immortal work, or that it will ever become so universally popular ; nor that in point of true sublimity it is to be compared for a moment with the *greatest* of all Handel's productions " ISRAEL IN EGYPT."

Since writing the foregoing, we have thought that the entire cast of the oratorio would be interesting to our readers who are in possession of *Elijah ;* and who is he, being a musician, who has not obtained a copy of this great work ?

PART I.

PROLOGUE, Herr Formes, " As God the Lord,"

DUET and CHORUS, Madame Castellan and Miss Williams, " Zion Spreadeth her hand." " Lord bow thine ear."

RECITATIVE and AIR, Mr. Lockey, " If with all your hearts."

RECITATIVE, Miss Dolby, " Elijah get thee hence."

DOUBLE QUARTET, Madame Castellan, Mrs. Bull, Miss Dolby, Miss M. Williams, Mr. Lockey, Mr. T. Williams, Mr. Weiss, and Mr. Smythson, " For he shall give."

RECITATIVE, Miss M. Williams, " Now Cherith's brook."

RECITATIVE and DUET, Madame Castellan and Herr Formes, " Give me thy son."

RECITATIVE and CHORUS, Herr Formes and Mr. Lockey, " As God the Lord."

RECITATIVE, Herr Formes, " Call him louder."

RECITATIVE and AIR, Herr Formes, " Draw near all ye people."

QUARTET, Madame Castellan, Miss M. Williams, Mr. Lockey and Mr. Weiss, " Cast thy burden."

RECITATIVE, Herr Formes, " O thou who makest."

RECITATIVE, Herr Formes and Chorus, " Take all the prophets."

AIR, Herr Formes, " Is not his word like a Fire ?"

AIR, Madame Viardot Garcia, " Woe unto them."

RECITATIVE, Mr. Lockey, " O man of God."

RECITATIVE and CHORUS, Herr Formes and Madame Castellan, " O Lord, thou hast overthrown."

PART II.

AIR, Madame Clara Novello, "Hear ye, Israel."

RECITATIVE, Herr Formes, "The Lord hath exalted."

SOLO, Madame Viardot Garcia, and Chorus, "Have ye not heard."

RECITATIVE, Mr. Sims Reeves, "Man of God."

RECITATIVE and AIR, Herr Formes, "It is enough, O Lord."

RECITATIVE, Mr. Sims Reeves, "See now he sleepeth."

TRIO, Madame Clara Novello, Miss M. Williams and Miss Dolby, "Lift thine eyes."

RECITATIVE, Miss Dolby and Herr Formes, "Arise, Elijah."

AIR, Miss Dolby, "O rest in the Lord."

RECITATIVE, Herr Formes and Madame Clara Novello, "Night falleth."

RECITATIVE, Miss Dolby, "Above him stood."

QUARTET and CHORUS, Madame Clara Novello, Mrs. Bull, Miss M. Williams and Miss Dolby, "Holy, holy, holy."

CHORAL RECITATIVE and SOLO, Herr Formes and Chorus, "Go, return upon thy way."

AIR, Herr Formes, "For the mountains."

AIR, Mr. Sims Reeves, "Then shall the righteous."

RECITATIVE, Madame Clara Novello, "Behold God hath sent."

QUARTET, Madame Clara Novello, Miss M. Williams, Mr. Sims Reeves, and Mr. Weiss, "O Come every one."

The amount of money received for this morning's performance was somewhat more than ELEVEN THOUSAND AND FIVE HUNDRED DOLLARS.

TUESDAY EVENING.—The weather was unpropitious, and the evening was cold and damp. The Hall was not much more than half filled. At no other performance during the Festival, was the audience so small as this evening. The concert commenced at eight, and the programme was as follows:

PART I.

OVERTURE, *Jessonda*...*Spohr*.

ARIA, Signor Belletti, "Sorgette." *Assedio di Corinto*.........*Rossini*.

TRIO, Miss M. Williams, Mr. T. Williams, and Mr. Lockey, " Vanne
a colei."..*Costa.*
ARIA, Mde. Castellan, " O luce di quest anima." *Linda.......Donizetti.*
DUO, Mdle. Anna Zerr and Mr. Sims Reeves, " Sulla tomba."
Lucia di Lammermoor.........................Donizetti.
ARIA, Signor Tamberlik e Coro, " Ah ! non temer." *Faust.......Spohr.*
ARIA, Miss Dolby, " Nobil Signor." *Huguenots..............Meyerbeer.*
DUO, Madame Viardot Garcia e Madame Castellan, " Per serbar
me fedel." *Prophéte..............................Meyerbeer.*
ARIA, Madame Clara Novello, " Deh vieni." *Nozze di Figaro....Mozart.*
FINALE, Madame Castellan, Mdlle. Bertrandi, Signor Tamberlik,
Mr. Lockey, Signori Polinini, Belletti e Coro, " Mi
manca la voce." *Mosé in Egitto......................Rossini.*

PART II.

" The First Walpurgis night."........................*Mendelssohn.*

PART III.

OVERTURE, *Guillaume Tell................................Rossini.*
AIR, Mdlle. Anna Zerr, Variations........................*C. Proch.*
ARIA, Herr Formes e Coro, " Possentti numi." *Il Flauto Magico..Mozart.*
DUO, (Violin e Violoncello,) M. Sainton e Signor Piatti.
ARIA, Madame Viardot Garcia, " Nacqui all affanno." *Cenerentola..Rossini*
TRIO, Madame Clara Novello, Miss Dolby, and Mr. Lockey, " O
dolce e caro instante."............................*Cimarosa.*
AIR, Mr. Sims Reeves, " Soft Airs" *Euryanthe...............Weber.*
DUO, Mde. Castellan e Signor Tamberlik. " Per te d'una sposa."
I Martiri.......................................Donizetti.
AIR, Mdlle. Bertrandi, " Robert, toi que j'aime." *Roberto....Meyerbeer.*
PREGHIERA E FINALE, "Numa del ciel." *Massaniello...........Auber.*

It hardly need be said that the great attraction of the evening was the cantata by Mendelssohn—" The First Walpurgis
night." The following explanatory note is from the programme of the evening. " The Germand legend, that witches
and evil spirits assemble on the night of the first of May (Walpurgis Nacht) on the summit of the Harz Mountains, is sup-

posed to have taken its origin in the heathen time, when the Christians tried by force to prevent the Druids from observing their accustomed rights of sacrificing in the open air, and on the hills. The Druids are said to have placed watches round their mountains, who, with their dreadful appearance, hovering round the fires, and clashing with their weapons, frightened the enemy, and the ceremonies were proceeded with." On this tradition Göethe founded the poem, which Mendelssohn has set to music. It begins with an overture, describing a Winter storm, and the gradually-approaching Spring. It is thoroughly Mendelssohn. The power of stringed instruments is wonderfully brought out, and the whole piece is most effective. A spring song of the Druids follow;

> "Now May again
> Breaks Winter's chain,
> The bud and bloom are springing !
> No snow is seen,
> The leaves are green,
> The woodland choirs are singing," &c.

This was finely given by Mr. Lockey and chorus. A solo by Miss M. Williams, " Know ye not a deed so daring," was sung as well as need be. Miss M. Williams has a charming alto voice (we repeat it) and sings finely. A chorus of Druid Guards, " Disperse, disperse, ye gallant men," brought out in a remarkable manner *pianissimo ;* it was whispered by both orchestra and choir. This is soon followed by a most extraordinary chorus, to the following words :

> " Come with torches brightly flashing ;
> Rush along with billets clashing ;
> Through the night-gloom lead and follow,
> In and out each rocky hollow.
> Owls and ravens,
> Howl with us, and scare the cravens."

Most brilliant and characteristic is the music; Mendelssohn seems to have felt at liberty to employ all the powers of instruments and voices, and he has done so, in his own masterly way. The sweep of the tempest, the howling of the winds, and the glare of the torches, the rush to the battle, the gloom of the thick darkness, and the screeches of the birds of night, though not attempted to be particularly described, are yet, in general, well portrayed. The *staccato* is admirably employed. The violins are fully occupied, the trumpets and brass instruments send forth their blasts of horror, the cymbals clash, the drums roar, and the yelling of voices is heard, altogether forming an aggregation of sounds as frightful as ever entered into the imagination of mortal man. It was brought out, one would suppose, according to the full intent of the composer, and the effect was terrific indeed. The " Legion," " from Satan's region," " in flames advancing," " on wolves and dragons riding," " *Imp and Devil*," having been successful in driving away their enemies, the cantata closes with a full chorus of Druids.

> " Unclouded now, the flame is bright,
>   Though faith from error sever ;
> Though foes may cloud or quell our light,
>   Thy light shall shine forever."

And thus they chant their hymn unmolested, in grand and solemn strains. The Walpurgis Night seemed to give great satisfaction ; and, for aught we saw, the people were as much delighted, and as well satisfied, with the success of the Druids, as with the triumphs of a more mild and rational religion, based on the revelation of Him who came to *save from sin*. The moral effect of song seems to be regarded as of much less importance than its artistic excellence.

The overtures, " Jessonda," and " William Tell," were played with great spirit, and the latter called out a hearty encore. The violoncello solo was finely done by Mr. Charles Lucas, successor to the veteran Lindley. Signor Belletti did himself great credit by his "Sorgette" of Rossini, which he sang with the same unerring certainty, good taste, and perfect execution as in America. Madame Castellan was quite at home in the evening concerts ; she has a great power of vocalization, sings well, and generally pleases. It has been remarked that she has much improved since she was in the United States. The duet from the Prophéte, "Per serbar me fadel," was well sung by Madame Viardot and Madame Castellan, but it was ineffective, and appeared quite out of place. It belongs to the opera, and loses its interest when taken out of its connection. This remark is also applicable to many of the pieces which were sung at this and at the other evening concerts. Most extracts from operas are quite dependent upon their relation to the general plot, or other musical pieces, with which they are originally connected. Madame Clara Novello sang very beautifully the Aria "Deh! Vieni, non tardar," from Nozze de Figaro, by Mozart. We should have been charmed with this, had we not heard Madame Jenny Lind Goldschmidt sing it both in New York and in Boston ; besides which, we have heard it by Madame Henrietta Sontag, in its regular place in the opera. It is hardly possible under such circumstances that any other performance of the same song should be satisfactory. The closing chorus in "Moses in Egypt" was well worth hearing, as done by Madame Castellan, Mademoiselle Bertrandi, Signor Tamberlik, Signor Polinini, Mr. Lockey, and Signor Belletti, with the full choir. The final chorus especially was animating in a high degree. This chorus was performed many years ago at the concerts of the Boston Academy of Music; it is very brilliant, and we always wondered why it should have been altogether omitted by the Boston Handel and Haydn Society when they sang the music to this popular opera of Rossini. Mademoiselle Anna Zerr sang a song requiring very difficult vocalization, and did it well; but it failed to please us, for we could not help making the comparison between the singer and SONTAG, whose powers of execution are much greater. Herr Formes sang the delicious melody "Possentti Numi," from Il Flauto Magico, by Mozart, to perfection; but the accompanying chorus was rather dull and heavy—not much so, indeed, yet so much as to be quite intolerable in the Birmingham Hall. One of the most interesting performances of the evening was a Duo (violin and violoncello) by Mr. Sainton and Signor Piatti, both artists of great excellence. We think we have never heard so beautiful a tone from the violoncello before, not even when in the hands of Romberg of Berlin.

An incident occurred towards the close of the concert that awakened some feeling. A duet near the beginning of the programme had been omitted, and, as was naturally supposed, on account of the absence of one of the singers. The duet was to have been sung by Mademoiselle Anna Zerr and Mr. Sims Reeves, and the supposition by some persons present (concert-goers) was, that Mr. Sims Reeves was the delinquent; consequently, when he came on the stage to sing a song, ("Soft airs around me play," by Weber,) he was received with a chorus of hisses. He looked up aghast, bowed, and retired. Mr. Costa immediately arose, and, turning to the audience, said: "It is not Mr. Reeves' fault—Mr. Reeves was here; it was not Mr. Reeves' fault." Loud cheers followed. Mr. Reeves reappeared, and, after greeting Mr. Costa by a warm shake of the hand, proceeded with his song; he was loudly applauded—recalled—bowed—and retired, amidst shouts of commendation, so long and loud as to make ample amends for the sibilants of his first appearance. The concert this evening closed at a quarter before twelve o'clock; the amount received was somewhat more than TWO THOUSAND AND ONE HUNDRED DOLLARS.

WEDNESDAY MORNING.—"CHRISTUS," "CREATION."—Although the night was dark and full of rain, the morning opened brightly. At a little past ten, the streets were full, and a long line of carriages extended nearly half a mile from the Hall, filled with ladies and gentlemen, making their way towards the grand scene of attraction. The streets were almost impassable, because of the crowd; we took care to have a hand on the purse, for some of these English rogues are expert at extracting the contents of one's pocket. The Hall was well filled at an early hour, and looked gayer in the bright sunshine of to-day than in the dark clouds of yesterday. Exactly at the appointed time, the immense organ threw out a volume of sound, in minor chords, majestic, sublime. Oh! that those little organists who delight in fancy stops, and play very sweet voluntaries from some Italian opera, on the flute, oboe, and claribella, could hear, and hearing, feel, tremble, be converted, and made to appreciate the greatness of their instrument, and its true uses in worship! Let the full and rich diapasons sound on the Sabbath morning, for it is they that tell of God, saying, "The Lord is in his holy temple; let the whole earth fear before him."

Thus far, the festival had been quite Mendelssohnian in its character; and this morning again the concert commenced with a new motet by our great modern composer.

> " Saviour of sinners, throned in glory,
>   Adoration, praise, and might be unto Thee.
>   Holy Redeemer, hear us in mercy!
>   Save and bless us, in mercy,
>   Lord, forgive our sins.
>   Lord, let thy mercy fall upon us,
>   Saviour of sinners, hear us in mercy!"

The motet is written in eight parts; its character is truly religious, and it seems well expressive of the words. The same subject as is heard in Handel's Hallelujah, at the words, " For the Lord God omnipotent reigneth," (a very common one,) is brought in, though its treatment is entirely different from that of Handel. The piece was not well performed. The chorus was not only unsteady, but sometimes out of tune. We think the piece itself was somewhat out of place, being adapted to a church rather than to a concert room. This was followed by a posthumous fragment of an oratorio, also by Mendelssohn, called " Christus." It consists of a succession of recitatives and choruses, relating to the birth and death of the Saviour. While it undoubtedly possesses great merit, we doubt whether Mendelssohn would have consented to its publication. It is a first sketch ; and it is well known how his first sketches had to yield to after-thoughts. Some of the critics, however, praise it very much, and say that it is an advance even on " Elijah." The string of recitatives and choruses is very peculiar, reminding one somewhat of "Israel in Egypt," yet there is no approach to similarity in the music. It is highly dramatic, and is full of striking passages. The composer makes great use of the minor, (as does every great writer,) for example ; a recitative, " Then said Pilate," in A minor, is followed by a chorus in D minor ; this again is succeeded by a chorus, highly dramatic, in G minor, attaining a climax in the following chorus, " Crucify him," in C minor. Two old German chorales are introduced, and treated in the masterly manner in which our author is wont to do such things. The " Christus" was well received ; and every one spoke well both of the composition and its first performance on this occasion.

This was followed by an anthem composed by Dr. Wesley. The anthem consists of a quartet, solo, recitative, and chorus, and is written with orchestral accompaniments. The words are from Isaiah, commencing, " The wilderness and the solitary place shall be glad," &c. The solo parts were by Madame Clara Novello, Miss M. Williams, Mr. Lockey, and Herr Formes. Dr. Wesley conducted the performance, but it was not well done. The fact is, no such thing can be well done with a single rehearsal; the singers were not sufficiently acquainted with it; consequently, there was a want of confidence; and a kind of zig-zag or here-and-there effect was the result. We will not pass judgment upon a composition that had not a fair trial; but we were decidedly pleased with the fine contrapuntal arrangement of the chorus. And now followed, as the last thing on the programme of the morning's performances, the " Creation" of HAYDN. We have never before heard it half so well done, either in the solo, chorus, or orchestral parts. The chaotic symphony, however, though exquisitely played, fails now to represent chaos. More modern authors have become so much more chaotic in their storms, and in various representations of fiendish passions, that Haydn's introduction seems like quite a plain piece of harmony. Perhaps we can hardly refer to a clearer illustration of the advance of musical science, than a comparison of this piece with some of Beethoven's or Mendelssohn's dark and labyrinthian harmonies. The solo parts were by Madame Clara Novello, Madame Castellan, Mr. Sims Reeves, Mr. Lockey, Mr. Weiss, and Herr Formes. Very slowly and distinctly were the recitatives uttered—more so than we are accustomed to hear them in the United States. Madame Clara Novello sang the two soprano songs as well, probably, as any living English vocalist can give them. Mr. Sims Reeves sang " In native worth" without fault, and Herr Formes performed his part in characteristic style; he is always good and great. The choruses all went superbly; we know

not to which to give the preference. The change in the time in
" The heavens are telling" was not so great as we have been
used to observe. The chorus, " Glory to his name," a very
fine fugue, was magnificently done; and indeed so were all the
other choruses. The concert this morning closed at a quarter
before three o'clock, and the amount of money received was
upwards of EIGHT THOUSAND AND TWO HUNDRED DOLLARS.

WEDNESDAY EVENING.—A large and brilliant assemblage was
waiting for half-an-hour before eight. Mr. Costa was greeted
as usual. The band appeared to be of good cheer, and the people full of expectation. The bâton moved, and we were listening to the symphony (Jupiter) by Mozart. It is said that this
great work of Mozart, together with two other symphonies, the
last he ever composed, were all written in the short space of
six weeks; yet they are regarded as among the finest compositions of their class; the *Jupiter*, in particular, being often quoted
as one of the finest specimens of contrapuntal writing extant.
The last movement contains four distinct subjects, which are
finally brought together and worked up with all the ingenuity
of one of the most brilliant musical geniuses that ever existed.
Every member of the orchestra was on the alert, and Costa was
everywhere; his eye or his gesticulations were in all the parts,
and his direction firm, steady, and energetic in the highest degree. The following is the evening's programme :

PART I.

SYMPHONY, "Jupiter."..*Mozart.*
ARIA, Miss M. Williams, " Paga fui." *Proserpina*...............*Winter.*
DUO, Madame Castellan e Signor Belletti, " Pronta io son."

    Don Pasquale...............................*Donizetti.*
ARIA, Mde. Clara Novello, "Come per me." *Somnambula*.......*Bellini.*
SOLO, (Pianoforte,) Herr Kuhe.
AIR, Madame Viardot Garcia, " Ah! mon fils." *Prophéte*.....*Meyerbeer.*

Serenata, Mr. Sims Reeves e Coro, "Com'è gentil." *Don Pasquale*....................................*Donizetti.*
Duo, Signor Tamberlik e Herr Formes, "Sara il mourir." *Massaniello* ....*Auber.*
Aria, Mde. Castellan, "Prendi per me." *L'Elisir d'Amore*.....*Donizetti.*
Air, Mr. Weiss, "The Wanderer."........................*Schubert.*
Grand Finale, Mde. Clara Novello and chorus. *Lorely*.....*Mendelssohn.*
[An unpublished posthumous Opera—first time of performance.]

PART II.

Overture. *Der Freyschütz*..................................*Weber.*
Aria, Mdlle. Anna Zerr, "Gli' angui." *Flauto Magico*..........*Mozart.*
Song, Mr. Lockey, "O beauteous daughter."...............*Beethoven.*
Trio, Signori Tamberlik, Belletti, e Herr Formes, "Trencar suoi di." *Guillaume Tell*........................*Rossini.*
Aria, Miss Dolby, "Ah rendimi quel cor."..............*Francisco Rossi.*
Duo, (Violoncello e Contrabasso,) Signori Piatti e Bottesini, on airs from *Puritani*............................*Bottesini.*
Scena, Mr. Sims Reeves, "Torn is the veil." *Fridolin*..........*F. Mori.*
Scena, Madame Viardot e Coro, "Chi mai dell' Erebeo." *Orfeo*.....*Gluck.*
Duo, Madame Castellan e Herr Formes, "Nella Notte." *Huguenots*......................................*Meyerbeer.*
Aria, Signor Tamberlik e Coro, "Re del Ciel." *Prophéte*....*Meyerbeer.*
Aria, Mdlle. Bertrandi, "Mi tradi." *Don Juan*...............*Mozart.*
Grand Finale, Signori Tamberlik, Polinini, Herr Formes e Coro. "Gugliemo sol per te." *Guillaume Tell*......*Rossini.*

The symphony over, Miss M. Williams sang, most simply and chastely, a very classical song by Winter; and this was followed by the humorous duet from *Don Pasquale*, by Castellan and Belletti. This was one of the most finished performances of the concert. Madame Clara Novello was encored in the succeeding song by Bellini; she answered with a courtesy, graceful and winning, giving way to Mendelssohn's concerto for the pianoforte which followed, and which was well played by Herr Kuhe, though we think we have heard a firmer, clearer touch. Garcia now sang "Ah! mon fils," from Meyerbeer's "Prophéte;" some parts of which were delivered with a plaintive tenderness that failed not to touch the heart. Garcia always touches the heart; she does not astonish one, or make one laugh, but she pierces the soul, and tears answer. "Com' e gentil" (Don Pasquale) by Mr. Sims Reeves received an enthusiastic encore. Castellan was brilliant in the song from "L'Elisir d'Amore," into which she threw much life and playfulness.

The great attraction of this concert was a part of the unfinished posthumous opera by Mendelssohn, "Lorely," or the "Spirit of the Rhine," which was now performed for the first time. It consists of a grand scene for soprano and chorus. All we know of the story is that the heroine of the opera, having been forsaken by her lover, seeks for aid or redress from the spirits of the Rhine. They bestow upon her irresistible charms, and a voice capable of inspiring deepest love, by which she is determined to be revenged on man. She then weds the river, to which she devotes herself, and promises she will dwell in its waters forever. Most Mendelssohnian is the music, especially the opening chorus in E minor and A minor. No one will doubt its authenticity. But notwithstanding its author's impress is so clearly stamped upon it, there is a vein of originality running through it, an originality, too, that seems not to have been studied or far-fetched, but which flows in a natural and easy manner; showing that all that is natural and melodious in music has not yet been exhausted. Madame Clara Novello sustained her part well, and the chorus and the orchestra exerted themselves to the utmost. The music gave great satisfaction, and was received with loud and continued expressions of delight.

The second part of the concert was opened by the overture to "Der Freyschütz," which was loudly encored, a deserved compliment, for it was done to perfection. Mademoiselle Anna

Zerr sang from " Il Flauto Magico," the very difficult Aria " Gli
angui d'inferno," in which she went up, clear and certain as a
flageolet, to F. An encore followed, and she sang it again,
even better than at first. Mr. Lockey, who is a real tenor, soft
and gentle, sang " O beauteous daughter," followed by the
splendid trio in *William Tell*, by Tamberlik, Belletti, and
Formes. Now came the ever interesting alto voice of Miss
Dolby, in a quaint old air of 1680 ; after which came a duet by
violoncello and double bass, reminding us of Lindley and Drag-
onetti. The performers were Piatti, the best violoncellist we
have ever heard, and Bottesini, who excels every one else on
the double bass. The scene from *Orfeo*, by Gluck, was full of
deep pathos. It was charmingly done by Madame Viardot
Garcia, who was well sustained by the chorus. It was past
eleven o'clock ; the people were fatigued, having listened to
piece after piece of beautiful music, admirably performed, until
they could give attention no longer ; and during the remaining
four pieces, one and another was going out, until there were
but few left. We pitied Mdlle. Bertrandi, pretty little lady,
and felt sorry that she must sing her song so finely to empty
seats ; but it could not be helped. The concert was too long,
quite too long, for it was after midnight before it closed. The
amount received for this concert was upwards of FOUR THOUSAND
AND THREE HUNDRED DOLLARS.

THURSDAY MORNING—THE " MESSIAH."—This was the grand
day—the climax of the Festival. This morning the musical
thermometer was at its highest point ; musical stock was in
great demand and brought a high premium. The tickets had
all been taken up, and now a standing place was sought for, at
a guinea, in vain. There is an astonishing rage for the *Messiah*,
in England ; it is always the great attraction at these Festivals,

Every place was occupied, and such a dazzling array of beauty and fashion one cannot often behold. It may interest some to know, that at the morning concerts the ladies all wore light silk bonnets, small, only covering the head, not the face; the greater number of these were white, but there was also every possible shade of yellow, pink, blue, &c., &c., &c. At the evening concerts, of course, no bonnets were worn, but every one was in full dress. On this day, there was a more rich and brilliant scene presented than at any other performance, since every available corner of the house was occupied.

At a quarter past eleven, the great organ, as if inspired, not so much by the brilliant auditory, as by the lofty subject of the oratorio, poured forth one mighty rush of sounds, filling the imagination with ideas of greatness and wonder. Mr. Stimpson, the organist, did his best, but yet he did nothing more than to give out the minor chord of D and its relatives. The object of this was threefold: it announced the pitch, covered orchestral tunings, and filled the mind with thoughts of the sublime.

Mr. Costa was a few minutes behind his time, but as soon as he took his place, the overture, in its commencing chords, was heard. It was most admirably played. Think of the fugue led off by twenty-six violins, and answered by as many more; think of the roar of thirty-six violoncellos and double basses, and the coming in of the other instruments; imagine every point to be taken up with the most perfect accuracy, and the subject carried on without the slightest wavering or doubtfulness! It was a fugue indeed. We have (we are ashamed to confess it) sometimes thought the overture unworthy of the oratorio, but it was because we knew it not. How often is a fine tune (in psalmody) in like manner, thought to be indifferent, merely because we have not the knowledge or the taste requisite to perceive its excellence. Many persons prefer Coronation to St. Ann's, or anything that is *soft and pretty* to the noble strains of the Old Hundredth or Windsor.

Mr. Sims Reeves sang the opening recitative and air, *Comfort ye my people*, &c. He did it with great care, and applied his most excellent voice to the music in fine taste. We have never before heard it so well sung. It seemed to satisfy even the old Brahamites, some of whom were near us. The word GOD—the last of the recitative—was uttered with wonderful power and propriety. The vocalization in the song was also clear and distinct. At the close of the song, the chorus, *And the glory of the Lord shall be revealed*, came forth with such truth and power as to confirm one's faith and nerve for action. After Jenny Lind had been introduced to Daniel Webster, she is reported to have said, "I have seen a man;" and so, after one has heard a chorus by Handel rightly interpreted, he may say, "I have heard a chorus." Haydn, Mozart, Beethoven, and Mendelssohn have written choruses, but Handel's *are* choruses. And now Miss Dolby rose and delivered the recitative, *Thus saith the Lord of Hosts*, in perfection; she sang the word *come* at the close of the first recitative, with very fine effect, an octave lower than it is written, F:—a dangerous experiment, but her splendid voice justified it. The following song, *But who shall abide*, she also sang in a most satisfactory manner. And thus has Handel been changed, and the alteration is universally approved. The recitative and song now sung by an alto, was originally written for a bass voice. Miss Dolby sang as if she had a proper idea of what she was doing, and several points were of remarkable force: for example, the great energy with which she uttered, *For he is like a refiner's fire*, and the most beautiful diminish on the words, *When he appeareth*, at the close. Her whole appearance, too, while singing, was solemn and dignified. We were sorry this solemnity of deport-

ment was not carried out by all the solo singers, when not engaged in singing. The whispering between them did not look
well; it was neither treating the audience, their own assumed
characters in the oratorio, nor the subject itself with proper
respect.

Solo singers, on such an occasion, should, in every look and
action, do honor to their office, which should be regarded as sacred as is that of him who ministers at the altar of religion.

The following charming chorus in G minor was given as it
deserved : *And he shall purify the sons of Levi, that they may
offer unto the Lord an offering of righteousness.* Miss M. Williams spoke the recitative, *Behold! a virgin shall conceive,* &c.,
as if she was making the declaration in the name of the Lord ;
and then, assuming a gentle smile indicating joy, gladness, and
confidence, both countenance and voice most appropriately
adapted themselves to the air, *O thou that tellest good tidings
to Zion.* All was perfectly natural and easy ; it was as if she
really *meant so,* and was only speaking forth the heart. Her
whole manner (as well as that of the other solo singers) indicated intellectual cultivation, without which, whatever vocal
talent one may possess, and however long one may study, success is impossible. We can hardly attach too much importance to this point : many parents and others seem to think that
a knowledge of music is all that is necessary to success, especially in one who has a fine voice, or who manifests a strong
love for the art. Now, nothing can be more certain, than that
a good musical education can only be acquired in connection
with general cultivation. A person who is not tasteful in dress,
for example, never can make a really good singer. And the
same may be said of manner generally. One whose walk is
awkward, whose movements are clumsy, whose bow or courtesy is ungraceful, whose gesticulation is untoward, or whose

speech is inelegant, can neither sing nor play well; for musical taste cannot be developed in any considerable degree, except in connection with general improvement of mind and manners. We wish we could say more on this point, and also, in connection, speak of the indispensable necessity of *intellectual improvement* in those who would become singers, teachers of music, or teachers of anything else; but this is not the place. Miss Williams made a grand point on the word LORD, to the tone C natural; the chorus which followed, on the same subject, was as good as the previous song.

But now comes Herr Formes;—*For, behold, darkness shall cover the earth, and gross darkness the people*, &c. How deliberate! How subdued! How distinct in utterance! The mouth is opened so that both tones and words flow freely. The very heart "runneth out at the mouth!" Aye, that is the secret of his success. Again, let it be repeated, for some one may read this who may hereafter sing the same thing, *nothing was hurried;* sufficient time was taken to utter every word, and for every sentiment to sink into the heart of the hearer. It was a good direction that Mr. Eliot used to give when he was President of the Boston Academy of Music: "Take sufficient time for the words." "But, sir, it is marked *allegro!*" "No matter what it is marked, be it *allegro* or *presto*, it is a plain matter of common-sense, that in vocal music time must be taken to give appropriate utterance to the words." Common-sense directions are often better than technical directions; or rather, perhaps, a little common-sense is necessary to enable one rightly to apply the technicals. *But the Lord shall arise upon thee;* here the crescendo is applied with great effect; so, also, on the words *His glory.* A grand climax was made on the word "KINGS." The accompaniment—it was so soft—was only the surrounding atmosphere aided by the violins, and breathing out sympathy to the great subject of song. *The people that walked in dark-ness have seen a great light,* followed in a length and breadth both of conception and execution truly grand. *For unto us a child is born,* was sung with an extraordinary degree of excellence *technically* considered. It commenced *pianissimo,* absolutely so; and both voices and instruments were kept down to this softest degree of power, until the violin passages leading to the word " WONDERFUL," and then in an instant came *fortissimo.* The contrast was very great; and this was repeated in the subsequent parts of the chorus. Considered as a mere musical exploit, it was most successful; but it seemed to us to be obtained at a sacrifice of the subject of the song. The sentiment requires no such sudden transition from soft to loud; and the gentle *crescendo* applied so as to lead gradually to the "WONDERFUL" is, we think, in much better taste. The chorus was finely brought out as it proceeded, presenting the sublime subject with amazing power, and calling up the response in the heart, " Even so, ride forth, mighty conqueror, until the enemy is destroyed, and the whole world is brought under the dominion of the Prince of Peace." During the singing of this chorus the people stood. The Pastoral Symphony followed, softly and gently; in close *legato* tones it flowed along, seeming to anticipate *Peace on earth and good will to men.* Madame Clara Novello delivered the succeeding recitatives as well as it is possible for them to be done; so perfectly pure is her voice, that one would suppose it must come from an angel indeed. She produced a thrilling effect on the words, *And they were sore afraid.* Joy was characteristic of the recitative, *And Angels said unto them, Fear not,* &c., and this arose to triumph as she came to the words, *Christ the Lord.* She dwelt very long upon, and thus made very emphatic, the word " CHRIST." Coming within the compass of her best and most powerful tones, the effect was most magnificent. As the chorus, *Glory to God in the highest*, was commenced, the people rose and remained standing as in *For unto us*.

We were sorry to see some of the solo singers leave their places and retire from the Hall at this point. It seemed to say " we are mere players or performers, having no more interest in the subject than to do our part." The incongruity was a little more apparent from the circumstance of the rising of the vast assembly at the utterance of the words, *Glory to God*, &c. For *appearance's sake*, if from no better motive, every singer should remain in his place throughout the performance. The song, *Rejoice greatly*, was sung by Madame Clara Novello ; and Miss M. Williams followed in the recitative, *Then shall the eyes of the blind be opened*. An attempt at expression was made on the words *the dumb shall sing*, which we could not approve. The words " *the dumb*" were sung in a very subdued manner, as if to describe dumbness, and the contrast in passing to the words "*shall sing*" (Forte) was great. Such attempts to paint *words* are, almost always, puerile. Sentiments may be expressed or colored, by musical tones, but not single words. *He shall feed his flock* (key of F) was most charmingly sung by the same artist; and the close was touching in the highest degree. Madame Clara Novello, in *Come unto him* (B flat) was equally good, that is, perfect. She took the liberty to raise her voice from F to B flat on the latter part of the word "*rest*," with a *pause* just before the final cadence, with good effect. Her voice is so perfectly clear on the tone B flat, that one could hardly believe it to be a material organ. The chorus *His yoke is easy*—and then an interval of twenty minutes.

PART II.—Listen to the organ ; again those minor chords, (slowly changing,) speak adoration, penitence, joy, love, gratitude ; they fill the soul with a delight which can only be expressed by musical tones. *Behold the Lamb of God that taketh away the sin of the world*; most vividly is he brought up to the mind, by the legitimate application or reception of Handel's music. Miss Dolby's "He was despised," was not susceptible of improvement; the last words, "*with grief*," were uttered with great tenderness. The chorus, *Surely he hath borne our griefs*, was taken in quicker time than it ought to have been; and the music, apart from the words, seemed too much to express the act of *inflicting stripes*, of *wounding* or *bruising*, or *chastising*; but in the second movement, the idea of *healing*, or of deliverance, was well expressed. *All we like sheep*, was hurried, yet not more so than a flock of sheep when they run away in a fright, if that was the idea intended; but deliverance from this unhappy adaptation came at the passage, *The Lord hath laid on him the iniquity of us all.* Recitative, *All they that see him*, by Mr. Lockey, was followed by one of the finest choruses in the oratorio, musically considered, in C minor. *He trusted in God that He would deliver Him*—it was sung slowly and with great firmness. Mr. Lockey, with his fine voice and perfect understanding of Handel, sang *Thy rebuke hath broken his heart*, and the air, *Behold and see if there be any sorrow like unto his sorrow.* The following recitative and song were by Castellan; she really did them well; though quite out of her appropriate sphere. *Lift up your heads* went admirably; if we except the hissing sibilants, in the words *heads* and *gates*; on which, according to the requirements of the rests, the vocal sound was cut off, but the hissing was continued. This is a common fault on both shores of the Atlantic. Mr. Lockey sang, *Unto which of the angels said He at any time*, and the chorus followed with great spirit, *Let all the Angels of God worship Him. Thou art gone upon high* was omitted; and the chorus, *The Son gave the word*, followed in a slower time than we have often heard it sung; yet not too slow. *How beautiful are the feet, &c.*, by Madame Castellan, and the admirable chorus, *Their sound is gone out*, were well done. The bass air, *Why do the nations*, by Mr. Weiss, was not very effective. Belletti sang it in America; he did the vocalizing passages with the neatness of a bassoon, but the style of the song is not adapted to his powers. I have heard our own Mr. Root sing it in better keeping, perhaps, than any one else. Signor Tamberlik, took the Recitative and song, *Thou shalt break them with a rod of iron.* We heard his performance of it extolled, but, notwithstanding his magnificent voice, we would almost prefer to hear this air played upon a flute. It was *minus* almost all appropriate expression—or at least, so we thought. We need not say that "The Hallelujah Chorus" was held up in a most perfect light, and seen and felt of every man. At its close, the President gave a signal for its repetition, which was immediately answered. The people stood during the performance of this chorus.

An interval of five minutes, and Madame Clara Novello sang *I know that my Redeemer liveth.* She did it well; but it did not come up to our *beau ideal* of this greatest song of the *Messiah.* *Since by death*, was by four voices, and *By man came also the resurrection of the dead*, by full chorus; the next two movements were treated in the same way. Herr Formes delivered the recitative, *Behold I tell you a mystery*, in a most masterly manner. "I never knew what recitative was," said an American gentleman to me, "until I heard Herr Formes;" it is indeed most powerful declamation in his hands. The following song was finely given; but the trumpet was so finely played, with soft and pure tones, and perfect intonation, as to draw one's attention. The whole song was most charmingly accompanied by the younger Harper. The several movements between this and the final chorus were omitted, and the oratorio closed with, " WORTHY IS THE LAMB THAT WAS SLAIN, AND HATH REDEEMED US TO GOD BY HIS BLOOD, TO RECEIVE POWER, AND RICHES, AND WISDOM, AND STRENGTH, AND HONOR, AND GLORY, AND BLESSING. BLESSING AND HONOR, GLORY AND POWER, BE UNTO HIM THAT SITTETH UPON THE THRONE, AND UNTO THE LAMB FOR-EVER AND EVER, AMEN." And what shall we say of the *Amen!* words fail ; it is utterly impossible to give anything like a cor-rect idea of the wonderful manner in which this great chorus was brought out. It was the grand climax ; unfettered by words, Handel soars into the spiritual regions of pure emotion and seems to carry one far beyond the reach of all sublunary existence. We say HANDEL soars, yet we do not believe Han-del himself had any adequate conception of the mighty power there was in this, and in some of his other choruses. He no more dreamt of the wonderful effects those choruses would pro-duce in the course of the progress of music in after ages, than did Dr. Franklin of the results of his experiments with his kite in the thunder and lightning ; and the latter would not be more surprised at the telegraphic communication of these latter days, than would Handel at the effects of his music at the Birming-ham festival. Where the great Apostle once was, not being able to tell whether in the body or out of the body, *there* this wonderful music takes us, and there we are left, until awaken-ing from the reverie, we look around upon gay colors and charming faces, hear the rustling of silken dresses, and the hum of gentle voices, and find that we are still members of the hu-man family, and inhabitants of the planet called Earth.

There is an astonishing rage for the *Messiah* in England ; it is always the great attraction at these festivals. It is beginning to become popular in America. We remember that a few years ago, a large Choral Society in an American city, came to us to ask advice as to what music they should procure. As they had not got the *Messiah*, we recommended it; but our recommendation was met by the objection, " it is too old-fashioned, it is out of date;" and, if we remember rightly, Haydn's *Seasons* was taken; and so they chose a shilling-piece when they might have had a gold sovereign. A few years after, they repented, took the *Messiah*, and hereafter it will be their most valuable oratorio. Whatever may be the reason, the *fact* is certain, that in England the *Messiah* is vastly more popular than any other oratorio. The best judges of music, professors and amateurs, the learned and the unlearned, the noble and the ignoble, the great and the little, those who ride in proud carriages with servants liveried with buff and scarlet, and those who walk through the rain with a cotton umbrella, the old and grave, and the young and gay, those who love music, and those who do not know whether they have any love for it or not;— all do homage to this mighty production of Handel. Handel is the Shakspeare of music; there has never been but one Handel, and it is not at all probable that there will ever be another. Handel has written but one *Messiah*, nor could he, had he lived until this time, have written another. He might have improved upon this, but another of equal merit, he could not have produced. This oratorio has been heard for a century, and it is as fresh and new now as ever; indeed the more it is heard the better it is apprectated. This oratorio, too, has done much for charity; it has succored the orphan, comforted the widow, and relieved the distressed. We think, indeed, that men should be willing, even without the luxury of an oratorio, or the gayety of a ball, to give their goods to feed the poor; and it is truly an expensive charity when one must give *five* pounds to get *one* into the poor box; but even in this case we must not suppose the four pounds to be thrown away; by no means, it encourages art and artists; and the festivals of England do a great work for the improvement and encouragement of musical knowledge and taste. In America, we need a less expensive music for the people, as in Germany; but here, where there is so much wealth, let the rich give of their abundance, bring together such an array of talent as can nowhere else on earth be collected, and let the results tell at once to the improvement of music, and to the relief of the distressed. But for the Birmingham Festival, the *Elijah* of Mendelssohn would not have been written; and Handel's *Messiah* has turned hundreds of thousands from the coffers of the opulent to the succor of the hungry and perishing.

The amount received at the performance of the *Messiah*, this morning, was somewhat more than THIRTEEN THOUSAND AND FIVE HUNDRED DOLLARS.

THURSDAY EVENING—BEETHOVEN'S 9TH.—At half-past seven the house was again filled. The concert was a very attractive one, and especially so because the Grand Choral Symphony constituted the first part. Solo parts by Madame Clara Novello, Miss M. Williams, Mr. Sims Reeves and Mr. Weiss; chorus by the whole choir. We had never heard this greatest work of Beethoven, having unfortunately missed it in several places in Germany. From its great reputation, we were more anxious to hear this than any other piece announced for the festival. The orchestra was in perfect order; all its members were in their places, and were fully awake to the task that was before them. Costa was received with more than an ordinary welcome; a little anxiety upon his brow was apparent. He looked around; every eye was fixed upon the baton;—it moved—and the revelations of Beethoven were being made known to an eager and closely-attentive multitude of listeners.

We are entirely incompetent to give any description of this

composition;—*first*, because we do not know it, and *secondly*, because we have not sufficient musical knowledge to do it. Suffice it to say, that whatever can be suggested to an awakened imagination, by the whole range of sounds which the vibrating atmosphere is capable of producing, or man's perceptive powers are capable of appreciating, is here brought to view, portrayed, delineated, exhibited, expressed. Handel has done nothing like this; great and unapproachable as he is, here is something in the world of sounds that is far in advance of anything that he has left recorded. We believe Handel to have been as great a genius as Beethoven; but it was reserved for Beethoven to go down into the deep, and explore more thoroughly the works of the Infinite, in this department. God is not yet fully known in his works; yet science is gradually revealing him; and in the kingdom of sounds, as well as in that of plants, and minerals, living things, and in surrounding worlds, he is manifesting himself in the researches and investigations of him whom he made in his own image. Beethoven is the great modern revealer of truth, as it exists in the region of sounds. He has extended the boundaries of science; and from the combinations and their successions, he has given to the world new views as to the variety and power of tones; so that modern musical science now rests essentially upon his works. We do not mean to exclude the Bachs, Mozarts, or even Mendelssohns, from the honored catalogue; but we only speak of Beethoven in this connection, and in this point of view, as him who stands pre-eminently great. A gentleman near to us, a learned musician, and a distinguished writer on music, who spoke to us of the first production of the Choral Symphony in England, said: "It was long before it could be understood or appreciated, and even now there are parts of it which are not understood." True, indeed; neither are the sun and the moon and the stars *understood;* but they shed down upon us their light and heat, and give life and bliss. Our own frame, how little it is understood, but yet it answers our purpose. Electricity is not understood, and probably never will be; yet something of it has been revealed by modern investigations, and we are beginning to know some of the laws by which it may be made subservient to him who is Lord of all below. Who understands the ocean, a tempest, or the everlasting hills? yet these things have great moral power over man, and may be made to minister to his happiness. Who comprehends immensity and eternity? But does it follow that, therefore, these may not fill the mind with aspirations after the Infinite, the source of all perfection and happiness? We may not understand, and yet may derive great pleasure and good from the musical forms of truth, which Beethoven or others have discovered. If God can be seen in his works; if ideas of beauty and sublimity can bring up any proper conceptions to the imaginations of the good and the true; then Beethoven has, in part, lifted the veil; but yet we may not fully understand; Beethoven himself might not have understood his own productions, for even human nature *restored*, purified, and raised to its highest degree of intellectual and moral greatness, can only appreciate *in part* the wonderful works of its own creation.

The Choral Symphony is in a key which has wrought wonders in the hands of many masters, viz.: D minor. It is divided into three parts. The first part comprises three movements, viz. :

I.—*Allegro ma non troppo, un poco maestoso.*

II —*Sherzo molto vivace.*

III.—*Adagio molto e cantabile.*

The third movement leads to the second or choral part of the Symphony, as follows :

    I.—Tenor Recitative—" Companions ! be wise."
    II.—Solo and chorus, bass—" Welcome, ye who pine in sadness."
    III.—Quartet—" Sweet content, our hope inviting."
    IV.—Quartet and chorus—" Oh ! may he whose soul is despairing."
    V.—Tenor solo, and chorus—" Oh ! thou bright fire !"
    VI.—Quartet and chorus—" Oh ! ye sons of earth !"

As we have already intimated, we dare not attempt any description of this music. We repeat, we have heard it but once ; but if we may judge of it by the feelings it produced in us, then it is certainly to be classed with the most powerful of all musical compositions. We do not know but, in years past we may have been as much moved and delighted with music, and if so, it was at the performance of Handel's *Messiah*, in the same hall in 1837. But this can hardly be regarded as a proper comparison, since the *Messiah* is not merely musical, or does not rest so much on musical power, but brings to its aid the wonders of man's redemption, as drawn from the divine word ; it tells of the birth, sufferings and death of the Saviour, as *the Lamb of God who taketh away the sins of the world ;* of the progress and universal triumph of His kingdom, and of the hallelujahs of the redeemed. But if we were as much moved on that occasion, and in part certainly by music, we did not suppose it possible ever again to feel its influence in so high a degree. We were almost foolish enough to suppose that so far as it related to our own experience, the powers of the art had been exhausted. Beethoven's 9th reproved us for this folly and unbelief, and carried us away, we know not whither. And not we alone, for the feelings of the whole audience were aroused, and such an enthusiam was manifested as we had hardly seen be-

fore. But we have said enough of this great work, for our
present purpose. We shall hear it ere long in New York or
Boston; but stay ye, who lead in these things, and do not attempt it until orchestra, solo, and chorus are fully prepared for
the mighty task of its performance.

The second part of the concert was opened by the overture
to *Zampa*, by Herold. What a contrast! Milton and Mother
Goose's melodies are not more unlike ! But yet we do not wish
to disparage the *Zampa*. It is a nice, comfortable, enlivening,
cheering, animating overture indeed; and the people needed,
by way of change, *something* which contained *nothing :* and so
they gave them *Zampa*. It was received in good faith, as it
was given, and called forth shouts of applause. Here is the
programme :

PART I.

GRAND CHORAL SYMPHONY in D minor, solo parts by Mad.
            Clara Novello, Miss M. Williams, Mr. Sims
            Reeves, and Mr. Weiss........................*Beethoven.*

PART II.

OVERTURE. *Zampa*......................................*Herold.*
ARIA, Mad. Castellan, "Ah! un amore." *Faust*................*Spohr.*
DUO, Mad. Viardot Garcia and Signor Belletti, "Al capricci."
            L'Italiani in Algeri..............................*Rossini.*
ARIA, Herr Formes, "In diesen heiligen Hallen. *Il Flauto
            Magico*...*Mozart.*
LIED, Mad. Anna Zerr,, "A Sträussli will i.".............*Carl Haas.*
DUO, Mad. Clara Novello and Mr. Sims Reeves; "Da quel di."
            Linda.......................................*Donizetti.*
SCENA, Signor Tamberlik, e Coro, "O muto asil. *Guillaume
            Tell*...*Rossini*
BALLAD, Miss M. Williams, "The Slave Girl's love.".............*Laud.*
DUO, Mad. Castellan e Miss Dolby, "Serbami ognor." *Semi-
            ramide*...*Rossini.*
SONG, Mr. Lockey, "O, give me back." *Pascal Bruno*..........*Hatton.*

We were so completely exhausted by the Symphony, that
we did not make many notes of the after performance. Mad.
Viardot Garcia sang twice, and, of course, with deep emotion,
for she never sings without this. Herr Formes gave a perfect
rendering of the popular song in Zauberflöte, *In dissen heiligen
Hallen*, &c. Mademoiselle Anna Zerr sang a song that reminded us of Jenny Lind's Bird Song, though far inferior in point
of execution. Madame Clara Novello and Mr. Sims Reeves
sang most delightfully a duet by Donizetti. Signor Tamberlik
sent a thrill through the hall by the full, clear and triumphant
manner in which, in chest voice, he went up to C, in the scene
from *William Tell.* Miss M. Williams and Miss Dolby sang
charmingly. The old Madrigal, said to be the best composition
of the kind in the world, *Down in a flowery vale*, was cleverly
done, without accompaniment. Signor Bottesini's contra basso
was truly wonderful.

It was twelve o'clock before the concert was concluded; and
every one was worn out, save, perhaps, Costa, who seemed as
fresh and vigorous as a son of the morning.

The amount received for this concert was somewhat more
than FIVE THOUSAND DOLLARS.

FRIDAY MORNING.—" SAMSON."—The following, from one of the books of the Sacred Harmonic Society, sets forth the argument of the drama :

PART I.

Samson, blind and captive to the Philistines, being relieved from his toil by a festival in honor of Dagon their god, comes forth into the open air. The priests of Dagon sing in praise of their idol. Samson, bemoaning his condition, is visited by his friends and his father, Manoah, who join in bewailing his degradation. Samson, acknowledging the justice of his punishment, predicts that Dagon will not be allowed to triumph over the God of Israel. Micah and his friends express a hope that Samson's prediction may be verified. Samson, however, declares his hopes to be gone, his nature declining, and his life drawing to a close. Upon which his friends recount to him the joy and peace that his spirit will realize in the eternal world.

PART II.

Micah and the Israelites call upon God to have pity on Samson. Dalila, his wife, then appears, and, pretending penitence and submission, entreats him to go home with her. He refuses to listen to her entreaties ; a scene of mutual recrimination ensues ; and they separate. His friends assert the ordained subjection of the wife to the husband. Harapha, a giant of Gath, then approaches, attracted by the fame of Samson's might, and boasts how he would have overcome him had he encountered him before his captivity. Samson dares him to a trial now, which he refuses, and is taunted by Samson with cowardice. Micah proposes as a test of who is the Supreme God, that Harapha should call upon Dagon, to try his power over Samson. The Israelites prostrate themselves before Jehovah, and supplicate his delivering aid. Harapha calls upon Dagon, and the worshippers of that idol appeal to him for succor and protection ; after which the Israelites and Philistines jointly, but in opposition to each other, celebrate the majesty, power, and supremacy of their respective deities.

PART III.

Harapha is sent, by the Philistine lords, to bid Samson attend their festival, to exhibit his strength before them, which at first he refuses to do. His friends, perplexed for his safety, call upon God for help. Samson, persuaded inwardly that this was from God, yields to go along with Harapha, who comes again with great threatenings to fetch him. Samson departs, invoking the aid of that Spirit with which he had formerly been inspired. His friends cheer him on, and declare him to be fulfilling the call, and under the guidance of Heaven. Manoah returns to tell his friends his hopes of obtaining Samson's release. The priests of Dagon are heard to celebrate the praises of their idol for subduing their foe. Micah and Manoah hear the shouts of joy, and the latter again manifests his paternal solicitude for Samson. An appalling, loud, and confused noise is heard, succeeded by wailings and cries for help. An Israelitish messenger arrives in breathless haste, and relates to the relations and friends of Samson the fearful news of his having pulled down the Philistine temple, and buried his enemies and himself in its ruins. Micah and the Israelites lament his fall. A Dead March is heard, and his body approaches on its way to the tomb; and Manoah and Micah and the Israelites perform the funeral rites.

It is said, that of all Handel's oratorios, this was his favorite. It was written when he was more at leisure than he was when many of his other works were produced, and after he had established his fame as the greatest living composer. It has received additional accompaniments, written after the example of Mozart, by Mr. Costa.

We will not dwell upon the performance of the different pieces, for we have already written perhaps more upon the Festival than will be read. The fine overture was admirably played, and we cannot but think that an overture of this pleasing, melodious character, easily appreciated and always pleasing, would sometimes be attractive at our orchestral concerts in America. The chorus, *Awake the trumpet's lofty sound*, was very brilliant. The sublime chorus, *O first created beam, and thou great word, Let there be light! and light was over all*—was also given most magnificently. We could not help comparing this chorus with the same subject as treated in the *Creation*, by

Haydn; and the superiority seems to be most decidedly on the side of Handel. Haydn merely excites surprise and astonishment; whereas Handel inspires with the deepest reverence and awe. *God said, Let there be light, and there was light!* Haydn treats it as if he wished to amuse his hearers; Handel seems to feel, and to express, the sublime thought. One is like a *child*, the other like a *man*,—one is *weak*, the other is *strong*,—one is *small*, the other is *great*.

Miss Dolby's " *Return, O God af Hosts*" was perfectly satisfactory. The chorus, *Fixed in his everlasting seat*, was taken slowly, and carried through in steady time, and with tremendous power. Madame Viardot Garcia was encored in the Air, *Ye sons of Israel now lament*, and repeated it. The chorus, *Weep, Israel, weep a louder strain*, was one of the most effective points in the whole oratorio.

When Handel first wrote Samson, he concluded it with the chorus—

> " Glorious hero, may thy grave
> Peace and honor ever have ;
> After all thy pains and woes,
> Rest eternal, sweet repose."

We think this is a much better close than that which is now attached to the oratorio, and which Handel wrote afterwards. The change is too abrupt; and we should much prefer to leave the quiet and gentle emotions produced by the funeral scene, (full of calm resignation and cheering hope,) unbroken, than to disturb them, even by the best trumpet song which was ever written.

> " Bring the laurels, bring the bays,
> Strew the hearse, and strew the ways,
> Glorious hero, may thy grave
> Peace and honor ever have ;
> After all thy griefs and woes,
> Rest eternal, sweet repose."

Here, then, we would stop, leaving the grave strewed with flowers, and the eye of faith fixed on that better land, where "the wicked cease to trouble, and the weary are at rest." But it was not so. "Let the bright seraphim," was finely sung. We are sorry to add, that it was greatly injured by a long cadenza, foreign and unmeaning. The final chorus, *Let their celestial concerts all unite*, was sung in a very spirited manner ; and this was the conclusion of the whole matter.

The cast of *Samson* was a most powerful one ; and we subjoin the programme, for the gratification of the members of Sacred Music Societies, and others interested in oratorial performances.

PART I.

RECITATIVE, Mr. Sims Reeves, "This day a solemn feast."

AIR, Madame Clara Novello, "Ye men of Gaza."

RECITATIVE, Mr. Sims Reeves, "Why by an angel."

RECITATIVE, Miss Dolby and Mr. Sims Reeves, "Matchless in might."

AIR, Mr. Sims Reeves, "Total eclipse."

RECITATIVE, Mr. Weiss and Miss Dolby, "Brethren and men of Dan."

AIR, Mr. Weiss, "Thy glorious deeds."

RECITATIVE and AIR, Mr. Sims Reeves, "Why does the God of Israel sleep."

RECITATIVE, Mr. Weiss and Mr. Sims Reeves, "For thee, my dearest son."

PART II.

RECITATIVE, Mr. Sims Reeves and Miss Dolby, "My evils hopeless are."

AIR, Miss Dolby, "Return, O God of Hosts."

RECITATIVE, Miss Dolby, Mr. Sims Reeves, and Mad. Clara Novello, "But who is this."

RECITATIVE, AIR, and CHORUS, Madame Clara Novello, and Chorus of Female Voices, "My faith and truth."

RECITATIVE, Mr. Sims Reeves, "Ne'er think of that."

DUET, Madame Clara Novello and Mr. Sims Reeves, "Traitor to love."

RECITATIVE, Miss Dolby and Mr. Sims Reeves, "She's gone—a serpent manifest."

RECITATIVE, Miss Dolby, Herr Formes, and Mr. Sims Reeves, " No words of peace."

AIR, Herr Formes, " Honor and arms."

RECITATIVE and DUET, Mr. Sims Reeves and Herr Formes, " Go, baffled coward, go."

RECITATIVE, Miss Dolby, " Here lies the proof."

RECITATIVE, Herr Formes, " Dagon, arise."

PART III.

RECITATIVE, Miss H. Williams, Mr. Sims Reeves, and Herr Formes, " More trouble is behind."

AIR, Herr Formes, " Presuming slave."

RECITATIVE, Miss M. Williams and Mr. Sims Reeves, " Consider, Samson."

RECITATIVE, Mr. Sims Reeves, Miss M. Williams, and Herr Formes, " Be of good courage."

AIR, Mr. Sims Reeves, " Thus when the sun."

RECITATIVE and AIR, Miss M. Williams, " The Holy One of Israel."

RECITATIVE, Miss M. Williams and Mr. Weiss, " Old Manoah."

RECITATIVE, Mr. Weiss and Miss M. Williams, " What noise of joy was that."

AIR, Mr. Weiss, " How willing my paternal love."

RECITATIVE, Madame Viardot Garcia and Mr. Weiss, " Your hopes of his delivery."

RECITATIVE, Mr. Weiss, " Heaven, what noise."

RECITATIVE, Mad. Viardot Garcia, Mr. Weiss, and Mr. Williams, " Where shall I run."

AIR, Madame Viardot Garcia, " Ye sons of Israel."

CHORUS, the Solos by Mr. Weiss and Madame Clara Novello, " Glorious hero."

RECITATIVE, Mr. Weiss, " Come, no time for lamentation."

AIR, Madame Clara Novello, " Let the bright seraphim."

TRUMPET OBLIGATO, Mr. Harper, jr.

The amount received on this last day was upwards of EIGHT THOUSAND FIVE HUNDRED DOLLARS.

We have given the amounts received in round numbers; we

suppose some hundreds of dollars, perhaps a thousand, might safely be added.

RECAPITULATION.

Tuesday morning	$11.500
Tuesday evening	2.100
Wednesday morning	8.200
Wednesday evening	4.300
Thursday morning	13.500
Thursday evening	5.000
Friday morning	8.500
Total	$53.100

We were not able to learn what were the expenses, and therefore know not how much went to the charity.

There were several things which we intended to say, when listening to the music, but which we find we have inadvertently omitted. It was a glorious performance, from beginning to end; the world has never seen a better; and in no place on earth can such a band and chorus be brought together, except in Birmingham. It is understood that arrangements are already in progress for the next Festival, in September, 1855.

LETTER XLIV.

Funeral Musical Performances—Messiah—Elijah—Smaller Musical Associations—The Oratorio Societies in London—Exeter Hall—Organ Performance.

LONDON, 1852.

On the week of the great funeral,* the "Sacred Harmonic Society" gave two public performances, appropriate, on the successive evenings of Wednesday and Thursday. The selection was the same on both evenings, as follows:

* Of the Duke of Wellington.

Dead March in Saul......................................*Handel.*
QUARTET—His Body is buried in peace........ ....*Handel.*
CHORUS—But his name liveth evermore...................,......*Handel.*
AIR—Oh, rest in the Lord (Elijah).....................*Mendelssohn.*
CHORALE—To thee, O Lord! (St. Paul)................... *Mendelssohn.*
AIR—Then shall the righteous (Elijah)................. ....*Mendelssohn.*
CHORUS—Happy and Blessed (St. Paul)................*Mendelssohn.*
QUARTET and CHORUS—Blest are the Departed.................*Spohr.*

Part Two embraced the recitatives and choruses composed
for the unfinished oratorio, Christus, by Mendelssohn. And
Part Three consisted of the entire third part of Handel's Messiah.

These performances were intended as a "tribute to the memory of the late Duke of Wellington," and the performers appeared in appropriate mourning.

Handel's Messiah was performed three or four times by
different societies at about Christmas time, and it is shortly to
be repeated. Nothing is so popular as this. The societies are
obliged to perform this oratorio, to enable them to perform
others, and to bring out new music. It is said to be the only
paying oratorio, and never fails to draw a full house. All the
singers know it by heart, so that a rehearsal for it is not needed.
Elijah, too, is so well known as not to need rehearsal. It is
often done. We heard it recently by the "London Sacred
Harmonic Society;" but the orchestra of this society was on
this occasion much inferior to that of either the other societies,
and then the whole performance contrasted much to its disadvantage with the grand representation of this oratorio at Birmingham.

In addition to the three great societies, there are frequent
performances of oratorios by smaller associations in some part
of London. We often see them advertised, but have not been
able to attend them.

There are now three large societies here for the performance of oratorios and the other smaller works of the great Masters. They are, "The Sacred Harmonic Society," under the direction of Mr. Costa; "The London Sacred Harmonic Society," under the direction of Mr. Surman; and "The Harmonic Union," under the direction of Mr. Benedict. The "Sacred Harmonic Society" is the original or oldest, and dates back to 1832. Mr. Surman, the present conductor of the "London Sacred Harmonic," was a leading man in its establishment, and was for many years its conductor. Some three or four years since, on the choice of Mr. Costa as conductor, Mr. Surman withdrew, and, in connection with others, formed a new society, which they called the "London Sacred Harmonic Society." Each of these societies commands a large chorus of from six to eight hundred performers; they each employ the best professional singers for the solo parts, and also a professional orchestra. They each have a weekly meeting for rehearsal of such music as they are about to perform in public. These rehearsals are sometimes under the direction of the conductor, and at others under that of a chorus-master. The "Sacred Harmonic Society" usually depend upon an organ accompaniment at their private meetings; the "London Sacred Harmonic Society" have an amateur orchestra, which plays badly enough on these occasions; and the "Harmonic Union" employs the grand piano-forte, sometimes under the hands of Mr. Benedict, while at others he directs to the playing of an assistant. I hardly need say that the piano-forte accompaniment is vastly the best for all the drilling or training purposes of such meetings. The orchestras employed by the "Sacred Harmonic Society" and by the "Harmonic Union" are much the most powerful and efficient, usually numbering say sixteen double basses, and other instruments in proportion. These societies all give their public performances in Exeter

Hall, and hold their rehearsals in an adjoining room, capable of accommodating some six or seven hundred persons. This room contains a small organ of ten or twelve stops. The large hall has lately been much altered, enlarged, ornamented, and improved, so that it is one of the best concert-rooms any where to be found. It seats comfortably three thousand persons, and by the aid of extra chairs and standing-places will accommodate a thousand more; so that it often contains a company of three thousand or three thousand five hundred hearers. The organ has also undergone very thorough repairs, and has been considerably enlarged. It was built by Walker, one of the best London organ builders, and in its improved state contains a little less than three thousand pipes. Its compass is from F to G, or sixty-three pipes. The pneumatic principle has been applied to this instrument; so the touch is easy, and the three rows of keys, when coupled, may be played with but very little extra power of the finger. The pedal organ has nine stops; there are also eight changing or coupling stops. Though not so large as some, it is very complete, has sufficient power for the hall, and is well adapted to the wants of the different societies. At the reöpening of the hall this season, an organ performance was given, under the direction of the "Sacred Harmonic Society," by its organist, Mr. J. L. Brownsmith. This performance commenced at eleven o'clock, A. M., and consisted of the following selections:

Lift up your heads..*Handel.*
Pastoral Symphony..*Handel.*
Et incarnatus est..*Mozart.*
Coronation Anthem.......................................*Atwood.*
German Hymn...————.
Dead March in Saul......................................*Handel.*
Movement from a Symphony..............................*Mozart.*

The Old Hundredth Psalm Tune..............................————.
Minuet (Samson)...*Handel.*
Fugue...*Leo*
Angels ever bright and fair...............................*Handel.*
Hallelujah..*Handel.*
God save the Queen..————

Perhaps nothing could more distinctly mark the difference of taste for organ music and style of organ playing between the Germans and the English than this performance, when compared with the similar organ performances one hears in the German cities. Here there was not a single organ piece, but the bill was mostly made up with extracts from the vocal compositions of Handel. However beautiful these may be, they are not adapted to organ playing, or certainly not to the exhibition of the powers of the instrument or the capacity of the player. Mr. Brownsmith is really an excellent organist, and we could not but regret that he should not have done himself the justice to play some of the great German organ music. But the public taste must be consulted, and unhappily there is too often amongst the musical profession a willingness to sacrifice their own taste, and the opportunity of ministering to the improvement of that of the public, by the performance of such music as will please rather than improve. We could see, too, by observing the countenances and movements of the company, that the lightest music pleased the most. For example, no one piece pleased more than the minuet from Samson. It was very tastefully and beautifully performed, and with the organist every one must have been delighted; so also the music is good in its place—nothing better. But, alas! that the poor organ should have to come down from its lofty eminence and be made a mere imitator of an orchestra. The minuet commanded universal attention, and the people were pleased. A fugue by Leo followed; and this afforded them a fine opportunity to express the gratification they had just received, as the old fuguist had no

tum, tum — | diddle, diddle dum | tum, tum — | diddle, diddle dum,

with which to produce the graceful waving of the head, and occasionally the foot-movement upon the floor. We are a little more Germanized in America; and I can hardly think it possible that a similar organ exhibition could be made in Boston or New York in which old Bach would not be heard. There is a greatness about the organ-playing of the Germans that is not known here. In the church service the difference is very great. In Germany we hear the lofty, grand, soul-inspiring strains of the full organ and of fugue; whereas in England the ornamental, gilded, spangled, fringe-trimming style too often prevails.

LETTER XLV.

St. George's Bloomsbury—St. Paul's Cathedral—Dr. Watts's Chapel—Pickle Shop— John Newton.

LONDON, 20th September, 1852.

REV. MR. VILLIERS, the clergyman of this parish, is not only a very popular, but a very excellent and evangelical preacher; he has a large congregation, and the service throughout, on Sabbath last, was highly interesting. Of course the common Episcopal liturgy is used. The psalms are read, but at the end of each psalm, as is very common here, the Gloria Patri is chanted. The Canticles are chanted; though this day the " Jubilate Deo " was sung in anthem form by the whole congregation. The music was very plain, and rather quick; that is, about as quick as it is convenient to speak the words and observe a distinct and solemn utterance. This Congregational anthem singing is not common, though it is quite practicable. The Canticles were chanted by the whole people, and quite well done. Cadences no slower than the utterance of the words on the chanting note. Both the chanting and the anthem singing this morning afforded sufficient proof of the practicability of these forms of music in congregations; but it must be understood that the anthem was, as we have already said, *very plain*. We know of but very few sufficiently plain, contained in our American singing books. Two metrical psalms were sung, both well done—everybody taking a part. The organ was not very well played; the organist seeming rather to adapt himself to choir than to Congregational singing, and making too much variation of stops and of piano and forte in different stanzas. The introductory voluntary was not more than three minutes in length, and there were no interludes between the stanzas of the hymns.

At three o'clock we attended service at St. Paul's. Mr. Goss very kindly gave us a seat in the organ loft—the most favorable place for observing the whole service.

In the evening we started to go to the chapel in which Dr. Watts used to preach, Bury Chapel, St. Mary, Axe. We looked and looked again, but could find no chapel; after walking down and up the street for several times, we found a man who could give us information, but alas! it was sad indeed to hear that the house so long occupied by him whose *praise* is in all the churches, and in whose words all the churches sing *praise*, is no longer used for public worship, but has been turned into a *pickle shop*. We do not know what has become of the congregation. We then went to St. Mary, Woolworth, Lombard-street, and attended service in the church where John Newton used to preach. Here we heard an excellent and faithful sermon. The spirit of Newton, or rather the spirit of the Gospel, is yet manifested within these walls. The singing was led by about a dozen charity children; the girls being dressed as the old ladies of New England used to dress half a century ago, each having a square handkerchief folded about the neck, a high white muslin cap, and a white apron. The chants were plain, and tolerably well done, and so were the tunes,—all the people singing. The organist played very long interludes; in several cases the interludes were *one quarter longer than the tune itself.* They were tedious, and in bad taste; otherwise the organ was well played. The exercises closed with the hymn, "May the grace of Christ our Saviour," sung to the tune *Sicily,*—quite home-like.

LETTER XLVI.

The Norwich Musical Festival.

London, September 30, 1852.

This, like the Birmingham Festival, is triennial. It was omitted last year on account of the absence of Mr. Benedict, its conductor, in America. Previous to the conductorship of Mr. Benedict, was that of the Gresham professor, Mr. Ed. Taylor, the friend of Spohr, who was instrumental of the introduction of the great German composer's oratorios into England. Indeed, Professor Taylor translated and adapted the English words to several oratorios and other vocal compositions of the Capellmeister of Cassel. The success of Spohr's oratorios was represented as having been entirely satisfactory, and we wonder why the directors of the Norwich Festival who had the honor of first bringing out these great works, should not, at least, cause one of them to be performed on every Festival occasion. There certainly must be other reasons than those of musical merit, since at the Festival, the present year, two original oratorios (so called) have been performed, which, to say the least, are vastly inferior to either of those of Spohr. The love of novelty is undoubtedly one of these reasons; the announcement of something new, or to be performed for the first time, always influences many, even though the newness should consist in *but the name of the thing*, as in the present instance. The great mass of people really know but little of true musical merit, even with respect to performance, and still less do they know of musical composition. Hence, let any ignoramus announce a new oratorio, and many will run after him and pay their money to listen to something which they suppose to be very wonderful. It is really astonishing to see the amazing presumption and self-complacency of some persons assuming to be oratorio composers. The fact is, there have, as yet, lived in the world but some two or three persons who have attempted to compose oratorios whose works have stood the test of time. That others will be raised up, we have no doubt; but modesty becomes a youthful aspirant to the distinction of composer of an oratorio.

The two new oratorios announced for this Festival were *Israel Restored*, by Dr. Wm. R. Bexfield, and *Jerusalem*, by Mr. Henry H. Pierson, and report had spoken so favorably of both of these that we felt a desire to go and hear. An engagement in London, however, prevented our attendance on Wednesday morning, when "Israel Restored" was performed. If we may judge by the reports of the musical men we have met, it is much the better of the two : possessing indeed some good points and effective pieces, both solos and choruses, yet undeserving, on the whole, of its dignified name, and sinking quite into insignificance by the side of Handel, or the popular writer already named, whose compositions were produced under the direction of the Gresham Professor.

We arrived at Norwich on Wednesday (four and a-half hours from London) in early season for the second evening concert. The performances were given in the St. Andrew's Hall, a large and convenient room, though greatly inferior in size and general arrangement to the Town Hall, Birmingham. The size of the room is one hundred and twenty-four feet by seventy-five. The roof is supported by twelve Gothic pillars, six on each side, which are injurious alike to hearing and seeing. The orchestra is fitted up at the West end of the Hall, and opposite to it, or at the East end, is the patron's gallery, occupied by the Lords and Ladies, or by such persons as choose to pay double price for their tickets. In front of the patron's gallery, stalls or reserved seats were fitted up at fifteen shillings each; to the space between these and the orchestra, the tickets were ten shillings and sixpence; but as these latter were unreserved places, it was necessary to be in previous attendance for half an hour or more at the outer door, and then to wait an hour inside after having fought one's way to a seat. The Hall is ornamented with pictures, and contains a very good organ.

The chorus was constituted as follows:

Female Sopranos	41
Boys　　do.	34
	—75
Female Alto	5
Men　　do.	47
	—52
Tenors	60
Basses	67
Total	254

THE ORCHESTRA CONSISTED OF

22 First Violins,	4 Bassoons,
20 Second Violins,	6 Horns,
18 Altos	4 Trumpets,
11 Violoncellos,	6 Trombones
11 Double Basses,	2 Ophicleides,
4 Flutes.	Double Drum,
4 Oboes,	Bass Drum,
4 Clarionets,	Side Drum.

—in all, 119 instruments beside the organ.

THE SOLO SINGERS WERE

Mad. VIARDOT GARCIA,	Mr. SIMS REEVES,
Miss LOUISA PYNE,	Mr. LOCKEY,
Madame FIORENTINI.	Signor BELLETTI,
Miss ALLEYNE,	Herr FORMES,
Miss DOLBY,	Mr. WEISS.
Signor GARDONI,	

THE INSTRUMENTAL SOLO PERFORMERS

Mons. SAINTON and Mr. BLAGROVE...............Violins.
Herr HAUSMANN..........................Violoncello.
Signor BOTTESINI.......................Double Bass.
Mr. HARECOURT............................Organist.
Mr. J. F. HILL........................Chorus Master.
Mr. BENEDICT.............................Conductor.

The number of performers was a little less than at Birmingham, but in effect about the same, with the exception of the soprano and the alto of the vocal chorus. These were much inferior. The soprano at Birmingham consisted almost entirely of the full-grown voices of females, whereas at Norwich, many of the female voices were quite young; and then there were boys enough to spoil almost any soprano. The consequence was that the soprano was sometimes harsh. The whole effect of the performance was also greatly marred by the boyish and girlish conduct witnessed in standing up and sitting down, in fanning one another with books, in laughing, talking, sending round papers, and general frivolity, unbecoming at any time and especially on such an occasion. But it was not strange to us; we have witnessed something like it before, both in Singing Societies and in Church choirs; showing that in some of the incidentals of choir life, the English do not differ materially from the Americans, and that lectures on correctness of deportment in choirs are equally necessary in both countries.

Again, the alto was composed mostly of men's voices. The effect was a harshness or roughness that has no mercy upon one's nervous system or musical sensibilities, and that, in the present instance, made one often curl or shrink away as if a severe blow had been inflicted; besides, in pressing up to the high tones, the men did not all quite reach the point; making altogether too much of that which the organ-tuners call "wolf" —a name applicable as well to *quality of tone* (howling) in this case as to *intonation*. With these exceptions (and they are important ones) the vocal chorus was highly effective. Mr. Benedict is a fine conductor, as is well known on both sides of the Atlantic, and he seemed to do his utmost (and with great success) to secure the proper results. We had the pleasure of meeting him; he seemed to be delighted to be reminded of his American tour, and spoke of kind treatment received, and endearing friendships formed. Both Benedict and Belletti looked like home, and brought up to the imagination Castle Garden, Tripler Hall, and Tremont Temple; but in vain we looked around for JENNY—she was not there; nor was there any one who could supply her place. We had, in another department, the VIARDOT; but she belongs to a different school.

The following was the programme for Tuesday evening:

PART I.

SELECTIONS FROM THE WORKS OF CLASSICAL COMPOSERS.

OVERTURE. *Oberon*..............................*C. M. Von Weber.*

NATIONAL ANTHEM, "God save the Queen." By the principal
singers and chorus.

QUINTETTO, "Sento o Dio." Miss Louisa Pyne, Miss Alleyne,
Signor Belletti, Mr. Lockey, and Mr. Weiss. *Cosi fan tutte*..*Mozart.*

ARIA, "Ah rendimi quel cor." Miss Dolby.......*Francesco Rossi* (1686).

SONG, "Fairer the meads are growing." Mr. Lockey.......*Mendelssohn.*

ARIA, "Ha, wie will ich triumphiren." Herr Formes, *Die Ent-
führung aus dem Serail*.............................*Mozart.*

DUETTO, "Bella ninfa." Miss Louisa Pyne and Sig. Gardoni.
Jessonda..*Spohr.*

SCENA with CHORUS, "Chi mai dell Erebo." Madame Viardot
Garcia. *Orfeo*.......................................*Gluck.*

ARIA, Mr. Sims Reeves. "Adelaide." Pianoforte, Mr. Benedict..*Beethoven.*

SERENADE, "Deh vieni alla finestra." Sig. Belletti. *Don Giovanni*..*Mozart.*

AIR AND VARIATIONS, Double Bass. Sig. Bottesini...........*Bottesini.*

QUARTET (unaccompanied), "Dors en paix." Sig. Gardoni, Mr.
Lockey, Sig. Belletti, and Mr. Weiss...........*C. M. Von Weber.*

SPANISH SONGS, accompanied by herself on the Pianoforte. Madame Viardot Garcia.

QUARTET AND CHORUS, "Alziam gli evviva." Miss Louisa Pyne,
Miss Dolby, Mr. Sims Reeves, and Herr Formes. "Euryanthe."..*Weber.*

PART II.

SHAKSPEARE'S PLAY of "A Midsummer Night's Dream," with the
incidental music, composed by......*Felix Mendelssohn Bartholdy,*
Read by Mrs. FANNY KEMBLE.

| OVERTURE. | SCHERZO. | FAIRY MARCH. |

DUETT WITH CHORUS, "Ye spotted snakes." Miss Louisa Pyne
and Miss Alleyne.

| INTERLUDE. | NOTTURNO. | WEDDING MARCH. |

FINALE AND CHORUS, "Thro' this house."

Report speaks highly of the musical performances, and especially of the singing of Madame Viardot. One of the papers spoke of her in the following terms: "In Madame Viardot we have art perfected by the highest intelligence and the deepest sensibility, affording an example not of the power which takes an audience by storm, and at once lifts itself to the very pinnacle of fame, but of that intrinsic excellence which, gradually increasing its power over the public, at length reaches the summit, and when there renders itself hourly more stable by its own strength. This is the position and the claim of Madame Viardot Garcia." The reading of the play, even by Mrs. Fanny Kemble, was regarded as out of place; and not even the artistic excellence of the reader, and the attractiveness of Mendelssohn's music, could hold the audience, who were evidently fatigued and impatient for rest. "The general feeling was that it ought to have been the first act, and that the musical selections should have been shortened."

We have already alluded to the Wednesday Morning's performance, the Oratorio of "Israel Restored" by Dr. Bexfield. We extract from the programme the following argument:—

"The overture (a sort of index to the work) having been performed, the first part contains the prophecies concerning the Israelitish nation, which are followed by God's awful threats and punishments for their disobedience and unbelief. At their scattered and desolate condition, 'all her people sigh!' They pray that God will 'make their way plain,' and that their prayers may 'enter his presence.' The prophecies are then gradually developed. Israel is to 'return and be at rest,' and 'God will wipe away all tears from their eyes.' The Israelites become a happier race; they gather themselves together and sing, 'Blessed is he that cometh in the name of the Lord,' acknowledging Him as their 'Father and Redeemer.' The great end is then accomplished;—Israel being restored in 'peace and glory' to their 'own land,' 'break forth into joy,' and exclaim "Marvellous are thy works, Lord God, Hallelujah! Amen.'"

At the close of the oratorio the following pieces from *Samson* were performed by order of the Committee of Arrangements, as a tribute of respect to the memory of the Duke of Wellington :—

SOLO—Madame Viardot Garcia.

> " Ye sons of Israel, now lament,
> Your spear is broke, your bow unbent,
>> Your glory's fled—
>> Among the dead
>> Our hero lies,
>> Forever closed his eyes."

>> DEAD MARCH.—Chorus.

> " Glorious hero, may thy grave
> Peace and honor ever have:
> After all thy pains and woes,
> Rest eternal, sweet repose."

" The simple solemnity, beauty, and pathos of the lament, by Madame Viardot," says an able critic, " surpassed all we can recall to mind. It was indeed the singing of the great artist— a great mind. To describe it would be impossible—but there was a holy inspiration in the union of sound and sense—a simple grandeur in the style which silently stole its way into every breast, for which tears came to their relief." Madame Viardot sang this same air of deepest pathos in the regular course of the oratorio of *Samson* at Birmingham. It was then given with very great power, and we can easily imagine that, affected, as she must have been on the present occasion, by the recollection of the recent death of the illustrious Duke, and by the circumstances under which she sang, she must have thrown into it a degree of feeling seldom witnessed. Suppose now, that on this occasion, the Trumpet Song, and the chorus, " Let their celestial concerts all unite," had been added! Every child in the room would have been struck with the bad adaptation, and the extreme inappropriateness of the music. Carry ourselves back as near to Samson as we are now to Wellington, and we think we have an illustration of the remarks made in our communication on the Birmingham Festival, in relation to the close of the Oratorio of *Samson*.

Our first attendance at Norwich was at the second (Wednesday) evening performance. The following is the programme:

PART I.

PASTORALE SINFONIA..*Beethoven.*
DUETT, "Folg dem Freunde mit Vertrauen," Madame Viardot
    Garcia and Herr Formes. *Faust*...................*Spohr.*
RECITATIVE and ARIA, "Chi per pieta mi dice." "Deh! parlate
    che forse tacendo," Madame Fiorentini. *Il sacri-*
    ficio d'Abramo...............................*Cimarosa.*
SCENA and AIR, "Soft airs around me play," Mr. Sims Reeves.
    Euryanthe....................................*C. M. v. Weber.*
VARIATIONS, "Ah! je veux briser ma chaîne," Miss Louisa
    Pyne. *Les Diamants de la Couronne*...............*Auber.*
TERZETTO, "Tremate, empi tremate," Madame Fiorentini, Sig-
    nor Gardoni, and Signor Belletti..................*Beethoven.*
AIR, "I am a roamer bold and gay," Mr. Weiss. *Son and*
    Stranger....................................*Mendelssohn.*
ARIA, "Oh cara immagine," Signor Gardoni. *Flauto Magico*.....*Mozart.*
ARIA, "Nobil Signor," Miss Dolby. *Les Huguenots*..........*Meyerbeer.*
CONCERTANTE for four violins, Messrs. Sainton, Blagrove, Day,
    and Cooper.....................................*Maurer.*
SCENA and ARIA, "Nacqui all' affanno." "Non più mesta,"
    Madame Viardot Garcia. *Cenerentola*............*Rossini.*
ARIA, with CHORUS, "Possenti Numi," Herr Formes. *Flauto*
    Magico......................................*Mozart.*

PART II.—MISCELLANEOUS.

SELECTIONS from *The Minnessinger*.....................,........*Benedict.*
(First time of performance.)

OVERTURE.

ROMANCE, "As weeping on my breast she lay," Mr. Sims Reeves.

HUNTING CHORUS, "To the chase."

BALLAD, "My home is in the peasant cot." Miss Louisa Pyne.

SONG, "O give me back," Mr. Lockey. *Pascal Bruno*..........*Hatton.*

ARIA, "Havvi un Dio," Madame Fiorentini. *Maria de Rohan*...*Donizetti.*

QUINTET, "Pour les attraits," Madame Viardot Garcia, Miss
        Louisa Pyne, Miss Dolby, Signor Gardoni, and Mr.
        Weiss. *Marie Stuart*......................*Niedermeyer.*

BARCAROLA, "Sulla poppa del mio brik," Signor Belletti. *La
        prigione d'Edinburgo*.............................*Ricci.*

SONG, "O bid your faithful Ariel," Miss Alleyne. *The Tempest*....*Linley.*

GLEE, "Blow gentle gales," Miss Louisa Pyne, Miss Dolby,
        Messrs. Sims Reeves, Lockey, and Weiss...........*Bishop.*

CORONATION MARCH. *Le Prophéte*.......................*Meyerbeer.*

The house was well filled though not crowded. Mr. Benedict met with a flattering reception on his entrance, as he did at every performance. The conductor is looked upon here, not as a mere time-beater, but as the responsible agent, an embodied representation of the whole *corps ;* to him the performers look for safe conduct, and to him the audience look for satisfactory results. He is cheered when he comes in, and this inspires him and all who depend upon his bâton with confidence, and is very likely to insure, at least, a good beginning. The Pastoral Symphony by Beethoven, one of his most picturesque and beautiful productions, was perfectly rendered throughout. The soft coloring of the pastoral scene, the singing of the happy birds, the dance of the rustics, the thunder and the tempest—

"At first heard solemn o'er the verge of heaven,"

and afterwards when the storm was over; when

> " Thro' the lightened air
> A higher lustre and a clearer calm,
> Diffusive tremble."

and

> " Nature stands revived "—

All seemed to say, the ideal of the immortal composer is realized, the spirit of Beethoven is here;—

> " 'Tis beauty all, and grateful song around."

The village dance and the storm especially chained the attention, and the audience listened with unmingled delight.   So it
is when Sontag or Jenny Lind pours out her enchanting strains,
filling the mind with lively forms of beauty, and the heart with
joy and gladness.   The influence of our Musical Fund Societies,
or such societies as are engaged in bringing out the grand symphonies of Mozart and Beethoven, is most important to musical
progress and taste.   Concerts where music of this description
is performed, by such competent bands as we now have in New
York and Boston, and I suppose in other more southern cities
also, are schools of taste, which every one ought to attend.
Parents ought to take their children to these concerts, and let
them, while young, form a taste for music so pure and truthful,
and thus prevent the evil, so extensive, that results from an
acquaintance more easily formed with coarser strains too often
found on handsomely-engraved sheets, with vignette ornamental.
There is music enough indeed to vitiate taste ; it is found in the
domestic circle, in the concert-room, and in church ; and the
work of corrupting is much easier than that of elevating and
refining a relish for good music, considered either with respect
to its intellectual or its æsthetic influences.   Success then to
those societies, by whatever name they are called, whose object
it is to bring out the great works of which we speak, which are

at once a school and the highest standard of musical excellence. Every one who loves music, nay, every one who loves his fellow-man, and desires to promote the cause of general cultivation and civilization, ought to patronize these societies. Let their season tickets all be taken, and at a price, too, which shall at once enable them to bestow the labor requisite for bringing out these works in a proper style, and also to live, at least from hand to mouth, while they do it. Public benefactors must not usually expect large pecuniary reward, but why should the musician receive less than the least of all others! We have got away from our subject, but we are glad of it, for we have happened to touch one of much practical importance to music's best influences.

The Duet from *Faust* was charmingly done, yet Herr Formes should have had a little compassion on his fair colleague, for his voice was too powerful for that of the Viardot. Madame Fiorentini is a brilliant soprano, and is indeed a fine singer, but is inferior to the two who outrival all others in the style in which she sings. The song by C. Von Weber, *Soft airs around me play*, a song in which Mr. Sims Reeves excels, was done in his very best style. Miss Louisa Pyne did herself great credit and charmed an attentive audience with the neatness and precision (almost Belletti-like) with which she sang the very difficult variations by Auber. A most animated and humorous song is that of the Pedlar, from a comic operetta by Mendelssohn, *The Son and Stranger*. Mr. Weiss' performance of it was irresistible, and a unanimous encore followed. The four violinists in the very brilliant Concertante drew forth immense applause. It is a fine concert piece of the lighter kind, and can never fail to please if well done. Madame Viardot Garcia was encored, as she deserved to be, in the Aria from *Cenerentola*, and Herr Formes concluded the first part of the concert by as

perfect a singing of the well-known air from Mozart as is possible to human organs. Majestic, dignified, and deliberate—
who but Formes could give it thus? In the second part several pieces were introduced from an unpublished opera by
Mr. Benedict, entitled the *Minnesinger*. First, the Overture,
which was finely played by the magnificent band, and drew
forth much applause. Then followed the song by Mr. Reeves,
the hunting chorus, *To the chase*, and the most pleasant ballad,
My home is in the peasant cot : the manner in which this music
was received must have been highly gratifying to the composer
and conductor, for it manifestly gave great delight. Mr. Belletti's performance of the Barcarola, *Sulla poppa del mio brik*,
was not surpassed by anything during the concert, or indeed
during the Festival. He has the most perfect command of his
instrument, and his performances are spirited and effective in
the highest degree. There are better voices than his, but indeed there is no better singer than Signor Belletti. The encore which followed this song, was given with a decision not to
be misunderstood. The Coronation March, Meyerbeer, was
played in a most spirited manner; and performers and hearers,
fatigued with the day's work, went home to seek for

" Tired Nature's sweet restorer."

THURSDAY.—It was a charming morning; the sun shone out
pleasantly, and it was neither too hot nor too cold. We took
a little walk round this old town before the Concert time.
Many of its streets are very narrow, only wide enough for a
single carriage, having sidewalks also so narrow that two persons cannot walk abreast. By mere accident we happened to
call in at the Book or Stationery Store of Mr. Bacon, formerly
the Editor of the Quarterly Musical Review, ten or twelve

volumes of which were completed about sixteen years ago, when the work ceased with the Editor's life. It was the most áble musical *review* ever published in England, and it is now very difficult to procure a copy. Bacon's "Vocal Elements," is also a very valuable work, well known here, though never reprinted in America. The establishment is now carried on by his son, who is also an able musical critic, and occasionally writes for some of the London papers.

The Hall was well filled this morning; the new Oratorio, "Jerusalem," was the more attractive from the fact that its author is well known, having resided here, as we were told, for some time past, attending the rehearsals and making the necessary preparation for the production of his work. Mr. Pierson is an Englishman, although he has heretofore assumed a German name as an author, having published several things under the name of Mansfeldt, and especially an opera at Hamburg. We have known of such things in our own country—that is, the publishing under an assumed name, for the apparent purpose of obtaining popularity, but it is an attempt at deception, and is dishonest. Let a man, if he pleases, publish anonymously, or assume a name that everybody knows to be assumed, (like Peter Parley, for example,) but let him not take a name for the purpose of leading the public to suppose that his own compositions are the productions of some great man, whose name is too difficult to be pronounced. Mr. Pierson was appointed professor of music in the University of Edinburgh, but resigned in consequence of some difficulties, after holding the office only for a short time. He is a clever musician, though not equal to the task he has undertaken. We have not seen the score of *Jeru-salem*, and only judge of it by a single hearing. It is very difficult both in its vocal and instrumental parts, but to us it seemed to be without form and void, and darkness rested upon the face of it throughout. We copy from the programme the following argument:

PART I.

Introduction of prologue. Christ foretells the destruction of Jerusalem. The crucifixion. Prophecy of Moses concerning the invasion and conquest of Judea by the Romans. Prophetic warnings and denunciations, chiefly from Isaiah and Jeremiah. The fall of Jerusalem depicted.

PART II.

The destruction lamented, the restoration promised.

PART III.

Prophecies concerning the recall of the Jews from all countries where they are now living in a state of exile. The great battle of Armeggeddon (in "the valley of Decision"), which will end in the total defeat of the armies attacking Jerusalem.

"The new Jerusalem. The last Judgment. The salvation of the righteous. Doxology."

The introduction or prologue is preceded by an overture consisting of a Maestoso Larghetto minor movement, an allegro, and a repetition of a part of the first movement, with different treatment. But it is not like an overture; it is constantly promising, but it never performs; bold in modulation, beautiful, occasionally, in instrumentation, it seems to be destitute of plan or design—except, indeed, it be the design of not having any plan, or of being different from any one else. The drums and trumpets may tell of the exposure and danger of the favored city, or of coming war, but beyond this we could not interpret, and the whole overture seemed to be dry and uninteresting. The introduction commences with an *Arioso*, "And Jesus said, Daughters of Jerusalem, weep not for me," &c.; which was well sung by the excellent tenor, Mr. Lockey; but he seemed like one wandering about in darkness, not knowing whither he was going. After the lament of the Saviour over Jerusalem, " O Jerusalem ! if thou hadst known it," we have a short *chorus-recitative* " And Moses spake unto all Israel," &c. We do not know how the leader of Israel came in here, but as Mr. Pierson seems to set at defiance all laws of *rhythm*, so for aught we know, he may treat *chronology* in a similar way. The introduction closes by an Aria, sung by Herr Formes, " The Lord shall bring a nation against thee from far," &c., parts of which are certainly fine, but there is a want of relation, or consistency, or decision of character, deeply felt throughout. Part I. commences with a *Recit-Arioso*, fragmentary and unsatisfactory ; this leads to a chorus, " How shall I pardon thee for this, O Jerusalem ?" A bird does not more depend upon its wings in flight, or a fish upon its fins for a propelling power, than our author does upon the orchestra for effect. He does not try to do much with the voices ; indeed a large part of the oratorio cannot be regarded as vocal music. We do not intend to intimate that, as a general thing, the author aims at *any definite effect*, for all is so vague, and wandering, that he cannot be thus charged. A terzetto follows for three female voices, " Cry aloud, spare not, lift up thy voice like a trumpet,"—a trumpet blast, of course, must be blown ; and although we did not like the introduction of the trumpet into this trio, yet we did like the manner in which the instrument was, and is ever, blown by Mr. Harper, jr., who always seems to do that which he intends. A chorus follows, " The Lord saith," &c., in some parts very difficult, (difficulties abound in Mr. P.'s music,) but in no place very good. An attempt at imitation on the words "I will scatter them," by difficult chromatic harmonies and modulations, but in which there was no scattering, unless it were in the performance of the music, brought to our minds by contrast, some of Handel's scatterings, in which, without resorting to chromatics, he by the plain diatonic scale performs the work to admiration, so that not a man of them is left. An air to the words, "Of the rock that begat thee," is very pleasant, it has some connection and form, and was charmingly sung by Madame Viardot Garcia.

In the succeeding *Aria*, our author wanders again in uncertainty. A piece representing the "March of the Roman army against Jerusalem" is feeble and ineffective. An air, "Blow ye the trumpet in Zion, and sound an alarm in my holy mountain," is much inferior to Jackson's setting of the same words. A chorus is introduced to the words, "Arise, and let us go by night, let us destroy her palaces;" in which there is an absence of all that dramatic character so necessary. How Mendelssohn would have set these words! When we listened to this chorus, amidst all the uncertainty and vagueness of the music, we thought of the answer of the youth whom Elijah sends to look out for rain, to the question, "Is there anything," &c. "No, nothing." Mr. P. has produced a very martial effect (never very difficult to do) upon the words, "I swear by myself, saith the Lord;" but unfortunately it is entirely out of place. What can be more awfully solemn than the thought of God's swearing by himself! Surely, if the music should express the emotions which the thought naturally excites, it must be slow, deliberate, and perhaps soft. This is not the only place in which the true feeling to be expressed seems to have been entirely misapprehended by our author. In the second part of the oratorio, the music to the words, "Because of the mountain of the Lord, which is desolate," would be better adapted to "Behold the mountain of the Lord, it is beautiful." A chorus, "O God, the heathen are come into thine inheritance," opens well; it is somewhat like Mendelssohn, and affords quite a relief; but it soon changes from Mendelssohn to Pierson, and the mountain becomes desolate indeed. In an *Arioso* which was sung by Madame Viardot, but which all her powers of performance could not render effective, the composer seems wholly to have mistaken the feeling to be expressed. The words are, "O Israel, thou hast destroyed thyself, but in me is thine help." Here, instead of expressing pity, compassion, or, of mourning over Israel, he has made the orchestral instruments to *scold* in blasts most inappropriate and offensive. A good chorus follows; in the latter part of which, to the words, "Break forth into joy," are some fine instrumental passages; but here again the *opening of the graves* has been depicted by a convulsive effort of the double drums. " When shall the Lord go forth," in the third part, is a spirited and good chorus.

There is a Hallelujah chorus, *Alleluia, for the Lord God Omnipotent reigneth.* This the Bishop ordered to a second singing, probably for the reason that Handel's Hallelujah is so popular. Surely, it could not have been because there is any merit in the piece encored. An air, by Madame Viardot, to the words, *God shall wipe away all tears from their eyes,* was the most popular piece in the Oratorio ; it was charmingly done, and was universally demanded a second time. Soft and gentle, it afforded a delightful relief from the continual trumpet blasts with which the Oratorio abounds. But in the succeeding Aria, the brass instruments are well employed on the words *The sea gave up their dead,* &c. A chorus follows this, after the manner of Mendelssohn's chorales in *Paul* and *Elijah ;* but instead of a grand and dignified chorale, the author has introduced a very feeble tune, composed by Dr. Madan, called *Helmsley,* and published in many singing books. We were surprised that such a hackneyed piece should have been chosen, in preference to a good chorale, of which there are many. Mr. P. has arranged it, however, (instrumented it,) exceedingly well. During the performance of this long oratorio, (upwards of four hours,) we often thought of a simile we once heard used by Hon. Horace Mann, when Secretary of the Board of Education, Massachusetts, by which he described some public address he had recently heard. "It was," said he, "like a nest of paper-boxes. We take up the nest; it feels heavy, and we suppose it contains something valuable. We open it carefully, but find another box. We now look with greater eagerness to ascertain the contents, and proceed to open the second, when we find only a *third* box; so we go on from box to box, with continually raised expectations, until we come to the last box, open it, and behold there is nothing there!" There are, however, several fine pieces in the oratorio, some of which we have mentioned; but as a whole, we can hardly conceive of a greater failure. It is surprising that the directors of the Festival should have admitted into their programme an oratorio so nearly destitute of merit. Many English oratorios have been produced; no one so great perhaps as *Palestine* by Dr. Crotch, but yet, not even this ever attained any considerable degree of popularity. They are born, speak once or twice perhaps, then die, are buried, and soon forgotten.

THIRD EVENING CONCERT.—THURSDAY EVENING.—The concert commenced with Mozart's Symphony in E flat; and the contrast between this music and that of the morning was sufficiently great. It was a pleasing change, indeed, to listen to the simple, natural strains of the great master; and every one appeared to be delighted. After the symphony, Mr. Sims Reeves sang a song, a tribute of respect to the memory of the late Duke of Wellington. Music by Mr. G. A. Macfarren. We enclose the words, thinking they may be interesting to your readers:

THE DEATH OF WELLINGTON.

Gloomy and dim the eventful morning broke,
Destined by Fate to crush a tyrant yoke ;
The adverse ranks with martial ardor glow,
And pant to view the signal flag unfurl'd ;
The rival chiefs prepare to strike the blow—
France for an Empire !—Britain for the world !

Fierce was the fight : the legions scorned to yield :
Conquest long hover'd o'er the field,
Unfix'd to whom 'twas due ;—
While dauntless hearts, the nation's pride,
For Britain bled—for Britain died—
Round Wellington at Waterloo.

At length the foe, in prowess quite outdone,
Despairing fled,
And Glory shone out with radiant hue.
" Cheerly, my hearts ! your ranks enlarge,
Victory smiles—the charge ! the charge !"
Cried Wellington at Waterloo.

Now, mourning o'er her fallen Hero's bier,
Grateful Britannia drops a tear,
And counts his deeds anew.
From pole to pole his praises ring,
And angels yet unborn shall sing
Of Wellington at Waterloo.

After the song, the pieces mentioned in the following programme were performed :

PART I.

DUETTO, Madame Viardot and Herr Formes.   *Fidelio*. . . . .*Beethoven*.
ROMANCE, " Vanne," Madame Fiorentini. . . . .*Meyerbeer*.
ARIA, " Fra poco," Mr. Sims Reeves. . . . .*Donizetti*.
TERZETTO, " Io diro se nel gestire," Mad. Viardot Garcia, Miss
    Louisa Pyne, and Signor Belletti. . . . .*Fioravanti*.

SONG, " Der Wanderer," Herr Formes....................................*Schubert.*
ROMANCE, " Oh, mon fils," Madame Viardot........................*Meyerbeer.*
CONCERTANTE, violoncello and double-bass, Herr Hausmann and
    Signor Bottesini.
ROMANZA, "Il Pescatore," Signor Gardoni............. ......*Donizetti.*
PART-SONG, " The wreath".....,........................*Benedict.*
DUETTO, Madame Fiorentini and Mr. Sims Reeves. *Ernani*....... *Verdi.*
SONG, " When midnight's darkest veil," Mr. Lockey ; corno ob-
    ligato, Mr. C. Harper.................................*Lachner.*
AIR, "By the rivers of Babylon," Miss Dolby................*S. Waley.*
FINALE, Miss L. Pyne, and chorus, *Lorely*..............*Mendelssohn.*

PART II.

OVERTURE, " Faniska".....................................*Cherubini.*
AIR, " Bravo, bravo, il mio Belcore," Signor Belletti..........*Donizetti.*
MADRIGAL—Song, " A poor simple maiden," Miss L. Pyne. Bal-
    lad, " Nan of Battersea," Mr. Weiss. *Charles II...* ......*Macfarren.*
TRIO, Miss L. Pyne, Miss Alleyne, and Mr. Lockey. *Don Gio-*
    vanni...*Mozart.*
SERENADE, " Young Agnes," Mr. Sims Reeves................*Auber.*
SCOTCH SONG, " Bonnie Dundee," Miss Dolby.
DUETTO, " Che vuoi di più," Madame Viardot Garcia and Signor
    Gardoni...*Donizetti.*
ARIA ESPANOLA. " La calesera," Madame Fiorentini.
GRAND MARCH. *Camp of Silesia*.......................*Meyerbeer.*

This was throughout a very pleasing concert, though too long.
The Terzetto by Madame Viardot, Miss Pyne, and Mr. Belletti,
called forth the most enthusiastic applause. It could not have
been better done. Schubert's *Wanderer* was sung to perfection
by Herr Formes. These and others were demanded a second
time. But the most attractive piece was the *finale* to Mendelssohn's opera, *Lorely*. This improves amazingly on a second
hearing. We were much more pleased with it than when we
heard it at Birmingham. The performance of it was very
spirited, and did great credit to band, choir, and conductor. It

was warmly applauded. But as we are in danger of too long a communication, we will only add, that the large company were held together from eight to twelve without restlessness, or the indication of impatience or fatigue.

FRIDAY MORNING—"THE MESSIAH."—It was very pleasing to us to have an opportunity of listening to this great oratorio of Handel twice in such close connection, performed as it was on both occasions (Birmingham and Norwich) by those who were so competent to do it justice. The popularity of this oratorio is wonderfully great. An hour previous to the time appointed for the commencement every seat and every standing-place, (with the exception of some of the reserved seats to which the occupants did not hasten at so early an hour,) was occupied. So full was the hall, that many men climbed up and obtained standing-room in recesses of the windows nearly at the top of the building outside. The hall presented a most splendid appearance. To what shall be attributed this great popularity of the *Messiah?* It is performed at every festival and never fails to sell every ticket. Can it be that it is because it is fully appreciated? Is it to be attributed to its musical excellence, to its religious character, or to fashion? Probably in part to each. It has been performed so much that it is better understood than any similar music; besides, Handel's music meets the wants of all classes; the learned and the unlearned are alike gratified in its performance; those who have made the greatest progress in art and science find enough in Handel to fill their minds and to draw out their feelings; and, like the poetry of Shakspeare, it so delineates human nature, or is so conformed to it, and is so common-sense-like in its character, that it can hardly fail to be appreciated even by a child. Handel is natural, always so, and his music is adapted to all classes of

people. Many, no doubt, are influenced by the religious
character of the *Messiah*. To the religious man, this oratorio
must be religious in its influences ; it falls in well with the general religious education, training, or habits of the English, especially of church-men, and the text (all from King James'
Bible) is regarded as not inferior to the Prayer Book itself.
Then there is the influence of habit, which has been handed
down and grown stronger from generation to generation.
Fathers tell their sons of Handel's *Messiah* with a kind of religious, national pride. Children are taught to regard it as the
greatest musical production the world has ever seen ; it is also
English, for although Handel was a German by birth, yet he
became an Englishman by adoption, and produced all his great
works here. It is the fashion also to hear it and to like it.
Everybody must hear it, and everybody must like it. Nor is
a single hearing sufficient ; it must be heard from year to year,
or as opportunity may occur, and of course the more it is heard
the more it is admired, as is the case with every work which is
at once based upon truly scientific principles, and adapted to the
truth or nature of man.

Mr. Benedict took his place two or three minutes before the
appointed time of commencement ; he was received with a
cheering welcome, both from the audience and from the performers—an indication that all is right, that good feeling abounds,
and that a good result may be looked for. With what majesty
and dignity the overture commenced ! Every man in the orchestra did his duty, and the effect was much heightened by the
full diapasons of the organ, and especially by the sub-bass. The
organ was not permitted in Birmingham, but it was a great mistake. It gives a fullness to the harmony, and is from association peculiarly religious in its character. It would not be appropriate in Covent Garden, at Her Majesty's Theatre, or on

any operatic performance; but it is well fitted for such an accasion as this, and Mr. Benedict was right in the application he made of its powers, Twenty-two violins led off the fugue; these were answered by the different stringed instruments in their turn, all moving with as much certainty and precision, as do the planets in their revolutions round the sun. The time was a little slower than at Birmingham, and the effect was much the better for it. The *bows* drew forth a rich volume of sound from the *strings*, most admirable in its consequences, and the whole overture was worthy of Handel and of his *Messiah*. *Comfort ye* was sung by Gardoni. We were more pleased with Mr. Sims Reeves on the whole, in this recitative, and in the air; though the vocalization of Signor Gardoni was more clear or articulate. The leading off of the first chorus produced a somewhat unpleasant feeling, for the tones of the men in alto struck hard upon the nerves, and musical taste was wounded in the house of its friends; but it soon recovered, as the parts came in and melted down the severe altos into one common mass of sound. Elsewhere, too, some suffering was produced by this austere, cutting severity of the alto. Let *men* sing the *tenor*, and let the lower voices of *females* sing alto; so shall this part have all the strength and firmness required, and yet be gentle, civil and kind in its approaches. The chorus was carried through in perfect time, slow and sure. The recitative, *Thus saith the Lord of Hosts*, and the following air, which were by a female alto voice at Birmingham, were here sung by Signor Belletti. It is not necessary to say that he sung them in excellent spirit and taste, for he has been heard in the same and other pieces in the *Messiah* in New York. The chorus, *For he shall purify*, was carried through with the greatest accuracy, and what is remarkable, the vocalizing passages here and in other choruses, were well done. Miss Dolby sang, *Behold! a virgin shall conceive,* and *O thou that tellest.* We cannot help remarking upon the most becoming appearance of the singer. She looked like one in earnest, as if she were really making these great declarations, and was wholly absorbed not in the music, but in them. The voice, the countenance, and the whole demeanor seemed to correspond, and all seemed to say that his name shall be, *Emanuel, God with us.* During the following chorus, too, she stood with the majesty and dignity of a Minister of State, (though always with a modesty becoming her sex,) singing *Arise, shine for thy light is come, and the glory of the Lord is risen upon thee.* This beautiful deportment on the part of Miss Dolby, was not carried out on the part of the choir, amongst whom there were some laughing and talking, and apparent congratulations, as soon as the chorus was over, which seemed to say, *we have done well.* If vanity must reign, if it cannot be subdued, do, singers, let us try and veil it for a moment, at least, during such a performance as this. Herr Formes sang (as at Birmingham) the next recitative and air; more need not be said. The chorus, *For unto us,* was much better at Norwich than at Birmingham. It was led off, not *Pianissimo,* but perhaps, *Mezzo Piano,* and there was a gradual *crescendo* all the way to the *fortissimo* on the word "wonderful." The great contrast made at Birmingham seemed like a kind of trifling. Handel has provided sufficiently for the grand climax in a contrapuntal way, and although the soft and loud are important, yet they must not be carried too far. The organ, notwithstanding the tardiness of its vibrations, greatly added to the magnificence of this chorus. The people stood during its performance. During the pastoral symphony, which was finely played, there was a general whispering and talking over the room; the singing had kept the people silent, and now that the music was merely instrumental, they felt at liberty to communicate their delights one to another. The organ was very effective in its holding-notes in this piece. The angel came, in the human form of Miss Louisa Pyne ; she hushed the noise of the great assembly as she told that *There were sheperds abiding in the field.* She spoke well, indeed she did ; yet Madame Clara Novello's delivery of the same and the following recitations was ringing in the ear to her disadvantage. The chorus, *His yoke is easy,* was too heavy. This chorus should float in the air ; it should not sink down to the earth. It should be light, buoyant, spiritual, not subjected to the laws of gravitation. Although we should not dare to say it, lest we might be regarded as musically heretical, yet we could not like Mozart's Trombones in this chorus.

"Behold the Lamb of God," went well as to time, but the voices were not kept down to *mezzo piano* as they ought to have been, nor were the *crescendo* and the *diminuendo* (so important in this chorus) well observed. Miss Dolby sang very effectively, *He was rejected and despised of men*—yet it had not so much the appearance of *singing* as of impressing the sentiment by the power of vocal utterance. The chorus, *Surely He hath borne our griefs,* was sung much better than at the Birmingham Festival, because of the *time,* which was considerably slower ; so also, *And with his stripes we are healed,* and the following, *All we like sheep,* each of which were given in a more steady, firm, and lofty manner. The grand chorus in C minor, *He trusted in God,* was most gloriously sung—time considerably slower than at Birmingham. The recitative, *Thy Rebuke,* and the air, *Behold and see,* were by Mr. Sims Reeves. The air especially, was given with great tenderness, and with deeply sympathizing tones and manner ; touching, indeed, was the utterance of the last words, *like unto his sorrow.* In the chorus, *The Lord gave the word,* the men's rough alto was like a saw-mill, when the saw strikes a nail ; how can this terrible grating be tolerated? The first part of the chorus, *Their sound is gone out*, was sung by four voices, and although the voices were perfect, yet the chorus was very much injured by the change. Here again Handel has made all the provisions for *soft* and *loud* required, and the chorus is vastly better when sung according to his intention. Signor Belletti sang, *Why do the nations*, and notwithstanding the great superiority of Herr Formes' voice, we think Belletti's performance the better of the two; his vocalization is perfect, like a good touch upon the Piano Forte; there is none better. Mr. Sims Reeves sang, *Thou shalt break them*, vastly better than Signor Tamberlik, yet we were not satisfied with its performance. We have heard this air, which Braham has made so famous, much injured by a mighty effort on the word "dash." Mr. Reeves made no violent attack upon this word; his effort rather was to give a proper character to the whole song, and not to depend so much upon the utterance of a single word. This was certainly in good taste. And now came the *Hallelujah*—the time could not have been better; Mr. Benedict's time in Handel is always without fault. The *alto* was again harsh on the passage by treble and alto in unison on, *A King of Kings and Lord of Lords*, but the chorus told admirably.

Madame Viardot Garcia sang, "*I know that my Redeemer liveth;*" it was transposed to accommodate her voice, but this was abundantly atoned for by the deep, appropriate emotion with which it was sung. Madame Viardot would excel in a song of this general character were it a *Mezzo Soprano*, or adapted to her voice; for she sings with a pathos and tenderness of feeling unheard, unfelt elsewhere. But "*I know that my Redeemer liveth*," as it stands, is beyond her reach. We have never yet heard justice done to this song. It requires a great voice, a great heart, and a finished singer. We need not particularize other pieces. The whole oratorio was sung, without omission, and although we think it may be better to abridge ordinarily, it was not now too long.

The closing "Amen" chorus, was given in slower time than we have usually heard it, and of course, as it was perfectly sustained throughout, carried with it great dignity and grandeur; it was like the rush of mighty waters, and towards the close, where the most remarkable contrapuntal passages occur, it was like the meeting of many seas. What an astonishing chorus is this! We must not omit to speak of the first violin passage in this chorus, leading off the principal subject in simple unison. It was a most beautiful thought of Handel, and on this occasion the passage was performed by twenty-two violins, all blending so as to form a perfect chorus, and given with a stability, compactness, solidity, and determination which cannot be expressed in words, and can only be imagined by those who have heard like effects. Great is Handel's oratorio of the *Messiah!* Great in its wonderful and soul-stirring themes! Great in musical inspiration! Great in its moral power! Ye choirs who seek for music of a high order in the oratorio form, purchase Handel's *Messiah!* There is nothing on earth like it! Be not satisfied with anything short of this! Study the sublime choruses; take the easier first, as, *And the glory of the Lord, The Lord gave the Word,* and *For unto us a child is born.* Then the *Hallelujah, Worthy is the Lamb,* and *Amen,* will soon follow; and also those which are still more difficult, as, *And he shall purify, Surely he hath borne our griefs, Behold the Lamb of God,* and others. The music is indeed difficult, it cannot be performed without labor, but the labor bestowed will be productive of rich reward. Instruments, too, are essential; but when or chestral instruments cannot be obtained, even a quartet of strings will help along very much. Or a piano forte (*if it be a piano forte*) may furnish a satisfactory accompaniment, but it must be *in tune,* and there must be *some one to play it.* Such practice as Handel's choruses will promote a healthy musical growth, general improvement, and good taste. It will render insipid much other music, contained in the *tune-books,* but it will lead to discrimination, and a psalm-tune which is at once based on true philosophy, and is yet so simple in its structure as to meet the wants of the people, will never suffer by being brought into close connection with Handel or Mendelssohn. The Old Hundredth, York, and Dundee, will live as long as anything that Handel has ever written; and although an acquaintance with Handel will certainly occasion a very large part of modern psalmody to appear insipid, foolish, or disgusting, tunes of the character of those above mentioned will stand firm and unmoved, and will be taken up after an hour with music of a higher scientific character, with new relish and increased delight.

LETTER XLVII.

The Tabernacle, Moorfields, Finsbury—Wickliffe Chapel, Commercial Road, East—
Rev. Dr. Reed.

LONDON, October, 1852.

WE attended the Tabernacle, Moorfields, in the morning. It is a large building, something like the Tabernacle in New-York, though incapable of seating so many persons. Whitefield formerly preached here, and it was here that Mr. Finney, of Oberlin, preached to multitudes of people about two years since. It is not always easy to obtain a seat in these houses of worship, so I went in and inquired of the sexton if he knew Rev. Mr. Finney from America. "Oh yes!" was the reply. "Well then," I said, "I wish you to give me a seat on his ac-

count, for I am an American, and know him well." Of course
he took me into one of the high places, if, indeed, there are any
such places there. Rev. Mr. Campbell, well known by his various publications, and especially by his Hymn Book, was un-
well, and did not officiate. He was present, however, and took
his seat in front of the pulpit, in the seat usually occupied by
the Precentor. A young man occupied the pulpit, and almost,
as a matter of course, we had a doctrinal sermon. Dr. Campbell added a few words at the close. The singing was led from
the gallery back of the preacher by a Precentor, who seemed
to have around him a few men-singers and women-singers whom
he called, perhaps, a choir; but there was no choir-effect, nor
was the Congregational singing as good as it is in most churches.
The lines of the hymns were read two by two, previous to
singing, as is the custom in many of the churches. The tunes
were bad. For example, a hymn beginning,

> " As the dew from heaven distilling,
> Gently on the grass descends," &c.,

was sung to Haydn's " God save the Emperor," or rather that
tune was attempted, for it is not proper to say that it was sung.

In the evening we went to the Wickliffe Chapel, Commercial
Road, East, Rev. Andrew Reed, D.D., pastor. Dr. Reed was
in America several years since, in company with Mr. Mathe-
son, now no more. In the singing exercises, the hymn was *lined
out.* The choir (so called) consisted of several men who occupied a square pew in front of the pulpit. The first tune was
Dr. Arnold's Wareham, abridged; the second was French
(Dundee), and the third I knew not, but it was unfit for Congregational use, as it went up to G and dwelt there considerably. No small effort was made by good people around me to

reach the lofty eminence, but in vain; most voices fell short
of the pitch, and vibrations inharmonious followed.   The hymn
was that beginning,

> "No more, my God, I boast no more,
> Of all the duties I have done."

The tune Hamburg, in the key of E flat, would have suited it
exactly.

The text was, "But now ye have no cloak for your sins."   It
was most faithful, and seemed to flow out of a heart filled with
love.   No abstract, scientific, theological discussion, as in the
morning, but it was the language of an affectionate parent, entreating his children, and urging them to the paths of truth and
virtue.

We have no cloak for our sins, first, because we live under
so gracious a dispensation of mercy.

Second, because of the land of liberty and of privileges in
which we dwell.   "Is there," said the preacher, "under the sun
a land where the gospel is so freely and so fully preached?
Indeed, we are highly distinguished above all others.   Religious privileges are nowhere so abundant and accessible to all
as here.   Who may not enjoy them?   The exertions in the
cause of Christian benevolence are greater here than anywhere
else.   Schools, from the infant school upward, are also more
abundant."   "You are a Briton," said Dr. Reed, "and you
glory in your name; be sure that you always associate this
with the religious advantages which your country affords."
"Sabbaths are better observed, and religious knowledge
abounds.   Is it nothing to live in such a land as this?   Is it
nothing to enjoy these Sabbaths?   Is it nothing that we
enjoy these houses of worship? these songs of praise? these
rehearsals by which we may be prepared for the music of

the heavenly choir?" He alluded, in this connection, in a very tender and appropriate manner to his own preaching among his people, saying that he never allowed himself to come into the pulpit without attempting faithfully and affectionately to point out to his hearers the way of salvation. There were other heads of discourse, which do not now occur to us. He closed with a most earnest appeal to his hearers not to attempt to cloak their sins, but to forsake them at once, and find deliverance and salvation.

Dr. Reed's manner is that of a tender parent; it contrasted strongly with that of the young man we heard in the morning. *He* was sometimes extravagant in his language, and his manner seems to be adapted rather to *drive* than to invite, encourage, and lead one along; there was a severity about it, forbidding, more apt to be found in a young man having great confidence in what he has learned in the seminary, than in one who seems to depend less upon the knowledge which he acquired at school than upon the wisdom which he has derived from experience. Dr. Reed's manner was all tender, gentle, affectionate; the spirit he seemed to manifest was that of love; such a spirit, who can resist? His manner of speech was also excellent; his voice is soft, yet every word was so distinctly uttered that it was heard throughout the house. We have heard sermons that would be called greater than Dr. Reed's, evincing, perhaps, deeper thought or stronger intellect; but we have not heard a finer pulpit exercise than on this occasion. What a sympathy there is between a faithful and affectionate manner in the preacher, a preacher throwing out his heart and entreating his hearers to reconciliation and Zion's songs? When with such preaching the organ, the choir, the people, the hymn, and the tune all sympathize, Zion is beautiful, the joy of all who dwelt therein. Mount Zion rejoices, and the daughters of Jerusalem are glad; they walk about Zion, they mark her bulwarks, and consider her palaces, that they may sing to following generations—"This God is our God, he will be our guide even unto death."

In going to and coming from church to-day, we have traveled upwards of ten miles.

LETTER XLVIII.

Moravian Church—Baptist Chapel, Lyon-street—Singing in Rev. Mr. Brock's Church.

LONDON, October, 1852.

WE attended the Moravian church with the expectation of finding a cultivated state of psalmody, with perhaps motets, chants and anthems. We have long known of the musical works and efforts of Rev. Mr. LATROBE, Moravian minister, whose six volumes of Church music are very valuable, and also something of his son, who is the author of the very valuable volume known as "Latrobe on Church Music." But the glory has departed from the Moravian chapel. The congregation was small, and the singing was drawled out very heavily. They have a small organ, poorly played; between every line was a transition passage, after the manner of some of the German churches. There was a small choir, but they attempted nothing further than to lead the congregation. The service was by a liturgy, but the responses were mostly said and not sung.

In the evening we went to the "Zion-street Chapel," Walworth. This is a Baptist chapel; the pastor was absent, and a young man, a student, filled his place. As a matter to be expected in such a case, there seemed to be some attempt at *eloquence ;* we almost invariably see it in a young man, and especially in a student. It is often somewhat trying to listen to the sermons of the theological students, and so it was on this occasion. The hymns were given out by the Precentor, who read them badly enough, applying the same accent, or general inflection, to each stanza. Perhaps the following may convey some idea of his manner of reading :—Let the first line be commenced on a high pitch, and let the pitch rise by a slide gradually until a climax very high is obtained by a strong pressure tone and upward slide or inflection on the last syllable but two ; then a sudden slide down, still on the same syllable, followed by still another upward on the last syllable, and this to be ex·actly the same in form, though differing a little in force in every couplet, or twice in each stanza :

> How sweet the name of Jesus sounds
>
> In a believer's ear ;
> It soothes his sorrows, heals his wounds,
>
> And drives away his fear.

We have seldom heard a hymn read in a more mechanical sing·song manner, or in worse taste. There was no choir, and the congregation generally joined in the singing. The people were all seated in prayer, and all stood in singing. They all took their seats merely for the benediction after the last singing. People in our own country are very much troubled that the custom of sitting in prayer should be increasing so much ; but it seems to prevail in a majority of the churches here. We did not learn much in relation to church music this day, either in the Moravian or Baptist chapel.

REV. MR. BROCK (Baptist) is the minister of Bloomsbury chapel, Bloomsbury street. He is a very popular preacher, and has a large and flourishing congregation. Not indeed like the great German congregations where we often see two or three thousand people assembled on a Sabbath morning, but there were not less, we think, than a thousand persons present at the Bloomsbury chapel last Sunday. The church is furnished with a very good-sized organ, though its tones are harsh, and especially so are the stops of small pipes, as mixture or cornet. There is no choir, but the singing is by the people, and seems to be very general. There was a chorus of many voices; a chorus not of musical attraction, but of religious edification—excellent and appropriate. Chanting had been introduced into this congregation, and is practised by the whole collected assembly with much success. We do not hesitate to say that the chanting by all the people in Rev. Mr. Brock's church is much superior to any of the cathedral choir chanting which we have heard. The chant itself was, indeed, unfavorable to the best results, being the well-known Dr. Dupuis in A; but notwithstanding the tune-like character of the chant, the effect was truly good, and seemed to furnish a most satisfactory answer to those objectors to chanting, who say that it is impossible for a large congregation to chant together. The words were, in general, deliberately and well delivered, and with a good degree of simultaneousness on the part of the congregation. Chanting is practised in public worship in many dissenting churches in London, and in other parts of the kingdom. Indeed, although it was introduced at an earlier period into our New England churches than here, yet it seems to have spread more here, and to have taken deeper root. One reason for this may be, that here it is made a *republican* thing; it is in the hands of the people, and *they* like it. The metrical psalms were also quite well sung, and the great importance of an organ in Congregational singing was made very apparent. A custom in giving out the hymn and tune is singular. The minister first gives out the number of the hymn, and immediately afterwards the organist plays over the tune. After this the minister, who stands in the pulpit during the playing, reads the hymn, and then the singing follows.

Mr. Brock has made a much-needed reform in relation to the public prayer. He has broken up the ever-so-long prayer, and instead of it has two shorter prayers. Rev. Mr. Binney of the Weigh House chapel has done the same. The devotional exercises occupied an hour, and the sermon that followed about forty minutes, after which the meeting was dismissed by the usual benediction.

LETTER XLIX.

Wesleyan Chapel, Great Queen Street, Lincoln's Inn Fields—Rev. Baptist Noel's Chapel —Lesson on Chanting, by C. C. Spencer—Anecdote—Stoke Newington—Dr. Watts' Monument and Inscription.

LONDON, October, 1852.

THE Wesleyan Chapel, Great Queen street, is a large building with double galleries. The Episcopal Church service is used, as it is in most of the Wesleyan congregations. The psalms were read by the minister, and intoned by the Precentor and others of the congregation, making a disagreeable mixture of speech and song. It was so likewise with other parts of the service, as the Lord's Prayer and the Creed. Four metrical hymns were sung, mostly to wretched tunes, and in a wretched manner. A small choir of boys surrounded the Precentor, but there was no organ. Next to me sat a young man who seemed to try and do his best, and the poor fellow would have done pretty well had the tunes been adapted to the circumstances; but when they went up as high as F or G, alas for him! He made the attempt indeed, which is better than not to try at all, but he fell; the leap was beyond his power. He tried to take the high parts of the tune an octave lower than the proper pitch, but in these attempts he often turned somersets, though he did not always come down upon his feet. It was really pitiable to stand by him and witness his efforts; but yet the easier parts of the tune he would get right. From this example, we obtained sufficient proof of what Congregational tunes ought to be: simple and easy, so that they may be within the reach of all. St. Ann, Phuvah, Tallis, are good examples, (Cantica Laudis, p. 307.) Yet they need not all be of this rhythmic character; Olmutz, Hamburg, Marlow, are always good. Had one of these tunes been sung at the Wesleyan Chapel, the young man would have been saved from many falls and bruises. In the evening we went to Rev. Baptist Noel's chapel, where one is always sure of edification from the sermon if not from the psalms.

We have recently had an opportunity of attending a lesson on chanting, given by C. C. Spencer to the Rev. Mr. Brock's (Baptist) congregation. Mr. Spencer is well known as a warm friend of old psalmody, and especially by his " Explanation of the Church Modes." His manner of chanting is good, quite a different thing from that of the Cathedral choirs. The words are delivered about as fast as in speech, and time in the cadences is almost wholly disregarded. His *beau ideal* seems to require the absence of all regular division of time, or all that which we commonly call measured rhythmic effect. He is favorable to the unisonous singing of the old church tunes, and the congregation tried some of them under his direction with good results. I insert one of these chants exactly as he teaches it, and as the people on this occasion sang it.

ANCIENT CHANT—TO BE SUNG IN UNISON.

ADAPTED BY C. C. SPENCER.

1. I will extol thee, my | God, O King;
   And I will bless thy name for | ever and ever.

2. Every day will I | bless–thee;
   And I will praise thy name for | ever and ever.

3. Great is the Lord, and greatly to be | prais–ed;
   And his greatness is un | search–able.

4. One generation shall praise thy works to an | o–ther;
   And shall declare thy | migh–ty acts.

5. I will speak of the glorious honor of thy | majesty;
   And of thy | won–drous work.

6. And men shall speak of the might of thy | terrible acts;
   And I will declare thy | great–ness.

7. They shall abundantly utter the memory of thy great | good–ness;
   And shall sing of thy | righteous–ness.

8. The Lord is gracious and full of com | pas–sion;
   Slow to anger, and of great | mer–cy.

9. The Lord is | good to all;
   And his tender mercies are over | all–his works.

10. All thy works shall praise | thee, O Lord;
    And thy saints shall | bless–thee.

11. They shall speak of the glory of thy | king–dom,
    And | talk of thy power;

12. To make known to the sons of men his | mighty acts,
    And the glorious majesty of his | king–dom.

13. Thy kingdom is an everlasting | king–dom;
    And thy dominion endureth throughout all gene | ra–tions.

14. The Lord upholdeth | all that fall ;
   And raiseth up all those that be | bow-ed down.

15. The eyes of all | wait upon thee ;
   And thou givest them their meat in due | sea-son.

16. Thou openest | thine-hand ;
   And satisfiest the desire of every | living thing.

17. The Lord is righteous in | all his ways,
   And holy | in all his works.

18. My mouth shall speak the | praise of the Lord ;
   And let all flesh bless his holy name for ever and | e-ver.

Mr. S. is giving a course of lessons to Mr. Brock's congregation on Chanting. It is but a few years since we had the honor of introducing chanting into some of the American churches (other than Episcopal) for the first time. At that time, perhaps some fifteen or twenty years ago, chanting had not been heard of in a dissenting congregation in England. Now it is common here to hear a congregation chant a Psalm. And it is often very well done, much better than we have often heard it by some four or six voices. It ought to be extended among the people, for its efficacy as a form of worship is most important. An anecdote related to me a few days ago is illustrative of this. When chanting was first introduced into the Weigh House chapel, (Rev. Mr. Binney's,) about four years since, it was received with almost universal favor from the first ; but there was one good old man who made strong objection to it ; it grieved him much ; but as the people were almost all in favor of it, he yielded in a good Christian spirit, looked on his book during the exercise, and tried to submit patiently to that which he could not approve. The sixty-seventh Psalm was, and is, often chanted. Indeed, they have but very few selections from the Psalms that they use, nor have they more than two or three chants. Tallis' chant is the principal. The few

Psalms that they use, therefore, with the tunes, are well engraved upon the memory of the people. A few weeks since the old man died. When on his death-bed, he sent for his minister. Mr. Binney immediately obeyed the summons, and as he entered the sick chamber found the old man on his deathbed, with his Bible open before him, trying to chant the sixty-seventh Psalm.

We have lately had the pleasure of lecturing in several churches on the subject of Psalmody, and among others, Rev. Mr. Jefferson's, Stoke Newington. Mr. Jefferson's chapel stands right opposite to the spot where Sir Thomas Abney formerly lived, in whose hospitable mansion Dr. Watts for many years found a home. Although his church was in the city, he often preached here, and here he wrote many of his beautiful hymns. He was buried in the Abney Park Cemetery, and a monument has there been erected to his memory. On the plinth on the pedestal is the following :—

In Memory

OF

ISAAC WATTS, D.D.;

And in testimony of the high and lasting esteem
in which his

Character and Writings are held in the great Christian Community
by whom the English language is spoken.

Of his psalms and hymns it may be predicted, in his own words,

Ages unborn will make his songs
The joy and labor of their tongues.

He was born at Southampton, July 17, 1674,
and died Nov. 25, 1748,

After a residence of 36 years in the mansion of Sir Thomas Abney, Bart.,
then standing on these grounds.

Below this is an extract from Johnson's Life of Watts. The monument was erected in September, 1845.

LETTER L.

Sacred Harmonic Society—Samson—Christus—Spohr's Last Things.

LONDON, Jan. 11, 1853.

IN a recent letter, we spoke of the different choral societies in London. Public performances by some one of them are very frequent; so frequent indeed, that we can find time for only now and then one. The first for the season was by the "Sacred Harmonic Society," under Mr. Costa, and consisted of a selection from "Samson," by Handel, Mendelssohn's "Christus," and "The Last Judgment," by Spohr. The death of the illustrious Duke gave a tinge to all the earlier concerts, and the "Dead March" ·in Saul was in constant requisition. On the present occasion, the selection from "Samson" consisted of the air, "Ye Sons of Israel," "Dead March," and chorus,

> "Glorious hero, may thy grave
> Peace and honor ever have."

The "Christus" by Mendelssohn, seems to be very popular, both among the singers and hearers. The chorale, "As bright the Star of Morning gleams," one of the best German chorales, and one that is very often heard in their churches, is brought in with fine effect after the chorus, "There shall a Star of Jacob come forth." Mendelssohn is always great in such choruses as "He stirreth up the Jews," "Crucify Him," and others in which he depends mostly upon orchestral effect, and in which he carries out his ideas of imitation or description with all the powers of modern instrumentation.

Spohr's oratorio was well given, the Gresham Professor himself being judge; for we had the honor of a seat by his side, and of listening to his remarks during the performance. Mr. Taylor was the first to bring out Spohr in England. "Die letzten Dinge," or "The Last Things," (which is a much better title for the oratorio than the one it now bears,) was composed about twenty-five years ago. It accidently came into the hands of Prof. Taylor, who translated the words, and first brought it out at the Norwich Festival in 1830. Since then it has been a standard oratorio, and is often performed. Prof. Taylor says: "It at once seized the public attention, and commanded the admiration of the most distinguished professors of every school. Its influences upon the feelings of an audience has been attested by expressions more decided and unequivocal than I ever remember to have witnessed. I speak not of the admiration which the musician derives from such a display of the power and the resources of his art, but of the homage which nature, though musically untutored, involuntarily yet willingly pays to genius. The throbbing heart, the moistening eye, the quivering lip, here bespeak the triumph of the composer." The solo parts were sustained by Mrs. Endersohn, Miss Williams, Mr. Lockey and Mr. Phillips.

We cannot enter into the detail of this performance; suffice it to say, that it afforded some of the best specimens of solo, quartet and chorus singing which we have ever heard. It was performed with admirable promptitude and exactness, as is everything else that is brought under the bâton of Mr. Costa.

LETTER LI.

St. Paul's Cathedral—Rev. Mr. Brock's.

THE organist at St. Paul's is a fine player. He played to-day as well as the canon read. He does not let himself and his instrument down to mere merry-making, or to a concert manner; but always preserves his own dignity and that of his instrument, and so plays as to promote the true end of music in worship. The contrast between the organ-playing of this morning and that which we heard on the last Sabbath, cannot be expressed in words. It was at a popular chapel attached to a large establishment where poor children are cared for and protected, and which is much visited by strangers coming to London. Here the organ-playing is frivolous, light and trifling, we had almost said, as is Jullien's Quadrille Orchestra in Drury Lane. It is amazing that any one who has musical knowledge should so pervert the powers of his instrument. But yet the organist has fine powers of execution; he plays with a rapidity of finger, with a clean piano-forte touch, producing the staccato with as much distinctness as stringed instruments, and at times almost the pizzicato. So it was on the occasion when we last heard him, when the song, "Why do the nations," from the Messiah, with the chorus, "Let us break their bands," were sung to an organ accompaniment as brilliant almost as that of a grand orchestra.

Congregational chanting is very good in some of the nonconformist churches; it was really excellent in Rev. Mr. Brock's church this evening. The chant was in unison, as follows:

Of course, the organist played full harmony. The fine old tune, Tallis, (Cantica Laudis, p. 307,) was sung to the 23d Psalm,

" My shepherd will supply my need."

The organ is very well played by an amateur ; yet he has the habit of stopping his instrument at the end of each stanza, so as to break up all flow of melody. We hardly know a worse habit than this, which we have heard in several places where the organ is used in non-conformist places of worship. An introductory voluntary was played, but no afterlude, or marching the people out. The congregation is always large at this church, almost every seat being occupied ; yet there are no congregations of three or five thousand people here, as we find in different parts of Germany.

We have been recently more than ever before convinced of the necessity of simple harmony for Congregational purposes. We have seen attempts to introduce, for example, some of John Sebastian Bach's harmony parts into congregations. Now, it is well known that Bach did not write harmony parts for Congregational singing, but for choir singing. In his church, the St. Thomas', Leipzig, all the people sing the melody, and the parts are sung (when sung at all) by the choir. Of course, Bach wrote such difficult harmonies as none but a choir, and a professional choir too, can sing well. Yet editors not knowing these circumstances have introduced these difficult harmonies into tune books designed for Congregational use. Congregations might as well undertake to sing Beethoven's Mass No. 2, as these chorals, with all sorts of complicated and difficult harmony parts. Oh that two things in relation to psalmody might be understood ! 1st. That Congregational singing cannot be good unless the tunes are very plain and easy ; and 2d,

That there are plenty of such plain and easy tunes which possess true musical excellence, and which are in all respects suited to the wants of a worshipping assembly.

LETTER LII.

Church Music in Holland—Haarlem Organ—Leyden—The Hague—Bells—Hats on—
Reading the Bible for a Voluntary.

During a recent tour through some of the principal places in Holland, we took care to hear the church-singing, and to learn what we could of the actual state of Psalmody. As the whole appearance of religious worship differs from that of Germany, so also does this particular branch of it. It is more like that of the Swiss churches, or like that of those German churches which border on Switzerland, and where the Reformation seems to have left more decided or clearer impressions than are generally seen in Saxony or other German States. The prevailing forms of worship are, so far as we have observed, more simple in Holland, or more like those of our New England churches. Now, the more simple the form of worship, the less, certainly, it is adapted to anything like artistic display, if not also to artistic excellence. As there are no pictures and no statuary in the Dutch churches, so there is no artistic music. There are no anthems, no motets, no solos or quartets; there cannot be, for there are no choirs. We do not know but there may be choirs in some of the churches in Holland, but we did not see or hear of any.

Holland is the country of BELLS; and the merry chimes are to be heard hourly, from almost every church-tower or steeple.

It is the country of ORGANS also. Every church is supplied with keys and pipes, as a necessary part of its furniture. The organs, too, are (many of them) large and excellent, but are only used as an accompaniment to the chorus of the people. Everybody has heard of the Haarlem Organ. It was for many years the largest in the world, and is famed for its size the world over. We thought it as *good* as it is *great*, and listened to its tones with delight. It is indeed very powerful, but its full power is seldom heard, and never in public worship. There are now several organs as large, or larger; for example, the organ in the Town Hall, at Birmingham; but although the Haarlem organ is now equaled in size, and although various improvements (especially within a few years past) have been made both in action and in pipes, yet there is not perhaps anywhere to be found, a more powerful chorus than that of this famous instrument. Dr. Burney took particular pains to examine and describe it, many years ago; and, in his " Musical Tour in Holland," he gives the details which have been often copied and published. The present organist has fine execution, and appears to understand well his instrument; but, it is a pity that, for the sake of pleasing his company, and confirming his hearers in a bad taste, he should employ its noble powers in battle-piece and thunder-storm representations; or, at least, that these should be made the principal feature of his exhibitions. There was a large congregation the Sabbath we were in Haarlem, and all united in great earnestness in the psalms. The movement was very slow—very nearly twice as slow as it is common to sing the Old Hundredth in our American churches, so that the time was easily described by counting four to each note, or eight in a double measure. No leading voice was heard; the organ alone seemed to lead, and yet the singing and the playing were so nearly together that no unpleasant effect was produced. It is always better that the organ should lead, than that a single voice should be heard ahead of others ; but, there is, indeed, no necessity for either, even in Congregational singing, and the idea that a single voice should lead a choir by being always a little in advance in time, is so entirely at variance with good taste that it is not to be tolerated. The singing was in unison, and the tunes seemed to be perfectly familiar. The tune was not played over upon the organ before the singing, but the organist played only a prelude of a few measures, when all the people joined at once in the hymn. The interludes were very short ; indeed, they could hardly be called interludes in the ordinary sense, since they were too short to include even a single phrase ; they consisted only of a passing chord or two, merely allowing time to breathe between the stanzas.

We have already intimated that the singing was very general in the congregation ; in this respect, we think the Dutch congregations are in advance even of the German ; for there was one universal burst of vocal sound from the beginning to the end of the hymn. No other musical form was attempted than that of the plain metrical tune, or chorale.

We were also present during public worship in churches at other places, as Leyden, and The Hague, but a description of one is a description of all. At Amsterdam and Rotterdam the same general style of church-singing prevails. There is one prevailing custom here, which strikes a stranger with surprise, and which seems to indicate a want of propriety, if not of reverence ; and that is, *the wearing of hats in church*. It is a custom in the Hollandish churches for the men to enter and remain with hats on, until the devotional exercises actually commence ; they then uncover their heads, but put on their hats again the moment the preacher begins his sermon. It looks strange to see the hats put on the moment the text is named. This custom also prevails in some parts of Switzerland.

There was another custom which we observed here, that we have not seen elsewhere. Very soon after the people began to assemble for public worship, an elder took his stand in front of the pulpit and commenced reading the Scriptures aloud. This he continued for perhaps fifteen minutes, while the people were assembling, or until the minister had arrived and was quite ready to commence the service. So that the reading of the Scriptures publicly, was treated with less appearance of reverence than are our organ voluntaries in New England; since it is not the general custom with us to commence the voluntary until after the minister has taken his place in the pulpit. But it seemed strange to see the public reading of the Scriptures employ the coming in of the people, the walking, talking, and other noises of disturbance, and at the same time to see the men with heads covered, or hats on, in the house of God.

LETTER LIII.

Dr. Bexfield's Lectures—English Glee and Madrigal Union—Oratorios—Sacred Harmonic Society—Judas Macccbæus—Concerts.

London, March 11, 1853.

DR. W. R. BEXFIELD, the author of the oratorio " Israel Restored," has been giving a course of lectures on music, and especially on the present state of music in England, at the London Institution. This is an institution which provides lectures, popular and instructive, annually, on many subjects. The present season there have been courses of lectures on Physiology, Physical Geography, Electricity, Geology, Poetry, and Music.

The musical course consisted of six lectures, on the following topics :

Lecture I. CHURCH MUSIC.—Chants, Psalms, Tunes, Services, Anthems, Voluntaries.

Lect. II. THE ORATORIO.—Requirements for writing one; Handel, Haydn, Crotch, Mendelssohn, Spohr.

Lect. III. THE CONCERT-ROOM.—Concertos, Violin, Clarionet, Overtures, Symphonies.

Lect. IV. THE DRAWING-ROOM.—Pianoforte; Mozart, Weber, Sterndale, Bennett, Mendelssohn's songs without words.

Lect. V. THE OPERA.—Beethoven, Mozart, Gluck, Spohr, Rossini, and others.

Lect. VI. Revival of taste for Glees and Madrigals, etc.

These have been accompanied with illustrations by various artists in the different departments. Indeed, it may be said that the illustrations have constituted the principal attraction (and the house has always been crowded), Dr. Bexfield not having given himself much to close analysis or description. Dr. Bexfield is quite a young man, but a fine musician, considered either as a composer or as a performer. He has a good command of the keys, and were he not otherwise occupied, *i. e.* as a composer, he might excel as a solo performer. He is a great lover of the old writers, is well acquainted with musical history and with the various excellences or peculiarities of all the musical composers, and seems ready to quote any of them from memory. His oratorio of "Israel Restored," though owing to peculiar circumstances it did not draw a full house on its second representation at the Norwich Festival, is regarded as a work of considerable merit. We have heard parts of it under the author's direction, and were much pleased. It is by some regarded as the best English oratorio which has appeared for many years.

The concert season is now coming on, and we have some kind of musical performance almost every evening. On Monday last we had the pleasure of listening to one of the " English Glee and Madrigal Union's" concerts. This Union consists of a number of the best English singers, say six or eight, who, by much practice together, bring glee singing to a great state of perfection. Messrs. Lockey, Hobbs, and Phillips, are of the number. The best glees sung on the present occasion were : " Mark'd you her eye of heavenly blue ?"—*Spofforth ;* " As on a Summer's Day"—*J. Stafford Smith ;* and " Under the Greenwood Tree"—*Arne and Bishop.* The best madrigal was, " Flora gave me fairest flowers." For the madrigals they have a chorus of about sixteen voices. Several songs were also sung, two of which excited some interest, viz. : " My Time, O ye Muses !" by Dr. Croft, sung by the most charming mezzo-soprano, Miss M. Williams ; and a song from Handel's opera of " Orlando," by Mr. Phillips, " Lascia amor, e siegui." There were also some very poor specimens of songs, glees, etc., which need not be mentioned. There are in almost all concerts things to be endured, as well as things to be enjoyed.

Mendelssohn's Elijah has been given this week by the Harmonic Union; so also the Hymn of Praise and Mozart's Requiem, by the Sacred Harmonic Society. The Messiah and Elijah are in constant demand, and, like Macbeth, never fail to draw a full house.

The Philharmonic Concerts are now soon to begin; but ere that we expect to be on our way towards home.

On Friday evening last, the Sacred Harmonic Society gave Handel's Judas Maccabæus. This is one of the most popular of Handel's oratorios, though less so than the Messiah. Nor as a work of genius can it be compared to the greatest work of the mighty composer, the "Israel in Egypt." It contains some very fine specimens of chorus writing, both contrapuntal and dramatic. It is an oratorio well known in Boston, having been performed frequently by the Handel and Haydn Society. The greatest attraction in the way of performers was the magnificent tenor of Mr. Sims Reeves. "Sound an Alarm" was perhaps never given with greater power and ·effect. Mr. H. Phillips sang in his usual excellent style. A new soprano, Miss Deakin, attracted considerable attention, and promises to become a popular singer. She was cordially received, as one almost always is who *looks prettily.*

On the Monday following, the Harmonic Union performed Handel's Messiah. The Societies are all obliged to perform the Messiah occasionally, otherwise they might not pay their expenses. This oratorio always insures a full house. Mr. Benedict proves himself to be fully adequate to the direction of Handel's music—no one can do it better—and the Harmonic Union have an efficient chorus and orchestra.

There are now many concerts of classical music. Mr. Sterndale Bennett is giving a series of concerts into which he introduces none but the finest compositions. He includes the modern German authors, and even Robert Schumann is heard at his rooms.

Mr. Lucas, the Professor of Harmony in the Royal Academy, is also giving a series of quartet concerts at his own residence, in which the first artists in London are employed, and the most classic works are introduced.

The Concerts of the English Glee and Madrigal Society, in which the finest English glees are performed in the very best manner by the most accomplished English singers, are highly interesting and instructive. The principal performers are Mrs.

Endersohn, Miss Williams, Mr. Lockey, Mr. Hobbs, and Mr. Phillips.

Other concerts of less interest are of daily occurrence; and the season is now coming when London will be full indeed of music, as it always is from April to July.

LETTER LIV.

York—Dr. Camidge—Roughness of boys' voices—Lord Murray—Neukomm's Psalms—
Rev. Mr. Guthrie's—St. Giles's Cathedral—Choral singing in Scotland.

EDINBURGH, March 29th, 1853.

I LEFT London on Monday 21st inst., at five o'clock, and arrived at York the same evening, at half past eleven. The next day I visited the cathedral, and had a pleasant interview with the organist, Dr. Camidge. He is a fine musician, and is well known by his various church compositions. Perhaps there is no cathedral town which one can visit with greater interest than this, and the service under the direction of Dr. C., is said to be as well performed as at any place in England. But still we find the same rapid style of chanting, or nearly so, and the terrible roughness of boys' voices. Of course boys' voices must be relied upon for such establishments, but it is enough to tear out one's soul to hear them. Just before leaving London, I called on Chevalier Neukomm, and in the course of conversation I asked him how he liked boys' voices on the soprano? "Boys' voices," replied he, "their voices are like cat's voices." Mendelssohn disliked the shrill and screeching feature of the English choruses in which boys' voices prevailed, and in which the alto is sung by men. I was sitting by him in Exeter Hall during the rehearsal of a part of his St. Paul, in 1837, when he said, " It is a pity that the English should not follow our (the German) custom of employing female voices for both soprano and alto."

There is a society in Edinburgh for the " revival of church music." It is under the principal direction of Lord Murray, from whom an introductory note from Chev. Neukomm procured for me a cordial reception. By the way, it will be interesting to many of your readers to know that the Chev. Neukomm, whose Oratorio of David has been so extensively sung in Boston and elsewhere, is now residing in London with the Prussian ambassador, who has long been his intimate friend, and who provides him with an excellent apartment in his magnificent residence. He is much troubled with his eyes, yet by the strongest magnifying glasses, he is able to see to write. He composes much church music, and has lately completed the music to twenty of the Psalms (Bible version) which have been published by the " Association for the revival of Sacred Music in Scotland." These Psalms (anthems) have been written for two choirs, or for a quartet and choir, so as to preserve their original responsive character. " The Psalms," says the Chev. Neukomm, " have been to me, during my long life, a very gratifying subject of meditation. I have set to music most of the Psalms, and many of them four or five times in different languages ; in Latin, in German, in English, in Italian, in Russian, in French, and even in Hebrew, and such is the spirit which lives in these sublime sacred poems, that the music to the very same Psalms takes in each of these languages a peculiar, but always a most high and admirable character." " For Congregational singing," says the Chevalier, " the Metrical translation (old Scotch) may be sufficient, provided this translation be sung to the ancient Psalm tunes, which are, in their unpretending simplicity, far preferable to modern adaptations from Haydn, Mozart, and other composers."

Psalmody is at a low ebb in the churches here. In Rev. Mr. Guthrie's church (he is one of the most popular preachers) the singing is led by a choir, or as it is called here, a Band (pronounced Bond), consisting of about eighteen or twenty voices. They sit together in front of the pulpit, facing the minister, and do not rise when they sing.

St. Giles is the old cathedral church where John Knox once preached. The building is so divided by partition walls as to accommodate three separate congregations, who all engage in the exercises of worship at the same time, yet without any interference. In one of these the Psalm was led off by a strong male voice, but the tune was bad, and the people did not very generally unite. In one of the other congregations in the same building, the precentor stood up with great dignity in his place, having on his black surplice, but I listened in vain for his voice. He seemed to be put up there for a show or display, since the lead of the singing came from a powerful female voice, sitting near him, but so as to be unobserved by the people. In the afternoon I attended church in a distant part of the city, where the singing was much better done, but where its general characteristics were the same.

Church singing in Scotland is, I believe, universally Congregational. It receives but little attention, there are but few good bands (choirs), and consequently it is in a low state. Almost as well might we expect the religious interests of a congregation to flourish without a minister, as the cause of Psalmody to prosper without a choir. Another reason for the low state of church-music in Scotland, may be found in the absence of organs. Choirs and organs are both necessary, not only to the greatest success of church-music, but also to the best style of Congregational singing.

From hence to Liverpool to-morrow, and from thence by the steamer America, on the 2d April, to Boston.

THE END.